How to
Understand
Financial
Statements

How to Understand Financial Statements

A Nontechnical Guide for Financial Analysts, Managers, and Executives

DISK INCLUDED

Kenneth R. Ferris
Kirk L. Tennant
Scott I. Jerris

PRENTICE HALL
Englewood Cliffs, New Jersey 07632

Prentice-Hall International (UK) Limited, *London*
Prentice-Hall of Australia Pty. Limited, *Sydney*
Prentice-Hall Canada, Inc., *Toronto*
Prentice-Hall Hispanoamericana, S.A., *Mexico*
Prentice-Hall of India Private Limited, *New Delhi*
Prentice-Hall of Japan, Inc., *Tokyo*
Simon & Schuster Asia Pte. Ltd., *Singapore*
Editora Prentice-Hall do Brasil, Ltda., *Rio de Janeiro*

10 9 8 7 6 5 4 3 2

Library of Congress Cataloging-in-Publication Data

Ferris, Kenneth R.
    How to understand financial statements: a nontechnical guide for
financial analysts, managers, and executives / by Kenneth R. Ferris
and Kirk L. Tennant with Scott I. Jerris.
        p. cm.
    Includes index.
    ISBN 0-13-051913-8
    1. Financial statements. 2. Corporations—Finance. I. Tennant,
Kirk L. II. Jerris, Scott I. III. Title.
HF5681.B2F426 1992
657' .3'024658—dc20   91-32534
                                                              CIP

ISBN 0-13-051913-8

PRENTICE HALL
Professional Publishing
Englewood Cliffs, NJ 07632
Simon & Schuster, A Paramount Communications Company

Printed in the United States of America

Acknowledgments

We gratefully acknowledge the constructive criticisms and suggestions of David Harvey (Tulane University), Keith A. Schmidt (NCNB-Texas), and Thomas Selling (Wake Forest University), who reviewed this manuscript at various stages. We would also like to thank Alice Doster for her contribution to its preparation.

K.R.F.
K.L.T.
S.I.J.

Introduction

Initially, we were puzzled. Why would major banking institutions and investment houses spend significant sums to recruit bright, well-educated students from the finest U.S. academic institutions only to then invest further company funds to retrain (or train, as the case may be) the new recruits in the fundamentals of accounting and finance? Weren't we—the business professors of U.S. academic institutions—doing our job?

After several involvements with in-house corporate training programs, the need for this retraining (or training) process became apparent: academic institutions were graduating students well armed with technical skills, but equipped with very few analytical or interpretive skills. Indeed, a review of our own classroom efforts revealed that a far greater percentage of the curriculum was devoted to the preparation aspects of accounting and the techniques of finance than was devoted to understanding just what the financial data revealed. In short, too few courses and too little classroom time were devoted to the critical review and understanding of accounting and financial data.

Thus, it appeared, to us at least, that the financial community was essentially forced to assume the responsibility for placing the finishing touches on the professional education of its new employees. The assumption of this responsibility was, on the one hand, quite natural as most companies maintained as a normal entry experience some form of in-house training program for the purpose of creating or instilling a corporate culture. The proliferation of these entry-level accounting and finance programs, however, revealed the failure of most academic programs to equip their graduates with the requisite skills to transition, without some further assistance, from the academic setting of the university to the "real world" of banking and finance.

After over a decade of working with financial institutions in assisting their recruits to make this transition, our colleagues in the financial community suggested that we put our experience into book form. In the pages that follow, we have tried to capture in nontechnical language and with as few references as possible to the mechanical aspects of accounting, the essence of corporate financial analysis and reporting. Where technical issues could not be avoided, we have tried to relegate them to footnotes or appendices. Our guiding objective throughout this effort was to assist the reader to become financial statement literate.

Several Premises

Before embarking on the following pages, we feel that the reader should recognize several premises, in fact realities, that underlie much of this book.

First, in order to teach students unfamiliar and sometimes difficult concepts, it is useful to make simplifying assumptions regarding the topic at hand. For example, in teaching the fundamentals of accounting, it is frequently expeditious to ask students to assume away the vagaries of the real world in order to more easily arrive at definitive solutions to problems and cases. In this way, students are able to learn a particular set of concepts; and, at a later date, the assumptions can be relaxed to enable the student to learn yet additional concepts. Many students, however, fail to reach the advanced stages of accounting and finance where such assumptions are (or may be) relaxed, and where the "real world" can be viewed.

One goal of this book is to portray financial statements as they really are—without any constraining assumptions. Thus, the reader is asked at this early stage to accept the notion that the reality of accounting is that "generally accepted accounting principles," or GAAP, constitute a menu of methods among which corporate managers must choose in order to present their company's financial results. As a consequence, when an analyst or investor reviews a company's annual report and reads that the company's net income was $100 million and its total assets were valued at $200 million, the reader must recognize that these apparently quite precise accounting figures are merely estimates of the company's net earnings and total assets. By definition, the reported figures are a function of the particular accounting methods selected from the GAAP menu. They are but one possible representation of the company's net earnings and total assets, with other representations equally possible and plausible. It is because other representations are equally possible and plausible that an analyst must be able to assess the quality of the reported earnings, assets, and cash flows. How "quality" is, or can be assessed, is a major theme of this book.

A second reality, or premise, is that when faced with the need to select from the GAAP menu, most corporate managers of public companies will choose those methods which tend to make the reported results of a company look their best. It is important to note that so long as the reported results are prepared using GAAP, the selection of those methods which place a company in a favorable light is in no way unethical. Indeed, the institutional reality is that management must make a decision as to what GAAP to use and they may choose any of the methods that are considered to be GAAP. Thus, "the system" requires that choices be made, and in most cases permits considerable diversity in the methods adopted.

The notion that corporate managers choose those reporting methods which make a company look its best is not all that surprising. Most executives do not share the belief that the capital markets are informationally efficient,[1] and instead hold the view that they can positively influence their company's stock and bond prices, or debt ratings as the case may be, by adopting those reporting methods which maximize reported earnings and assets.[2] Thus, GAAP is often selected with the explicit intent, or at least expectation, of producing a positive security price reaction. Further, the managerial decision to use "liberal" accounting methods may also be self-motivated. For example, if corporate executives are compensated on the basis of current earnings, it is only natural to expect those individuals to employ methods which maximize a firm's reported earnings, and hence maximize their own current compensation. Finally, as we will document in subsequent chapters, the decision to adopt particular accounting methods may also be driven by debt considerations and the desire to avoid covenant violations. The bottom-line is that for whatever reason, managers often select the most liberal reporting methods available, and the analyst must recognize this as a fact of life in the financial community and develop as thorough an understanding of GAAP as possible.

---

1. It is well documented that the securities markets are informationally efficient with respect to all publicly available information. That is to say, security prices reflect all publicly available information, and when new information is released to the market, the information is very quickly reflected in the security's price. It is also well documented that the market understands GAAP and is not often fooled by accounting method changes that increase reported earnings without also increasing cash flows. By implication, the market is capable of seeing through the veneer of alternative accounting methods to assess a company's underlying economic value. These views have become sufficiently well-documented that they are relied upon by the U.S. Supreme Court in decisions involving financial markets.

2. One executive expressed the following viewpoint: "If you can fool some of the people some of the time, then do it."

An end product of these realities is that the financial statement analyst bears the ultimate responsibility for understanding and interpreting the reported financial results. The purpose of this book is to facilitate that understanding, and so, let us begin.

K.R.F.
K.L.T.
S.I.J.

Contents

PART III
The Balance Sheet / 81

APPENDIXES

PART I

Overview

This book is about understanding financial statements, and by implication, the accounting rules and conventions used in the preparation of those statements. Many financial statement users inappropriately equate the analysis and interpretation of financial data with ratio analysis. This book, however, adopts a broader perspective. In our view, ratio analysis is but one aspect of the analytical process of understanding financial statements. The process also includes the analysis of cash flows, the development of pro forma statements, and an understanding of the accounting measurement rules used to prepare the financial statements being analyzed. Thus, it is inadequate, for example, to calculate an inventory turnover ratio without first understanding the inventory valuation method being used (e.g., FIFO, LIFO, weighted average) and the likely effect of that method on the ratio itself. As we shall see throughout the following chapters, financial ratios are substantially influenced by the accounting methods in use.

Thus, in this book we take a holistic approach to financial statement analysis and assume that a principal aspect of an analyst's investigation is to gain an understanding of the quality of reported earnings, assets, and cash flows. We consider not only the ratios themselves, but also the accounting methods used to prepare the numbers that are being compared and contrasted by the financial ratios. Finally, we consider this information against the backdrop of a company's cash flows, for it is well recognized that dividends and debt repayment are made from cash flows, and not earnings flows.

As a point of departure, this section considers the institutional environment in which financial statements are prepared, and thus in which the analysis of such statements must occur. We consider by whom and how accounting rules and conventions are set, and how the integrity of those rules and conventions are preserved. These issues are important to the analyst in that not only do they help explain why certain methods appear on the GAAP menu, but they also help the analyst to understand the review process that audited financial data must undergo before being publicly disseminated.

As a supplement to this book, a checklist of the key analytical issues raised in each chapter is presented (see Appendix 4). Not only can this checklist help organize the analyst's approach to financial statements, but it can also serve as a means of reviewing one's understanding of each topic.

CHAPTER ONE

The Institutional Environment

Financial Reporting Standards

In the Introduction, we observed that a company's management is required to make a number of accounting policy decisions before financial statements can be prepared and disseminated to the public. Indeed, it is corporate management, and not the external independent auditor, who decides just what generally accepted accounting methods will be utilized. But by whom and how are these generally accepted accounting standards set?

Until 1973, the accounting standard-setting process in the U.S. largely fell under the aegis of the American Institute of Certified Public Accountants (AICPA). This professional organization of CPAs legislated GAAP through two separate but related organizations: the Accounting Principles Board (APB) and the Division of Research. The APB issued "opinions," thereby creating GAAP, based on the conclusions and findings of the Division of Research. During its existence, the APB issued 31 opinions (see Appendix 1), some of which remain in force today.

After receiving considerable criticism in the early 1970s over the way in which accounting standards were set, the AICPA appointed a committee to review the standard-setting process. The work of this committee, known as the Wheat Committee in honor of its chairman (former Securities and Exchange Commissioner Francis Wheat), led to the creation of the Financial Accounting Standards Board (FASB) in 1973.

The FASB was to be an independent, private sector organization, consisting of seven full-time members having no business or government-related affiliations. FASB members were to represent diverse backgrounds, while also possessing a knowledge of accounting, finance, and business. Members were (and still are) appointed for five-year terms and are eligible for reappointment for a second five-year term. In theory, the FASB was created to ensure that the standard-setting process would operate without bias or pressure from external constituencies. In reality, however, the FASB was, and is, subject to considerable lobbying by various business and political interest groups.

The process of standard setting adopted by the FASB is both lengthy in duration and intentionally open for public involvement. Once an accounting issue is placed on the FASB's agenda, a task force of FASB staff employees is created to study the issue. The task force reviews existing literature, briefs the FASB members on identified issues, and then assists in the development of a "discussion memorandum." Task force meetings, as well as those of the FASB, are open to the public.

A discussion memorandum is designed to present both the pros and cons of the various accounting treatments under consideration by the FASB. It is also used as a forum to generate written comments from such external constituencies as the financial community at large, public accounting firms, academics, and the government. A public hearing is then usually held to consider the submitted comments. On the basis of both the written and oral comments received by the FASB, and the original discussion memorandum, the FASB then prepares an "exposure draft" which sets forth a proposed reporting standard. The exposure draft is publicly disseminated to solicit yet another round of written comments, often followed by one or more public hearings.

When the FASB is satisfied that all available information and viewpoints have been considered, a vote of its seven members is then taken. Initially, the FASB required (at least) a 5-to-2 vote to approve a new accounting standard; however, for a number of years, in an effort to expedite the standard approval process, the FASB followed a simple majority rule vote. Beginning in January, 1991, the FASB returned to a 5-to-2 vote for new standard approval.

The official pronouncements of the FASB (see Appendix 1) are entitled Statements of Financial Accounting Standards (SFAS); however, the FASB also issues Interpretations and Technical Bulletins to help clarify or explain existing GAAP. Accounting guidance may also be obtained from reports issued by the Emerging Issues Task Force, and from the industry and audit guides issued by the AICPA.

———————— **The Securities and Exchange Commission** ————————

The catalyst for much of today's securities market regulation was the market crash of 1929, and to a lesser extent various accounting and reporting abuses that existed at that time. In an effort to prevent a recurrence of those abuses, the U. S. Congress passed the Securities Act of 1933, which established financial disclosure requirements for corporations issuing shares of stock to the public. In the following year, a second act was passed, the Securities Exchange Act of 1934, which created the Securities and Exchange Commission (SEC) and empowered it to oversee the activities of the various securities exchanges and their broker-dealers. Today, these two acts (as amended) form the nucleus of the securities laws of the United States.

A major aspect of the Securities Act of 1933 was that it gave the SEC authority "to prescribe the form or forms in which the required information shall be set forth, the terms or details to be shown in the balance sheet and the earnings statement, and the methods to be followed in the preparation of accounts." In effect, Congress delegated the authority for accounting standard-setting in the U.S. to the SEC. Since its creation in 1934, however, the SEC has itself largely delegated the responsibility for accounting standard-setting to the AICPA, and more recently the FASB.

Although accounting standard-setting occurs in the private sector, the SEC maintains a comprehensive set of regulations that prescribe the form and content of the financial statements and disclosures that must be filed with that agency. For example, companies that wish to issue (or have issued) securities under either the 1933 or 1934 acts, must file an annual report (Form 10-K) with the SEC's Division of Corporation Finance. In addition to a complete set of financial statements and an accompanying independent auditor's report, Form 10-K requires the following nonfinancial information disclosures:

- A description of the company's principal business activity, highlighting any recent developments or changes.
- A description of any pending or ongoing legal proceedings.
- A description of any matters submitted to the shareholders for a vote during the fourth quarter.
- A management discussion and analysis of the company's financial condition and results of operations.
- A description of any disagreements with the company's independent auditors regarding accounting or financial disclosure.
- A description of the background of all directors, executive officers, or other persons exercising significant control over the company.
- The compensation levels of the principal executives.

In addition to Form 10-K, public companies must also file Form 10-Q, a quarterly reporting document, with the SEC. The purpose of the 10-Q is similar to that of the 10-K, but the required disclosures are not as extensive. For example, the 10-Q financial statements do not have to be audited by an independent auditor, and the nonfinancial disclosures are limited to material developments or events. The 10-Q is filed only for the first three quarters, since fourth-quarter data is presented in the annual 10-K filing.

When significant events occur between 10-Q filing dates, a Form 8-K may be used to inform the SEC and the company's shareholders of these recent events. For example, the SEC requires that a Form 8-K be filed within 15 days of any of the following events:

- A change of control or ownership in the company.
- An acquisition or disposition of company assets that is material in amount.
- A bankruptcy filing by the company.
- A resignation of a board member as a consequence of a business disagreement.

Forms 10-K, 10-Q, 8-K, and others, are all documents in the public domain, and thus are available for review by any interested party. Because many of the nonfinancial disclosures required by the SEC do not appear in a company's annual report, analysts should avail themselves of these public documents to more fully understand the investment or credit risk associated with public companies.

As a concluding observation on the SEC, it is noteworthy that the role of this agency is to ensure corporate compliance with the objectives of "full and fair financial disclosure." By controlling the form and content of financial disclosures, the SEC hopes to enable the public to make informed credit and investment decisions. However, while the responsibility for accounting standard-setting effectively resides with the FASB, the SEC maintains, and indeed has exercised, the right to overrule the FASB with respect to the final form of GAAP accounting rules and conventions.[1]

Corporate Accountability

As noted earlier, the primary responsibility for the preparation of all corporate financial reports resides with the corporation itself and, by extension, its management. Hence the extent to which reported accounting data are objective, reliable, and unbiased is directly under the control and influence of corporate management. Some companies publicly acknowledge this responsibility by including a "management letter of responsibility" in their annual report. Still others acknowledge this stewardship role through the adoption of a corporate code of conduct with respect to a company's accounting and reporting activities.

While neither of these statements is currently required by either the SEC or the FASB, the inclusion of a statement of responsibility is certainly viewed as desirable and is quickly becoming a normal inclusion in the published annual report. Exhibit 1.1 contains an example of a management letter of responsibility as presented in the Valhi, Inc. annual report, while Exhibit 1.2 contains an example of a corporate code of financial conduct, as presented in the J. C. Penney Co. annual report.

The ability of some companies to effectively discharge their reporting responsibilities has in recent years, however, been called in question. In the early 1970s, for example, Mattel, Inc., a large toy manufacturer, admitted issuing false and misleading financial statements.[2] According to an SEC filing by Arthur Andersen & Co., Mattel's independent auditor:

> Through false financial reporting which was part of a calculated scheme directed by certain officers of Mattel and others, Mattel substantially overstated its pre-tax income for fiscal 1971 and substantially understated its pre-tax loss for fiscal 1972. This scheme involved, directly or indirectly, a large number of Mattel officers and employees from the most senior executives to clerical personnel. The fraud was perpetuated by, among other things, the preparation of forged or falsified records and accounting entries, and a pattern of false representations and responses by Mattel personnel which misled AA & Co.

In 1971, Mattel common stock reached a high of $52\frac{1}{4}$. By June, 1973, following the disclosure that the financial statements had been falsified, the Mattel shares were trading at $5.

More recently, the SEC charged seven executives of Crazy Eddie, Inc., with engaging in a "massive financial fraud" to overstate the company's earnings from 1985 through 1987.[3] According to an SEC lawsuit, executives of this discount electronics retailer attempted to artificially inflate the

---

[1] One classic example demonstrating the SEC's ultimate right to establish accounting standards occurred in 1977 with regard to SFAS 19, which required oil and gas producing companies to adopt the successful efforts method of accounting for exploration costs. The SEC opposed this decision by the FASB on grounds that the successful efforts method might have adverse securities market consequences for smaller oil and gas companies. Under pressure from the SEC, the FASB issued SFAS 25 in 1978, which rescinded SFAS 19 and permitted oil and gas companies to utilize either the successful efforts method or the full cost method.

[2] For a complete discourse on the Mattel, Inc. case, the interested reader is referred to "Mattel, Inc.," a case study by E. Richard Brownlee, Darden Graduate School, University of Virginia (Charlottesville, Virginia).

[3] A. S. Hayes, "SEC Suit Charges Crazy Eddie Ex-Chief, Others With Fraud Linked to Share Sales," *The Wall Street Journal* (September 7, 1989).

Exhibit 1.1 ———————————————————————————————————

MANAGEMENT LETTER OF RESPONSIBILITY

To the Stockholders of Valhi, Inc.:

The Company's management assumes responsibility for the integrity and objectivity of the financial information contained in this summary Annual Report, including the statements covered by the independent accountants' report. The Company maintains an accounting system and related controls to provide reasonable assurance of the integrity and objectivity of accounting information and for the safeguarding of assets. The fair presentation of the Company's financial position and results of operations, in conformity with generally accepted accounting principles, is reported on by the independent accountants. In addition to the accounting and controls systems and the use of independent accountants, the Company utilizes internal auditors who conduct internal control audits as well as special audits, coordinating their activities with the independent accountants. The Company has an Audit Committee of the Board of Directors. The Committee consists exclusively of directors who are not employees of the Company, and will meet as required, but at a minimum, two times a year. The Committee has been established for the general purpose of satisfying itself as to the integrity of the Company's accounting and financial reporting, maintaining communications between the Board of Directors and external and internal auditors, continuously emphasizing the need for internal financial controls, and instigating special investigations as deemed necessary. The independent accountants and the internal auditors have full and free access to the Audit Committee and meet with it, with and without management being present, to discuss all appropriate matters.

Harold C. Simmons
Chairman of the Board

Michael A. Snetzer
President

———————————————————————————————————

company's market value to enable the executives to reap substantial profits through personal stock sales. For example, Mr. Eddie Antar, former chairman of the company, reportedly sold 5.6 million shares of Crazy Eddie stock for a profit of over $60 million. The SEC lawsuit alleged that, under the direction of Mr. Antar, Crazy Eddie overstated pretax earnings by $20.6 million, $6.7 million, and $2.0 million, for fiscal years ending 1987, 1986, and 1985, respectively. The lawsuit charged that the fraudulent profit figures were achieved by understating accounts payables, overstating inventories, and falsifying debit memos.

And finally, after a six-month internal investigation by outside directors in 1989, Miniscribe Corporation concluded that "senior management apparently perpetuated a massive fraud on the company, its directors, its outside auditors and the investing public." According to the directors' report, the apparent fraud covered the period 1985 through 1988 and "re-

Exhibit 1.2 ————————————————————————————————

CORPORATE CODE OF FINANCIAL CONDUCT

J. C. Penney Co., Inc.

The results of operations of our company must be recorded in accordance with the requirements of law and generally accepted accounting principles. It is company policy, as well as requirement of law, to maintain books, records and accounting which, in reasonable detail, accurately and fairly reflect the business transactions and disposition of assets of the company. In order to carry out this policy and assure compliance with applicable laws, no Associate should take, or permit to be taken, any action in a manner whereby the company's books, records, and accounts would not accurately, fairly and completely reflect the action taken. No false or misleading entries should be made in any books or records of the company for any reason, and no fund, asset or account of the company may be established or acquired for any purpose unless such fund, asset, or account is accurately reflected in the books and records of the company. No corporate funds or assets should be used for any unlawful purpose.

———

quired the active participation of many company personnel." The directors' report alleged that senior officials of the disk-drive manufacturer:[4]

- broke into locked trunks containing the auditors' workpapers and inflated inventory values;
- packaged bricks as disk-drives and shipped them to distributors as a means to inflate revenues;
- accumulated scrap and obsolete parts that had been previously written off and reported them as part of inventory; and,
- packaged over 6,000 contaminated disk drives in order to inflate inventory levels.

In early January, 1990, Miniscribe filed for bankruptcy under Chapter 11 of the federal bankruptcy code. After restating its financial results for the prior three years, the company's negative net worth exceeded $150 million. The remaining assets of the company were liquidated in late 1990.

Unfortunately, these cases do not appear to be isolated incidents. Whether the level of fraudulent financial reporting in the U.S. is actually on the increase or whether the financial community's ability to detect such fraud has improved is unclear; however, what is evident is that the incidence of identified deceptive financial reporting has clearly grown over the last decade.

————————————

[4] A. Zipser, "Miniscribe's Investigators Determine That Massive Fraud Was Perpetuated," *The Wall Street Journal* (September 12, 1989).

In an effort to check the growth of deceptive reporting, both the SEC and the AICPA have undertaken a number of initiatives. The SEC, for example, has sought increased authority from the U. S. Congress to impose significant financial sanctions on disclosure regulation violators and to obtain greater criminal prosecution authority for fraudulent reporting cases. Similarly, the AICPA has adopted professional guidelines for its members requiring them to place greater emphasis on, and to effectively assume greater responsibility for, the detection of financial fraud.

The Independent Auditor

With the exception of the SEC's Form 10-K, there is no legal obligation for a company to issue audited financial statements.[5] However, since most financial statement users have come to view the independent auditor's opinion as an essential component of any financial report, many companies prepare and distribute audited financial statements in the normal course of business.

The purpose of the independent auditor's report is to inform statement users as to whether the presented financial data were prepared using GAAP and whether the reported results fairly present the company's financial position, results of operations, and statement of cash flows. The value of the auditor's report derives from the fact that the auditor is a professionally licensed, independent accounting authority. Thus, the auditor's report represents an objective assessment of the fairness of the financial information contained in the financial statements.

Not all financial statements, however, are issued with an accompanying auditor's report. Interim financial reports, for example, are rarely audited, although in some cases a company may employ an independent auditor to review (but not audit) these quarterly reports. In this latter case, the independent auditor will frequently issue what is commonly called a *comfort letter*, which should not be confused with the auditor's opinion issued in conjunction with the Form 10-K filing.

An auditor's report (see Exhibit 1.3) typically contains (at least) three paragraphs. The first paragraph is a statement of the scope of the audit examination actually performed, and a brief statement differentiating management's responsibility for the preparation of the financial statements from the auditor's role in expressing an opinion on them. The second paragraph states whether or not the audit was performed in accordance with

---

[5] One reference that should be part of every analyst's library is *Understanding Audits and the Auditor's Report: A Guide for Financial Statement Users* (AICPA, 1989). This guide addresses many of the misconceptions concerning the role and function of the audit process as it relates to financial statement analysis.

Exhibit 1.3 —————————————————————————

INDEPENDENT AUDITOR'S REPORT

We have audited the accompanying balance sheets of X Company as of December 31, 19X2 and 19X1, and the related statements of income, retained earnings, and cash flows for the years then ended. These financial statements are the responsibility of the company's management. Our responsibility is to express an opinion of these financial statements based on our audits.

We conducted our audits in accordance with generally accepted auditing standards. Those standards require that we plan and perform the audit to obtain responsible assurance about whether the financial statements are free of material misstatement. An audit includes examining, on a test basis, evidence supporting the amounts and disclosures in the financial statements. An audit also includes assessing the accounting principles used and significant estimates made by management, as well as evaluating the overall financial statement presentation. We believe that our audits provide a reasonable basis for our opinion.

In our opinion, the financial statements referred to above present fairly, in all material respects, the financial position of X Company as of [at] December 31, 19X2 and 19X1, and the results of its operations and its cash flows for the years then ended in conformity with generally accepted accounting principles.

Source: AICPA Auditing Standard Board, *Statement on Auditing Standards No. 58*, "Reports on Audited Financial Statements" (New York, 1988).

——

generally accepted auditing standards (GAAS), and briefly explains what an audit entails.

The third paragraph is a statement of opinion as to whether the financial statements have been prepared on a consistent basis with prior years using GAAP, and whether the statements as a whole fairly present the financial position, cash flows, and results of operations.

Four different types of audit opinions may be issued. An *unqualified*, or "clean," opinion is issued when a full audit examination is undertaken and indicates that the reported results are fairly presented using GAAP on a consistent basis. A *qualified* opinion, on the other hand, indicates that the auditor is unable to express a clean opinion. A qualification may be issued for any number of reasons: the scope of the audit investigation was limited; the company changed its method of accounting and the auditor disagrees with the change; the statements were prepared using non-GAAP methods; or possibly because of the existence of uncertainties or pending events that might materially affect the company's financial condition.[6]

The final two types of opinions, the *adverse* opinion and the *disclaimer* of opinion, are rarely encountered. When an adverse opinion is issued, the auditor's objections are so material that a qualified opinion is not even justified. In this case, the auditor is likely to conclude that the financial statements "do not fairly present" the company's financial position, results of operations, or cash flows. Finally, a disclaimer is issued when the auditor is unable to issue any of the three preceding types of opinions.

As noted above, it is extremely unusual to encounter an adverse or disclaimer of opinion, in part because of the practice of *opinion shopping*. Opinion shopping occurs when management and the independent auditor irreconcilably disagree on the financial accounting or disclosure to be used in a company's financial statements. The resolution of this conflict is frequently the dismissal or resignation of the independent auditor, providing management with the opportunity to solicit an alternative, and possibly more favorable opinion on the accounting issue.

It is important to note that opinion shopping is neither illegal nor unethical. However, where the interpretation of an economic event leads to polarized accounting viewpoints on the part of management and the independent auditor, the possibility for questionable, and even deceptive financial reporting has historically been very high. Thus, it is always in the analyst's best interests to investigate the circumstances surrounding a change in independent auditors. Under current SEC regulations, a company must notify the Commission within five business days of a change in auditors and the circumstances leading to the change via a Form 8-K filing. To ensure that both sides of a conflict are publicly aired, the independent auditor must also file a letter of explanation with the SEC within ten days of engagement completion or termination.[7] Both documents fall in the public domain, and thus are available for review by any and all interested parties.

As an illustration of the kind of auditor-management conflict that can exist, the firm of Deloitte & Touche was dismissed by A. J. Ross Logistics, Inc. in August, 1990, over the accounting for two transactions. In their SEC filing, Ross officials noted that disagreement existed over the classification (i.e., current versus noncurrent) of $800,000 in loans to Ross's President,

---

[6] The question of just what constitutes a "material" event is, and probably always will be a matter of professional judgment. Most public accounting firms adopt various rules of thumb to judge whether an event is material or not, and thus whether financial statement disclosure is warranted. For some accounting firms, a material event is one that produces a change in total assets of 3 percent or more, whereas for other firms a material event might be a change in earnings of 5 percent or more. Unfortunately, there is little consensus within the accounting profession as to just what thresholds define materiality.

[7] The time lag between engagement termination and the required SEC filing by the independent auditor was recently reduced from 45 days, in large measure due to the ZZZZ Best Co. scandal in 1988. According to the SEC, ZZZZ Best's auditor, Ernst & Whinney (now Ernst & Young), resigned on June 2, 1988, suspecting that one of the company's major contracts was fraudulent. E & W then waited the maximum allotted period of 45 days before informing the SEC of its suspicions, during which time the company negotiated several new loans and then filed for bankruptcy under Chapter 11 of the federal bankruptcy code. See L. Berton and D. Akst, "CPAs May Soon Have to Report Fraud Earlier," *The Wall Street Journal* (January 12, 1989).

and the company's recognition of a tax benefit from an operating loss carryforward. According to Ross's SEC filing, both issues "were resolved to the satisfaction of Deloitte & Touche"; however, a reading of Deloitte's parallel SEC filing revealed that, contrary to Ross's SEC statement, the auditors were not in agreement with the final position adopted by the company. Tabb & Co. was chosen to replace Deloitte and Touche as Ross's independent auditor.

Unfortunately, an audited set of financial statements is rarely the panacea that most analysts expect it to be. In 1982, for example, only three months after receiving a clean opinion from Peat, Marwick, Mitchell & Co., the Penn Square Bank of Oklahoma filed for bankruptcy. Also, in 1985, only seven months after receiving a clean opinion from Arthur Andersen & Co., Beker Industries filed for protection under Chapter 11 of the Bankruptcy Code. In short, there is no substitute for diligent analysis. For all financial data, the analyst would be wise to adopt the attitude of *caveat emptor*.

Investigation of Fraud

Because of the apparently increasing incidence of financial fraud, the independent auditor has been called upon to assume a more active role in the investigation and detection of financial irregularities. Under recently adopted AICPA auditing standards,[8] the independent auditor must design an audit "to provide reasonable assurance of detecting errors and irregularities that are material to the financial statements." In addition to identifying and correcting accounting errors, and disclosing material irregularities, the independent auditor is also responsible for identifying and reporting illegal acts by a corporation or its management. Illegal acts encompass such events as illegal political contributions, kickbacks, and other violations of U.S. laws and regulations. To help deter illegal acts, the U. S. Congress enacted the Foreign Corrupt Practices Act in 1977, which established criminal penalties for U. S. companies and their management if convicted of making payments to foreign agents or officials in order to obtain or retain business.

To help understand why it is possible for financial fraud to occur, the analyst must remember that the contents and preparation of the financial statements are under the immediate control of corporate management. Thus, in most companies, senior executives will have some degree of access to a company's computer system and financial records. It is also noteworthy that, because of time and personnel constraints, the independent auditor rarely investigates 100 percent of a company's records. Instead, the auditor utilizes sampling techniques to examine a (hopefully) representative sample

---

[8] AICPA Auditing Standards Board, *Statement of Auditing Standards No. 52*, "The Auditor's Responsibility to Detect and Report Errors and Irregularities," (AICPA, 1988).

of accounts. If the sampled accounts are substantially correct, the auditor will rely upon theories of inference to deduce the likelihood of accuracy for the remaining unsampled accounts. In this way, the auditor is able to conduct a timely, cost efficient, and statistically sound examination of accounting records. Nonetheless, since each and every account balance is not verified, the possibility of error exists, although the likelihood of such error is minimized.

Conclusions

The preparation, and hence the fairness, of a company's financial statements are the direct responsibility of corporate management. The role of the independent auditor is to provide financial statement users with an objective opinion as to the integrity of the accounting system used in the preparation of the statements, and by extension, the fairness of the data contained therein. Institutional and financial constraints prevent the auditor from examining all accounts, and thus the possibility of error in the accounts exists, particularly if such error is part of an intentional effort to deceive. So long as corporate management perceives some economic benefit to exist from deceptive financial reporting, the problem of financial fraud will continue to exist. Thus, the analyst must use all available information sources and investigative tools when assessing the quality of a company's reported earnings, assets, and cash flows.

While it is relatively easy to perpetuate a financial deception for short periods, it is much harder to sustain a deception beyond one year (i.e., through a thorough audit investigation). Nonetheless, the presence of financial irregularities is often revealed by simple ratio analysis or by a comparison of accrual and cash earnings. Thus, the analyst is not completely defenseless, and it is wise to pay heed to the financial indicators of low quality earnings and cash flow, to which we now turn.

PART II

The Income Statement

Companies issuing audited financial statements are required to provide three basic financial statements: a balance sheet, a statement of cash flows, and an income statement. Each statement provides a relatively unique view of a company's financial condition, and thus all three must be considered in order to obtain a complete picture of the relative financial health of a company.

In this section, we focus on the income statement, which describes a company's recent operating performance. We examine the principal elements of the income statement, namely revenues (Chapter 2), cost of goods sold (Chapter 3), and income taxes (Chapter 4).

The income statement, like the balance sheet and the statement of cash flows, presents information that is essentially historical in nature. It describes what has happened, rather than what will happen. Investment and lending decisions, however, should not be made exclusively, or even principally, on the basis of historical data, in that a company's future prospects are at least as important, if not more so, than its past performance. Thus, a significant aspect of financial statement analysis involves predicting future results on the basis of existing financial data. Admittedly, predicting the future under almost any circumstances is a risky endeavor, but a company's recent operating performance, as reported in the income statement, is an excellent departure point.

15

CHAPTER TWO

Revenue Recognition

In the words of one financial wag, the income statement is:

> An accounting report which includes actual or anticipated cash flows selected by the accountant as applicable to the time period covered. Those which have occurred but are not selected and those which are selected but have not occurred are stored on the balance sheet.[1]

While this definition of the income statement is not generally accepted, it does emphasize two important characteristics of this accounting statement. First, the income statement is prepared on the basis of accrual accounting concepts, and not on the basis of cash flow concepts. Second, the income statement measures the performance of a company for an arbitrarily selected period of time.[2]

---

[1] Michael W. Sperry, Bankers Trust of South Carolina.

[2] While monthly or even weekly income statements may be prepared for internal reporting purposes, quarterly or annual statements tend to be the norm for external reporting purposes. Most external reports include comparative operating data for the prior quarter or year (and perhaps more), in addition to the current period results.

In its simplest form, the income statement contains two broad categories of items: revenues and expenses. *Revenues* represent the level of accomplishment of a company, whereas *expenses* represent the level of effort expended to attain that level of accomplishment. More succinctly, revenues represent the actual or expected inflow of assets, or settlement of liabilities, from a company's primary business activity, whereas expenses represent the consumption of assets, or the assumption of liabilities, to produce the revenue inflow.

Most corporate income statements, however, provide more information than simply revenues and expenses. GAAP requires, for example, that the income statement reflect an all-inclusive view of a company's operations, such that all transactions, operating and nonoperating, which increase or decrease owners' equity during the period (with the exception of dividends and capital transactions), be reported in the income statement. As a consequence, corporate income statements frequently contain up to four different categories of income (or loss): operations, other, unusual, and extraordinary.

Consider, for example, Exhibit 2.1, which contains the comparative income statements of Dresser Industries, Inc. for 1987-88. For 1988, Dresser reported "earnings from operations" of $151.3 million. This measure indicates, overall, how successful the *primary* business activities of the company have been. Whether this figure is exceptional or poor, acceptable or not, must be judged in some context, for example against 1987 operating earnings (i.e., $24.3 million) or perhaps relative to some standard such as total assets.[3]

Regardless of the standard adopted, this category of earnings is, without question, the most important in that it is the best evidence available for predicting a company's future operating earnings. When this earnings figure is low or negative, it begs the question as to whether the company should be discontinued or dismantled, or whether management is just doing a bad job. Thus, judging the adequacy of operating earnings becomes a significant aspect of financial statement analysis.

The second principal category of income, "Other Income," summarizes the income and expenses, and gains and losses, from a company's *secondary* business activities.[4] Examples of this type of income include interest income on outstanding loans to other companies or individuals, rental income or royalties from properties under lease to others, and on the expense side,

---

[3] The ratio of operating earnings to total assets for Dresser in 1988 was 5.2 percent. The merits of this ratio, and others, must also be evaluated in the context of some previously established standard, such as the prior year's ratio, the ratio of a close competitor, or some minimum accepted threshold. See Chapter 12 for a discussion of traditional ratio analysis.

[4] Many analysts confuse the distinction between *expenses* and *losses*. It is useful to remember that while both represent a reduction in a company's assets, expenses are incurred while attempting to generate revenues, while losses occur without any parallel revenue generation.

interest expense on the general borrowings of the company. In 1988, Dresser's various secondary business activities produced net earnings of $27.3 million, a significant amount when compared to the company's net earnings from primary operations of $151.3 million.

The two final income categories represent those income (or loss) items that are unusual or extraordinary in nature. In most cases, these items are only peripherally related to the recurring operations of a company. For example, income from a discontinued division, subsidiary, or line of business —an *unusual* item—is fundamentally operational in nature, but more importantly, is also nonrecurring; and thus, the analyst should disregard this type of income (or loss) when assessing a company's future earnings potential. *Extraordinary* items, on the other hand, reflect those special events or transactions that are distinguished by their unusual nature and their infrequency of occurrence. Extraordinary items, like unusual items, tend to be single-period, nonrecurring transactions that have minimal future credit or investment value.

In 1988, Dresser reported an unusual gain from discontinued operations of $22.7 million and an extraordinary gain from recognized tax credits of $11.3 million. Together these two items represented over 21 percent of Dresser's total net income after tax. While these two events represent important sources of income and cash flows for Dresser in 1988, it is naive to expect these particular flows to recur in future years; and thus, when projecting either pro forma earnings or cash flows, these events and transactions like them should be ignored, unless the objective is to measure the liquidation value of a company's various assets or divisions.

Before departing these final categories of income (and loss), two items deserve special mention—the *minority interest in earnings of consolidated subsidiaries* and the *equity in earnings of unconsolidated subsidiaries*. Both of these accounts relate to subsidiary or affiliate companies and are given separate disclosure because they are unrelated to the operations of the parent company (e.g., Dresser). Both accounts are also by-products of the GAAP rules and conventions followed when accounting for subsidiary or affiliate company operations (discussed in detail in Chapter 6).

The minority interest account refers to the ownership interest of individuals or other corporations in subsidiaries predominantly owned by Dresser, and whose results have been consolidated with those of Dresser. This income statement account reflects the portion of the consolidated subsidiary's earnings (or losses) accruing to these other investors—an amount which is deducted from (or added to) Dresser's consolidated earnings and added to (or deducted from) the minority interest account on the balance sheet. The equity in earnings account, on the other hand, represents the proportionate share (i.e., less than 50 percent) of the earnings of Dresser-affiliate companies whose results have not been consolidated into Dresser's financial statements. These earnings (losses) are not only added to

Exhibit 2.1 _____

DRESSER INDUSTRIES, INC.
CONSOLIDATED STATEMENT OF EARNINGS
(in millions of dollars, except per share data)

	(years ended October 31)	
	1988	**1987**
Sales revenues	$ 3,226.7	$ 3,030.9
Service revenues—Notes C and D	715.0	88.8
Total sales and service revenues	3,941.7	3,119.7
Cost of sales	2,253.0	2,154.4
Cost of services	651.0	88.4
Total cost of sales and services—Notes D, E and N	2,904.0	2,242.8
Gross earnings	1,037.7	876.9
Selling, engineering, administrative and general expenses—Note N	886.4	852.6
Earnings from operations	151.3	24.3
Other income (deductions)		
Interest expense	(46.6)	(97.1)
Interest earned	41.5	35.6
Royalties earned	19.4	9.7
Pension plan settlements—Note M	13.6	88.9
Partnership operations—Note B	1.0	(36.8)
Other, net—Note N	(1.6)	14.7
Total other income	27.3	15.0
Earnings from continuing operations before income taxes, minority interest and equity earnings	178.6	39.3
Income taxes—Note G	(64.1)	(48.0)
Minority interest in (earnings) losses of subsidiaries—Note C	(6.3)	15.2
Equity in earnings of unconsolidated subsidiaries and affiliates—Note B	14.6	9.8
Earnings from continuing operations	122.8	16.3
Discontinued operations—Note B	22.7	26.7
Earnings before extraordinary item	145.5	43.0
Extraordinary item—tax benefits from loss carryforwards—Notes B and G	11.3	5.9
Net earnings	$ 156.8	$ 48.9

(deducted from) Dresser's consolidated earnings, but are also added to (deducted from) a balance sheet account entitled "investment in unconsolidated subsidiaries."

Whether these two income statement accounts should be considered by the analyst when generating pro forma financial statements is a matter of debate; however, our opinion is that the pro forma statements of the parent should reflect the minority interest of outside shareholders in the consolidated results of subsidiaries, but not the equity in unconsolidated subsidiary earnings. The former is a situation in which Dresser, the parent company, has a controlling interest in the operations of the subsidiary, and the latter is not.

The classification of income (and losses) into its various categories enables the analyst to more fully understand the relative contribution of each income category to a company's "bottom-line" net income. Knowing whether a company is being kept afloat by operations or by unusual and extraordinary items is essential to investment and credit decisions. In some financial statements, a segmentation of income into its various components will not be presented, and where this is the case, the onus falls upon the analyst to examine each income statement item and to properly classify them. Moreover, because of the possibility of diverse interpretation of various economic events and the latitude in reporting such events under GAAP, we believe that the analyst must assume a proactive posture in the review of income statement accounts, reclassifying items where justification exists. At a minimum, the analyst must clearly identify the recurring and non-recurring income (and loss) items. Earnings that can be expected to recur in the future are far more valuable to a firm, its owners, and its creditors than are nonrecurring profits.

In short, the analyst must consider the financial statements as a source of information that can be restructured or reformatted according to his or her needs. Throughout this book, a common prescription will be repeated: be prepared to restate the financial statements to conform to your own set of assumptions. Indeed, in many cases, the financial statements contain sufficient information to adequately restate the reported figures. In other cases, there will be insufficient data, and consequently the analyst will need to make reasonable assertions and assumptions. A goal in what follows is to help guide the analyst through the restatement process.

————————— Revenue Realization and Recognition —————————

As noted above, *revenues* represent the actual or expected inflow of assets, the settlement of liabilities, or both, from a company's primary business activity.[5] In general, GAAP stipulates that revenues should not be recorded, or *recognized*, in a company's financial statements until those revenues have been earned, or *realized*. Unfortunately, just when revenue realization occurs is a matter of judgement, and often debate; and, as a consequence, there is considerable diversity in revenue recognition practices between industries, and even within industries.

For a typical retail company, revenue recognition normally occurs at the *point of sale*, when a customer commits to purchase a product at an agreed upon price. Although the collectibility of cash from the customer may ultimately be in question, at the point of sale it is clear that an arms' length transaction has been concluded at a known selling price and cost. Thus, in spite of further concerns over cash collection, the retailer is justified in recognizing revenue at this time under the accrual basis of accounting. If the retailer's concerns over cash collectibility exceed those normally associated with any ordinary credit transaction, it may be prudent for the retailer to abandon the accrual basis, and instead consider deferring recognition of at least a portion of the sale revenues using the *installment* method. Under the installment approach, revenues and the related inventory cost are deferred and recognized only as cash payments are received from the customer.[6]

For a manufacturing company, revenue recognition may occur at any one of several points in the operating cycle: during the production process, when production is complete and the product is shipped, at the point of sale, or at the point of cash collection. (We are unaware of any circumstances which would permit a company to recognize revenue at a point preceding the initiation of production.) Since the primary objective in measuring revenues is to assess the level of accomplishment achieved by a company, one

---

[5] There is fairly widespread acceptance of the definition of revenues. One noteworthy exception, however, concerned Peabody International Corporation, a manufacturer and installer of pollution-control equipment. In 1979, Peabody included in its fourth quarter results a portion of the anticipated damages from two pending lawsuits against subcontractors who had failed to complete previously contracted-for work. The hoped-for awards represented 42 percent of Peabody's fourth quarter earnings of $.71 per share.

In general, contingent events that might result in gains are never reflected in a company's financial statements since to do so might cause revenues to be recognized before they are realized. Peabody's independent auditors, Peat, Marwick, Mitchell & Co., however, defended the company's accounting treatment of the pending lawsuits on reasoning that Peabody "didn't include the proceeds of the lawsuits; they've taken some costs on the project that they incurred and figured that they'll be covered by the lawsuits." See R. A. Joseph, "Firm's Action Raises Issue of Including An Expected Court Award in Earnings," *The Wall Street Journal* (January 15, 1980).

[6] A conservative version of the installment method is the *cost-recovery-first* method. Under this approach, no income is recognized on a sale until the full cost of the product sold is recovered through periodic cash payments by the customer. Thereafter, any cash payments received flow directly to the company's bottom-line as income, since all product costs have been previously recovered.

widely accepted GAAP convention is that (some) effort must be expended first before revenues can be recognized.[7]

Once production is initiated, however, circumstances may warrant the recognition of revenues. Consider, for example, companies in the defense industry producing military products for the U.S. and other governments under contract. Given that a known customer has legally committed to purchase the product at an agreed upon price, so long as the defense contractor can estimate the production costs with a reasonable degree of accuracy, revenue recognition may occur during the production process. However, if no guaranteed contract to buy exists, or if the contractor is unable to reasonably estimate the future costs of production, revenue recognition during the production process would not be justified.

Revenue recognition during the production cycle is thus often encountered where long-term contracts are present, for example in the commercial construction industry. The method by which revenue may be estimated under these contracts is called the *percentage of completion* approach. Under percentage of completion accounting, a company estimates the amount of contract revenues to be recognized in a given period on the basis of the amount of work actually completed during the period. In this way, the total expected contract revenues can be allocated to the various periods covered by a contract. Estimating the amount of work completed, and hence the revenues earned in a given period, can be accomplished in several ways: (1) using production cost ratios (i.e., the ratio of costs incurred in the current period to the total estimated project costs), or (2) using completion estimates provided by independent consulting engineers. Given the likelihood that cost estimates may be in error, our preference, and that of most financial institutions providing interim construction or production financing, is for completion estimates provided by independent consultants.

An alternative, and more conservative, approach to the recognition of contract revenues is the *completed contract* method. Under this approach, the recognition of contract revenues is postponed until all necessary work under a contract is substantially or fully completed (e.g., until all necessary safety code inspections have been completed and approvals obtained). Thus, unlike the percentage of completion approach, the completed contract method does not attempt to allocate contract revenues to the various periods covered by a contract. Instead, revenues are deferred until the project is completed. It is important for the analyst to note, however, that a construction company involved in many on-going projects may use a combination of

---

[7] A good illustration of this point involves revenue recognition by franchisors. SFAS 48 requires that a franchisor complete "substantial performance" on the terms of a franchise agreement before any initial franchise fees can be recognized as revenue. Thus, GAAP effectively requires that effort be expended before revenues may be recognized.

these methods when preparing its financial statements. Typically, the completed contract method is used for shorter-term projects, where revenue and cost allocation problems are minimized, while the percentage of completion method is used for longer-term projects.

Perhaps the most common method of recognizing revenue by manufacturing companies is the *shipment* approach. Under this approach, revenues are recognized when production is complete, when the product is made available for final consumption (as evidenced by its shipment, unless terms are FOB-shipping point), but before a legal sale transaction has been consummated. This recognition approach evolved largely in response to institutional market conditions that characterize many product markets. Because the market for most products is quite large and geographically dispersed, few manufacturers attempt to establish their own retail outlets, and instead, find it more efficient to concentrate on the wholesale side of an industry. Moreover, because of competitive industry conditions, many manufacturers are forced to "sell" to retailers under quite liberal terms (e.g., little or no cash up-front, with a three to six month right-to-return privilege).

Consider, for example, the highly competitive personal computer industry. With the exception of such industry giants as AT&T and Tandy, few computer manufacturers maintain their own retail outlets, finding it more efficient to sell to independently owned computer retail stores. Given the high cost of computers, and the very competitive nature of this consumer-products industry, many manufacturers provide inventory to retail outlets on (effectively) a consignment basis, but nonetheless book revenues when the units are shipped. While this accounting convention is indeed industry-accepted, it is a somewhat riskier approach to revenue recognition than, say, if revenues were deferred until the refund or return period has expired. If, for example, an economy-wide recession occurred, causing a parallel downturn in the computer industry, computer manufacturer profits might be adversely affected by larger than anticipated product returns. This, in turn, might necessitate a write-down of previously prematurely recognized revenues under the shipment approach.

Front-end Loading

The recognition of revenue at the point of shipment, where a final consumer has not yet been identified, often constitutes an industry-accepted form of front-end loading of revenues. *Front-end loading* refers to the practice of recognizing revenues in a period prior to the actual consummation of a sale transaction. In essence, this practice has the effect of improving the appearance of current period results, but potentially at the expense of future periods. So long as sales continue at the rate of growth indicated by current period sales, front-end loading would not appear to be misleading; however, there are few, if any, companies that can sustain sales growth indefinitely. Consequently, if front-end loaded revenues are used as a basis for projecting future revenues, there is some risk that an analyst's future revenue, earnings, and cash flow projections will be overstated.

If, on the other hand, a more conservative view is adopted that, unless a binding contract to buy is present, revenues should not be recognized until a sale to the final consumer occurs (of course, in some cases the "final consumer" may be the retail outlet), any recognition of revenue prior to this point would constitute front-end loading. As reported above, however, GAAP does permit some instances of front-end loading where industry-accepted practices so dictate. It is important to note, nonetheless, that from a quality of earnings perspective, any revenues (and thus earnings) recognized before a final sale has been consummated are subject to some degree of risk. Of concern to the analyst, then, is the degree of risk to which the reported revenues are exposed.

In general, there are two types of risk associated with revenues: (1) risk that the revenues have been booked too early and that the final sale will not be consummated; and (2) risk that, once consummated, the sale will not yield the anticipated level of cash inflows. The first type of risk can be minimized by adopting a conservative revenue recognition policy (e.g., recognition at the point of sale), or where a liberal recognition policy is adopted, by establishing a sufficient reserve to cover any future sales returns.[8]

The second type of risk (i.e., cash collection risk) can be minimized by adopting a conservative credit-granting policy or by establishing a sufficient reserve to cover any future uncollectible accounts. The need for this reserve is estimated at the end of each accounting period, usually on the basis of a process known as *aging the accounts receivables*. The aging process assumes that the older a receivable is, the lower the probability that the receivable will be collected. This estimation process enables management to deduct from current revenues an amount (i.e., the "provision for bad debts") representing the cost of extending credit during the current period. A parallel reserve account, the allowance for uncollectible accounts, appears on the balance sheet as a contra-accounts receivable account. (This topic is discussed further in Chapter 5.)

Unfortunately, there are many case examples where front-end loading, even when industry-accepted, has proven to be disastrous. Consider, for example, the case of Topper Toy, Inc. In 1970, Topper was the second largest

---

[8] The reserve for sales returns is a contra-revenue account commonly called the "sales returns and allowances" account. This account represents management's best estimate, based on prior period sales experience, of the amount of current period sales that will be negated in future periods due to product returns. This estimate is deducted from current period revenues to arrive at "net revenues." The parallel entry for this reserve is another contra-account, the "allowance for sales returns," reported on the balance sheet as a reduction in accounts receivable. (See Chapter 5)

U.S. toy manufacturer, with sales in excess of $60 million. Consistent with industry practice, Topper recognized revenue at the point of shipment, despite the fact that retail customers had from five to eight months to pay or to return unsold inventory. In 1971, Topper revealed that due to an unanticipated economic slow-down, product returns exceeded $14 million, or approximately 25 percent of 1970 sales. As a consequence, Topper was forced to write-down both its receivables and its reported prior revenues by $14 million. By early 1973, Topper filed for bankruptcy.[9]

The Topper Toy case is a good illustration of the hazards associated with using a liberal revenue recognition policy. In this case, despite using industry-accepted GAAP, Topper's financial statements for 1970 were overstated because of the company's inability to anticipate significant swings in the economy and parallel changes in the general purchasing behavior of consumers.

Another concern, however, is that liberal recognition policies are often associated with questionable management behavior. Consider the case of Datapoint, Inc., a Texas-based manufacturer of office equipment and computers. Prior to the third quarter of fiscal 1982, Datapoint had recorded 39 consecutive quarters of record earnings. In the early 1980s, however, Datapoint responded to increasing market competition by doubling its salesforce and instituting a lucrative incentive system for its sales personnel. Like Topper, Datapoint utilized the industry-accepted practice of recognizing revenues at the point of shipment. Unfortunately for Datapoint and its shareholders, unscrupulous sales personnel exploited the company's accounting system by shipping unordered and unwanted equipment to Datapoint retail distributors as a means to achieve incentive system quotas. Further, to facilitate future product "sales," marketing personnel placed large, unjustified orders with the company's production division, thereby creating the appearance of significant demand for the company's products. In short, Datapoint was being bled of its cash to pay commissions to its sales personnel and to build and ship unordered inventory.

In large measure, this rip-off was possible because Datapoint recognized revenue at the point of shipment. An internal investigation by Datapoint's independent auditors, Peat, Marwick, Mitchell & Co., revealed that approximately $15 million in 1982 sales had been unjustified, and were subsequently reversed out against third quarter 1982 results. Following the investigtion, Datapoint's share price fell from a high of over $67 in 1981 to a low of $11 in 1982—a decline of over $56 per share.

In another recent case, the SEC charged Stauffer Chemical Co. with overstating its 1982 earnings by $31.1 million as a result of improperly ac-

---

[9] For more information on the Topper Toy case, the interested reader is referred to E. K. Littrell, "Toying with Disclosure—A Christmas Parable." *Management Accounting* (September, 1980).

counting for certain product sales and for changes in its inventory valuation procedures.[10] Stauffer relies on agricultural chemical products for more than half of its total earnings, and when faced with a depressed market in 1982, the company allegedly initiated a plan to accelerate sales of certain products to its retail dealers. According to the SEC complaint, Stauffer offered its dealers special incentives to purchase goods during the fourth quarter of 1982, and as a consequence, enabled the company to book $72 million in revenues that ordinarily would not have been recognized until the first quarter of 1983.

The SEC charged that Stauffer enticed the early purchases by offering 100 percent refunds on any unsold products taken in 1982. By the Spring of 1983, Stauffer had refunded nearly 40 percent of its 1982 agricultural chemical sales. The SEC charged that, under the guaranteed refund program, product sales were effectively consignment sales, which shouldn't have been recognized as revenue in 1982.[11]

Fraudulent Revenues

While front-end loading is the most common form of revenue manipulation, the creation of fraudulent or fictitious revenues is also a concern for financial statement analysts. The most notorious case of this involved the Equity Funding Corporation of America (EFCA), a mutual fund and insurance sales company. From 1964 through 1973, EFCA falsely recorded receivables and fee income from mutual fund shares to nonexistent customers. A subsidiary of EFCA, the Equity Funding Life Insurance Company (EFLIC), also falsely recorded receivables and fee income from insurance policies written to insure the fraudulent mutual fund loans (i.e., receivables) issued by EFCA. By 1973, the value of the fictitious assets created from these transactions amounted to over $185 million; and, in April of 1973, EFCA filed for bankruptcy.

Several aspects of the Equity Funding scandal make it noteworthy. First, it was one of the earliest cases of recorded transactions involving nonexistent customers, and thus the scam involved not only the creation of ficti-

---

[10] L. E. Wynter, "Stauffer Profit Overstated in '82, SEC Says in Suit," *The Wall Street Journal* (August 14, 1984).

[11] In another case of front-end loading, the SEC charged AM International, Inc. in 1985 with issuing false and misleading financial statements for fiscal year 1980. According to the complaint, AM International offered favorable terms to certain foreign distributors, effectively transforming some sales into consignment sales that should not have been recognized as revenue in 1980. The SEC also charged that AM International routinely kept its books open after the end of each month in order to record revenues on late shipments. See T. E. Ricks, "AM International Ex-Aide Agrees to SEC Settlement," *The Wall Street Journal* (April 13, 1988).

tious accounting data, but also fraudulent customer documentation (e.g., names, dates and place of birth, employment records, medical histories, and even deaths and death certificates). Second, it extended beyond the operations of EFCA, in that EFLIC effectively sold the fraudulent insurance policies to legitimate reinsurance companies. Third, the deception lasted for nearly a decade, thereby revealing some of the inadequacies of generally accepted auditing practice of that era. Indeed, an important outcome of the Equity Funding scandal was the revision of many generally accepted auditing procedures.[12]

Since Equity Funding, the financial community has witnessed a number of similar revenue-based deceptions, such as the Stirling Homex Corporation case involving sales of modular homes, the National Student Marketing case involving sales of marketing services by college students, as well as such contemporary examples as Crazy Eddie, Inc. and Miniscribe, Inc. (see Chapter 1). Given the continued presence of these questionable and/or fraudulent revenue recognition practices, the analyst must be capable of identifying the various warning signs associated with these practices.

It is instructive to note that in each of the above mentioned scandals, the level of credit, and not cash, sales was manipulated. In essence, it is far more difficult to "manage" cash sales than it is to "manage" credit sales. Thus, when assessing the quality of a company's reported earnings, the analyst should focus particular attention on a company's credit sales. There are several key factors that should always be considered in this regard: (1) the cash flows from operations (and, in particular, the cash collections from revenues and receivables), and (2) the average receivable collection period.

Although cash collection will naturally lag a related credit sale, particularly during a period of sudden or rapid growth, the growth in cash flows should, within 30 to 60 days for most companies, begin to track any growth in credit sales. Where a growth in cash collections fails to eventually parallel a growth in recorded sales, one of several factors may be indicated: (1) a material change in the credit-granting policies of the company, usually involving a reduction in the company's credit standards; (2) a change in the method of recognizing revenue, usually involving a switch to a more liberal revenue recognition approach; or (3) a problem, and possibly a deception, involving the existing revenue recognition approach. In our opinion, each of these factors indicates a lower quality of reported revenues, although there is rarely sufficient information in published financial statements to determine just which factor is present.

The *receivables collection period*, on the other hand, refers to the average number of days that an account (or note) receivable is outstanding be-

---

[12] The interested reader is referred to the American Institute of Certified Public Accountants, *Report of the Special Committee on Equity Funding*, (AICPA, 1975).

fore cash is collected. A widely accepted measure of this asset-based quality indicator is:

$$\text{Receivable Collection Period} = 365 \text{ days} \times \frac{\text{Average Balance in Accounts Receivables}}{\text{Net Credit Sales for the period}}$$

In general, the larger the average collection period in days, the lower the quality of the receivables and/or the credit-granting policies followed by a company. When comparing this ratio over time, however, it is always important to remember that because of seasonal fluctuations, comparisons for similar time periods (i.e., first quarter 1990 versus first quarter 1991) are most effective.

The analyst should note that there is a one-to-one correspondence between credit sales and receivables, and thus it is possible to evaluate the quality of revenues on the income statement by investigating the quality of receivables on the balance sheet.[13] Thus, if a company's credit-granting policies are substantially unchanged, the receivable collection period should remain relatively stable, even in a period of substantial growth via credit sales. Hence, where the collection period is substantially extended in duration, concern over the revenue recognition approach and the quality of revenues (and receivables) may be warranted.[14]

Consider, for example, the case of Stirling Homex Corporation, a manufacturer of modular housing. In 1970, the company went public, and the financial statements presented as of July 31, 1970, revealed that the average receivable collection period was a lengthy 246 days. According to an SEC lawsuit, Stirling Homex recorded fictitious revenues totalling $27.7 million (or 75 percent of total recorded revenues) during fiscal year 1971. The July 31, 1971, financial statements revealed that the receivable collection period had grown by an astonishing 41 percent to approximately 348 days. In addition, an analysis of the cash flows from operations (not reported by the company) revealed that while Stirling Homex reported accrual net earnings in excess of $3.1 million, the underlying cash flows from operations exceeded negative $19 million.[15]

For analysts uncertain of their analytical abilities with respect to cash

---

[13] Accounts and notes receivable are important to the analyst not only because of their relation to sales, but also because they constitute an important source of working capital and liquidity. Suffice it to say at this time that if the quality of revenues is low, by definition the quality of receivables will also be low, and consequently the levels of working capital and liquidity will be in doubt. Receivable valuation is considered in detail in Chapter 5.

[14] T. O'glove writes in *The Quality of Earnings* (Free Press, 1987) that one of the two most revealing indicators of the quality of a company's earnings is the receivable turnover ratio (i.e., accounts receivable/credit sales), a measure imbedded in the receivable collection period.

flows, it is noteworthy that the FASB adopted SFAS 95, effective for fiscal years ending after December 15, 1988, which requires the inclusion of a statement of cash flows in audited financial statements. Thus, even for the analyst with few analytical skills, cash flow data is currently readily available in audited financial statements. The development of a statement of cash flows, and the topic of cash flows, is discussed in detail in Chapter 11.

As a concluding observation, it may appear that public companies only overstate their reported revenues and earnings. This, however, is not necessarily the case. In 1979, for example, the H. J. Heinz Co. revealed that certain of its senior employees had engaged in a profit-juggling scheme to constrain the level of reported profits.[16] The company disclosed that certain officials had improperly accounted for sales and prepaid expenses, causing as much as $8.5 million in profits to be transferred into 1979 from prior years. According to Heinz executives, the intent of the profit-switching was to "smooth out earnings increases to create the appearance of consistent, orderly growth."[17] The understatement of earnings is also commonly observed among private companies, typically through an understatement of ending inventory. Private companies, unlike public companies, rarely keep multiple sets of accounting records, and available financial statements usually reflect their desire to minimize taxable income.

Conclusions

This chapter focused on assessing the quality of reported revenues, and by extension, net income. It was noted that the quality of revenues could be evaluated in the context of two types of risk: (1) risk that the revenues were booked too early and thus that a final sale would not be consummated; and (2) risk that, once consummated, the sale would not produce the anticipated level of cash inflows. For most companies, the first type of risk can be minimized by using a conservative recognition policy—one that delays recognition until a final consumer has been identified, until substantial performance has been completed, and until any refund or return period has expired. Where a less conservative policy is followed, risk can be minimized

---

[15] The interested reader is referred to the "Stirling Homex Corporation" case by M. E. Barrett and K. R. Ferris, American Graduate School of International Management (Glendale, Arizona).

[16] T. Petzinger, "Heinz Discloses Profit-Switching at Units Was Much Broader Than First Realized," *The Wall Street Journal* (September 13, 1979).

[17] In another case of profits deferral, Firestone Tire and Rubber Co. pleaded guilty in 1980 to federal charges of defrauding the IRS of approximately $12 million in taxable income earned between 1966 and 1971, but not reported until 1972-1973. According to U.S. attorneys, Firestone hid the profits for use in lean years. See G. Getschow, "Slick Accounting Ploys Help Many Companies Improve Their Income," *The Wall Street Journal* (June 20,1980).

by establishing a sufficient reserve for sales returns. The second type of risk (i.e., cash collection risk) can be minimized by adopting sound credit-granting policies and by establishing an appropriate reserve for uncollectible accounts.

Where either type of risk is high, both the quality of revenues and the quality of receivables will be low, and the expected cash flows from operations in jeopardy. Evidence regarding these risks can be obtained by:

1. Reviewing the "Summary of Significant Accounting Policies" adopted by management in the preparation of the financial statements. This footnote can provide the analyst with information concerning just how and when revenues are being recognized. Hopefully, the adopted method will be an industry-accepted practice, and where it is not, the analyst should investigate whether special circumstances exist to warrant deviation from industry norms.

2. Comparing the cash flows from operations (and cash collections from sales) with sales revenue or net income. While there is always a lag between the growth in credit sales (and earnings) and the subsequent growth in cash flows, unless the credit-granting policies of a company have changed, the lag period should not exceed 30 to 60 days; and, following that period, the growth in operating cash flows should mirror the prior period's growth in sales. Where the lag period exceeds 60 days, the analyst is cautioned to investigate why.

3. Examining such asset-based quality indicators as the average receivable collection period. This ratio indicates the average time required to collect an outstanding receivable, and can provide important insights regarding not only the quality of receivables and the quality of the credit-granting policies followed by a company, but also the quality of its revenue recognition policy.

While most deceptive reporting situations involve the manipulation of revenues and receivables, the analyst is not without tools to help identify the presence of such reporting problems. Even where a deception does not exist, but where a company is merely using aggressive financial reporting practices, the analyst should be equipped to assess the degree of risk exposure of a company's revenues.

CHAPTER THREE

The Cost of Operations

This chapter focuses on the expense side of the income statement, with the exception of income taxes which are examined separately in Chapter 4. In this chapter, we consider the two principal expense items composing the cost of operations—the cost of goods sold and depreciation/amortization. In addition, we examine one of the principal expense-side reporting abuses, namely the rear-end loading of expenses.

The analyst's task as it relates to the analysis of expenses is essentially the reverse of that involving revenues. With respect to revenues, we saw that the principal tendency of most companies was to overstate the level of earned revenues, and thus the analyst was faced with the problem of assessing by how much revenues might be overstated. On the expense side, the problem is just the opposite—companies tend to understate the level of expenses incurred. For most companies, the analyst can view the level of reported expenses as a minimum estimate of the actual level of expenses incurred. And thus, the problem faced by the analyst is to determine to what extent the reported expenses might be underestimated. Thus, in regards to expense recognition, the "quality" of reported earnings and assets can be assessed with respect to the extent of understatement of expenses, and the parallel resulting overstatement of assets.

Cost of Goods Sold

For many companies, the cost of goods sold is the largest income statement deduction; consequently, it is important that the analyst understand how this figure is arrived at. A second aspect of this expense is its balance sheet counterpart, namely "inventory" or the cost of goods not sold. Inventory on the balance sheet is frequently the largest single current asset, and in some cases, the largest single asset account. Thus, how the cost of goods sold is determined affects not only a company's earnings, but also the level of its current assets, total assets, working capital, and liquidity. Indeed, the effects of inventory valuation problems can be quite pervasive.

To help illustrate the analytical issues associated with the cost of goods sold, we examine inventory data from Lakeside Enterprises, Inc. Apart from disguising the name of the company, changing the figures, and providing details about inventory purchases normally not available to the analyst, the case is drawn entirely from published financial reports. Before considering the Lakeside data, a brief overview of the various alternative inventory costing methods is in order.

Inventory Costing Methods

The valuation of inventory, and hence the calculation of the cost of goods sold, is effectively a three-stage process (see Exhibit 3.1). Stage one involves determining the total cost of goods available for sale during a given period. This stage may simply involve adding the cost of the beginning inventory with the cost of any purchases for the period, as in the case of a merchandising company, or alternatively, involve a complex cost accumulation procedure, as in the case of a manufacturing company.

One important valuation issue at this stage is whether fixed manufacturing overhead costs are treated as a *product cost*, and hence included in the cost of goods available for sale, or instead are treated as a *period cost*, and hence deducted against earnings as a selling and administrative expense. The former view is called *absorption* or *full costing*, whereas the latter is called *direct* or *variable costing*. The analyst should note that variable costing produces a lower cost of goods sold and a lower balance sheet value for ending inventory than does absorption costing. For audited financial statements, only absorption costing is permitted under GAAP.

Once the management accounting system has determined the total cost of finished goods available for sale, the value of those goods actually sold can be calculated. Stage two requires, however, that corporate manage-

Exhibit 3.1

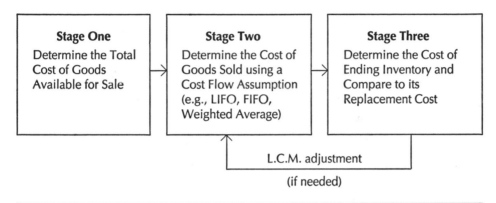

INVENTORY VALUATION AND THE CALCULATION
OF COST OF GOODS SOLD

Stage One	**Stage Two**	**Stage Three**
Determine the Total Cost of Goods Available for Sale	Determine the Cost of Goods Sold using a Cost Flow Assumption (e.g., LIFO, FIFO, Weighted Average)	Determine the Cost of Ending Inventory and Compare to its Replacement Cost

L.C.M. adjustment
(if needed)

ment first select from the GAAP menu an inventory costing approach, such as Last-in, First-out (LIFO), First-in, First-out (FIFO), or a weighted-average cost approach. The purpose of these methods is to systematically assign cost values from the inventory of goods available for sale to the units actually sold. This decision is necessary because unless all inventory and labor costs are stable over time and unless the labor force is uniformly efficient, cost variances will occur even amongst homogeneous, mass-produced goods. Thus, some systematic approach must be adopted to assign these varying costs to units as they are sold.

With few exceptions, most products actually flow from the inventory warehouse to the consumer on a FIFO basis. Nonetheless, for financial statement purposes, management may select any one of the GAAP costing methods. In short, the accounting flow of costs need not parallel the physical flow of goods. While a company should consistently apply whichever cost method it adopts, it is acceptable for a company, for example, to use LIFO for one inventory item, FIFO for another, and weighted average for a third.[1]

Management's decision to select one costing method over another may be based on a variety of considerations. If inventory costs are rising, LIFO will assign the most recent, higher inventory costs to the cost of goods sold, and consequently the older, lower costs to the inventory remaining on the

---

[1] Another inventory costing approach is known as the *specific identification* method. This method is very costly and time-consuming, and is used only in those rare cases where the finished product is relatively unique, few in number, and expensive. Where a product is relatively homogeneous and produced in large quantities, it is normally cost-beneficial to utilize LIFO, FIFO, or weighted average.

balance sheet at the end of the period. Thus, using LIFO results in a higher cost of goods sold, but lower net earnings. If management is concerned about maximizing the level of reported profit, they would surely want to avoid the LIFO method. But, while LIFO does result in lower net earnings, if it is also used for tax purposes, the level of taxes payable to the IRS will be minimized and the company's cash flows preserved.[2]

The FIFO method, on the other hand, assigns the older, yet lower inventory costs to the cost of goods sold, and the more recent, higher costs to the ending inventory on the balance sheet. Thus, using FIFO results in a lower cost of goods sold, but higher net earnings. If management is concerned about the level of reported earnings and the level of reported inventory, FIFO will be the method of preference. Unfortunately, if used for taxes, the higher FIFO earnings will also be associated with higher income taxes and a reduced cash flow position.

The weighted-average method, as its name implies, makes no cost flow assumption whatsoever, and instead assigns a cost value to each unit sold based on the average of all prices available in inventory, weighted by the number of units available at each respective price. By virtue of the averaging process inherent in this method, it produces a cost of goods sold figure that will effectively lie between the extremes of FIFO cost of goods sold and LIFO cost of goods sold. Similarly, the balance sheet values for ending inventory under weighted-average will also fall between the extremes of LIFO and FIFO values. (Although extremely large fluctuations in product cost from one period to the next may force the average cost to be higher or lower than FIFO or LIFO-calculated cost, these exceptions are so rare that the analyst may ignore this possibility.)

If inventory costs are stable, it makes very little difference which of these methods is adopted since each will yield an equivalent cost of goods sold and ending inventory. However, the faster inventory prices rise or fall, the greater will be the difference between these methods. Exhibit 3.2 summarizes the effects of these costing methods on reported earnings, assets, and cash flows.

Let us now return to the valuation process depicted in Exhibit 3.1. Once a cost flow method is adopted and the cost of goods sold calculated, the third and final stage (i.e., determining the cost of ending inventory on the balance sheet) will be predetermined. For most companies, stage 3 will simply be the residual of stage 1 minus stage 2. However, for a small minority of companies, approximately 5 to 10 percent of those companies listed on

---

[2] There are few examples where an accounting method used for IRS purposes must also be used for financial statement purposes. One exception, however, involves the LIFO method. According to the *Revenue Act of 1939*, if a taxpayer elects to use the LIFO method for tax purposes, the taxpayer may not use any method other than LIFO in financial reports to shareholders.

the New York and American stock exchanges, the third stage involves yet one final aspect—a comparison of the cost of the ending inventory (calculated using LIFO, FIFO, or weighted-average) with its replacement cost.

This final task in the inventory valuation process involves the application of the *Lower of Cost or Market* method, or L.C.M. The purpose of L.C.M. is to insure that the calculated cost of ending inventory does not exceed its underlying economic value, namely the cost to replace it by purchase or production. (Note that the word "market" in L.C.M. refers to the input market price of the good rather than its output market or selling price.)

For most companies, inventory costs are strictly increasing, and consequently the calculated cost of inventory will always be less than its replacement cost. However, if inventory costs are strictly declining or are in a state of fluctuation, the calculated cost of ending inventory may exceed its replacement cost. Under these circumstances, L.C.M. would require that the calculated cost figure be adjusted downward to reflect the lower replacement cost. Where the L.C.M. adjustment is immaterial in amount, it is usually added to the cost of goods sold.[3] Where the L.C.M. adjustment is material in amount, a separate loss account may be disclosed on the income statement.

Analytical Issues

There are a number of special issues that analysts should consider when evaluating the cost of goods sold and ending inventory. First, it is essential to remember that the various alternative inventory costing approaches are merely cost allocation methods. Each requires that a different assumption be made regarding the flow of costs from the inventory stockpile to the cost of goods sold; and none attempts to pattern the flow of costs after either the actual cash or product flows. Where inventory prices vary, we have seen (in Exhibit 3.2) that these methods produce very different effects on the balance sheet and the income statement. Consequently, they will also produce (possibly substantially) different effects on the typical balance sheet and income statement ratios used by analysts.

Consider, for example, Exhibit 3.3, which presents the income statement and selected financial ratios for two economically identical compa-

---

[3] The accounting journal entry to record an immaterial L.C.M. adjustment is:

Debit: Cost of Goods Sold	$X	
Credit: Allowance for Decline in value of Ending Inventory		$X

The allowance for decline in value is a contra-asset account much like the allowance for uncollectible accounts. This account is rarely, if ever, disclosed in published financial statements. Instead, the inventory account is reported net of the allowance account, with the original cost of the inventory reported in parentheses. For example:

Inventory, valued at L.C.M. (Cost $XXX)	$XX

Exhibit 3.2

A COMPARISON OF THE EFFECTS OF ALTERNATIVE INVENTORY COSTING METHODS

If inventory costs are rising...

LIFO (results in)	FIFO (results in)
• Higher Cost of Goods Sold	• Lower Cost of Goods Sold
• Lower NIBT	• Higher NIBT
• Lower income taxes	• Higher income taxes
• Higher cash flows (if used for taxes)	• Lower cash flows (if used for taxes)
• Lower balance sheet value in inventory	• Higher balance sheet value in inventory

(If inventory costs are falling, the effects will be reversed, and if inventory costs are stable, there will be no difference between the methods.)

nies—FIFO Company and LIFO Company—which differ only in regard to the accounting method used to value the cost of goods sold and ending inventory. A review of this financial data reveals that since inventory costs are rising, FIFO Company appears to be financially better off than the LIFO Company—earnings are higher by $7.8 million, the liquidity indicators of working capital and the current ratio are higher, the borrowing capacity (as measured by the debt-to-equity ratio) is greater, and the profitability indicators of return on sales, return on equity, and return on assets are superior. Only the inventory turnover ratio appears to be better for the LIFO Company. But are these indicators really depicting economic reality?

Holding the question of taxes aside, the answer to our question is a resounding "No!" The companies are economically identical, in spite of what the financial ratios indicate. In effect, the different cost allocation assumptions inherent in LIFO and FIFO mask the real economic performance of the two companies, which is equivalent. If we now add the dimension of taxes and assume that each company uses the same costing approach for both IRS purposes and financial statement purposes, then our conclusion is even more startling: the LIFO company is actually superior in economic performance to the FIFO Company because greater cash flow is preserved in the LIFO Company due to the lower taxable earnings. Thus, contrary to our financial indicators, the LIFO Company may actually be a superior credit and investment risk.[4]

A second analytical consideration concerns those companies using the LIFO method. One adverse outcome of LIFO concerns the quality of the

Exhibit 3.3 ———————————————————————————————————

INVENTORY COSTING METHODS AND FINANCIAL STATEMENT ANALYSIS

Presented below are the income statements and selected financial ratios for two companies that are identical in every respect except with regard to the method of inventory costing and the cost of goods sold:

	FIFO Company	LIFO Company
Sales	$75,000,000	$75,000,000
Less: Cost of Goods Sold	(34,500,000)	(42,300,000)
	$40,500,000	$32,700,000
Less: Other operating expenses	(15,000,000)	(15,000,000)
Net income before tax (NIBT)	$25,500,000	$17,700,000
Selected financial ratios:		
Earnings per share	$ 2.55	$ 1.77
Current ratio	1.67:1	1.57:1
Working capital	$10,800,000	$ 3,000,000
Inventory turnover	2:1	3:1
Debt-to-equity ratio	1:5.17	1:4.91
Return on Assets	10.8%	8.0%
Return on Equity	14%	12.1%
Return on Sales	34%	24%

inventory valuation reported on the balance sheet. Under LIFO, the most recent inventory costs are assigned to the cost of goods sold, while older inventory costs are assigned to the ending inventory on the balance sheet. When inflation is present, the cost values reflected in the LIFO inventory account may be substantially understated relative to their actual replacement cost. Thus, not only will the LIFO inventory account be understated,

———————————————

[4] This discussion highlights a special issue for credit analysts. When evaluating a company against accepted ratio levels, FIFO Company will more likely exceed or satisfy those ratio levels than LIFO Company, making it appear as if the FIFO Company is a superior lending opportunity. In fact, holding tax considerations aside, the two companies are equivalent opportunities. When setting debt convenant ratios, the FIFO Company will more easily satisfy such ratios, suggesting that a standard ratio limit should not be applied to all companies, but rather the actual convenant ratio be established as a function of the accounting methods used by the company, and hence its ability to satisfy such covenant restrictions. See R. Reilly, "LIFO Adoption and a Firm's Ability to Meet Indenture Covenant Restrictions," *Credit and Financial Management* (September, 1982).

but also the level of working capital and such ratios as the current ratio which include the understated inventory account.

Concerned that LIFO inventory values may be substantially understated, the FASB and the SEC adopted a requirement in 1978 that audited financial statements using LIFO include in the inventory footnote a LIFO reserve figure. The *LIFO reserve* measures the difference between the current (or replacement) cost of ending inventory and its calculated LIFO cost. Thus, by adding the LIFO reserve to the LIFO cost of inventory, the analyst can obtain a more accurate assessment of the fair market value (i.e., current cost) of the ending inventory. Similarly, a more realistic value for working capital and the current ratio may also be determined. Finally, for those analysts interested in comparing LIFO earnings to FIFO earnings, the LIFO reserve is a useful tool for such comparisons. By adding the change in the LIFO reserve from one year to the next to the NIBT under LIFO, the analyst can approximate the FIFO NIBT.[5]

A third analytical concern, also relating to companies using the LIFO method, involves LIFO base stock liquidations. A *LIFO liquidation* occurs when the inventory levels of a LIFO company fall below a base level, normally the beginning inventory, causing old, understated inventory cost values to be charged into the LIFO cost of goods sold. When this occurs, the level of NIBT will be artificially inflated by the lower cost values charged into cost of goods sold.[6] This increase in NIBT is purely a "paper profit" in that the cash flows from operations are not equivalently increased. In fact, the cash flows from operations are actually decreased under a LIFO liquidation in that the paper profits are subject to income taxation. Consequently, in the eyes of most analysts, LIFO liquidation profits are of questionable quality.

To gain some appreciation for the magnitude of these potential paper profits, consider Exhibit 3.4, which presents survey data for the oil and gas

---

[5] The LIFO reserve may be thought of as an approximation of the difference between LIFO ending inventory and FIFO ending inventory. It is also an approximation of the cumulative difference between NIBT under FIFO and NIBT under LIFO. Thus, by identifying the change in the LIFO reserve from one year to the next, yearly LIFO income statements can be restated to approximate the FIFO income statements. In this way, an analyst can determine the "earnings reserve" that a LIFO company has hidden on its balance sheet.

Another way of interpreting the LIFO reserve is as a barometer of the effects of inflation on the inventory of a company. Obviously, if inflation is significant for a given company, the size of the LIFO reserve will be large and growing rapidly, a fact we will see illustrated shortly in the Lakeside Enterprises case. As a general observation, it is worth noting that inflation in inventory prices is only a problem if the inflated prices cannot be passed on to consumers, and the LIFO reserve is effectively a measure of the profit reduction due to such price increases.

[6] Since 1976, for example, U.S. Steel has reported $1.7 billion in LIFO liquidation profits as a direct consequence of the company's shrinking of its steel business (See F. Worthy, "Manipulating Profits: How It's Done, *Fortune*, June 25, 1984).

Exhibit 3.4 _____

LIFO LIQUIDATION PROFITS: OIL INDUSTRY SURVEY

Company	NIAT 1981 *	Percent of 1981 NIAT	NIAT 1982 *	Percent of 1982 NIAT
Exxon	$ 294	6%	$ 1,092	20%
Mobil	179	8	193	14
Texaco	454	20	503	39
Standard Oil of California	100	4	397	29
Standard Oil of Indiana	71	4	110	6
Gulf	194	16	360	40
Atlantic Richfield	190	11	120	7
Phillips	14	2	72	11
Tenneco	50	6	24	3
Amerada Hess	FIFO		FIFO	
American Petrofina	25	34	19	35

* Figures are in millions of dollars.

Source: K. R. Ferris and M. E. Barrett, "Assessing the Quality of Reported Earnings in the Oil and Gas Industry: Some Guidance for Credit Analysis," *The Journal of Commercial Bank Lending* (February, 1984).

_____

industry from 1981 and 1982. Beginning in the early 1980s, the oil industry experienced a world-wide excess supply. In response to this over-supply condition, major domestic oil companies reduced the level of their base stock of oil inventory. Since all of these companies (with the exception of Amerada Hess) utilized LIFO costing, they experienced, to varying degrees, LIFO-liquidation profits.

Exhibit 3.4 reveals the percentage of 1981 and 1982 net earnings after tax (NIAT) represented by the liquidation profits. At the extreme, over 16 percent of 1981 NIAT and over 40 percent of 1982 NIAT of the Gulf Corporation were LIFO liquidation profits. When a company experiences a LIFO liquidation, it is required to disclose this fact and the magnitude of the liquidation on its net income in its footnotes. Thus, by carefully reading the inventory footnote, the analyst should be able to ascertain whether a LIFO liquidation occurred and to what extent reported profits were inflated by the liquidation profits.

As a final point, the analyst should note that LIFO liquidations largely occur in the context of *unit* or *quantity* LIFO. Because of the extensive clerical effort associated with maintaining unit LIFO cost data for hundreds, and perhaps thousands of different inventory items each year, many companies find it cost-advantageous to use *dollar-value* LIFO. Under dollar-value LIFO, cost data is maintained for "pools" of inventory items, rather than for individual inventory items. One positive outcome of this approach is that the cost decreases experienced by some inventory items in a pool will be offset by cost increases in others, consequently decreasing the likelihood of LIFO liquidation profits within a given pool.[7]

Dollar-value LIFO, however, is not without its own limitations. In 1984, for example, the SEC charged Stauffer Chemical Company with overstating its 1982 earnings, in part by improperly structuring its dollar-value LIFO "puddles."[8] The SEC alleged that Stauffer selectively tailored its inventory pools, occasionally into very small inventory groups called puddles, in order to maximize the effect of certain product LIFO liquidations. The effect of the puddling, according to the SEC, was to increase 1982 earnings by $16.5 million.

To resolve the problem, the SEC required Stauffer to recombine eight of its 288 inventory pools, thereby restating (i.e., lowering) its reported earnings.

An Illustration: Lakeside Enterprises

Lakeside Enterprises is a manufacturer of parts used mainly in lawn mowers and other small machines.[9] For many years, the company manufactured these parts in several states across the U.S. Early in 1984, however, one of the company's principal customers announced its intentions to buy machines completely ready for assembly from Japan. The news forced Lakeside to close its Kentucky plant and to dispose of its inventories at that location.

Several years earlier, in 1981, Lakeside had changed its method of accounting for inventory from FIFO to LIFO. The footnote to the 1981 financial statements detailing the method change is presented in Exhibit 3.5.

The company's 1984 annual report, which appeared in early 1985, disclosed that the closure of the Kentucky facility had precipitated a dramatic deterioration in business, accompanied by a significant liquidation of inventories. Exhibit 3.6 presents the footnotes to the 1984 financial statements describing these facts. Selected financial data for 1981 through 1984 are

---

[7] Unlike unit or quantity LIFO, which determines actual increases and decreases in the quantity of inventory on hand, dollar-value LIFO relies on price indices of the entire pool of inventory to determine inventory quantity changes. For more information, the interested reader is referred to Chapter 7 of E. Brownlee, K. Ferris, and M. Haskins, *Corporate Financial Reporting* (BPI/Irwin, 1990).

[8] G. Smith, "Puddle Muddle," *Forbes* (October 8, 1984).

[9] For more information, the interested reader is referred to M. F. van Breda and K. R. Ferris, "Lakeside Enterprises," Cox School of Business, Southern Methodist University (Dallas, Texas).

Exhibit 3.5 _____

LAKESIDE ENTERPRISES
FOOTNOTE DATA FROM 1981 ANNUAL REPORT

NOTE 2—CHANGE IN INVENTORY VALUATION METHOD

In 1981, the company adopted the last-in, first-out (LIFO) method of determining costs for substantially all of its U.S. inventories. In prior years, inventory values were principally computed under the lower of cost or market, first-in, first-out (FIFO) method.

The effect of the change on the operating results for 1981 was to reduce net earnings after tax by $4,714, or 25 cents per share. The inventory balance at December 31, 1981, would have been $7,365 higher if inventory costs had continued to be determined principally under FIFO, rather than LIFO.

It was not practical to determine prior year effects of retroactive LIFO application.

Exhibit 3.6 _____

LAKESIDE ENTERPRISES
FOOTNOTE DATA FROM 1984 ANNUAL REPORT

NOTE 1—SUMMARY OF SIGNIFICANT ACCOUNTING POLICIES

Inventories are stated at the lower of cost or market value. Cost of inventories is determined by the last-in, first-out method [LIFO] which is less than current cost by $87,609 and $55,592 at December 28, 1983, and December 30, 1984, respectively.

During 1984, inventory quantities were reduced resulting in a liquidation of LIFO inventory quantities carried at lower costs prevailing in prior years as compared with the 1984 cost of production. As a result, income before taxes was increased by $62,310, equivalent to $2.10 per share after applicable income taxes, of which $26,190 before tax, equivalent to $0.88 per share after applicable income taxes, was reflected in cost of product sold and the balance was included as a reduction of the shutdown/disposal provision (see Note 6).

NOTE 6—SHUTDOWN/DISPOSAL PROVISION

In the third quarter of 1984, a provision was recorded for the closing of the Kentucky facilities which are to be sold or otherwise disposed of. The after-tax provision of $55,595 is equivalent to $2.93 per common share and covers estimated losses on the disposition of property, plant, and equipment, and inventories and employee severance and other costs. Net sales or products from these facilities included in consolidated sales totaled $92,465 in 1982, $121,012 in 1983, and $147,554 in 1984.

Exhibit 3.7 —————————————————————————————

LAKESIDE ENTERPRISES
SELECTED FINANCIAL DATA

	1981	1982	1983	1984
Revenue	$ 1,053,422	$ 1,236,092	$ 1,421,526	$ 1,277,107
Cost of Sales	797,232	958,210	1,085,134	971,550
Gross margin	256,190	277,882	336,392	305,557
Selling and Administration	192,775	207,332	209,884	212,567
Loss on write-off (net)	-0-	-0-	-0-	55,595
Income tax	24,629	25,398	45,543	33,476
Net income	43,785	45,151	80,965	3,919
Inventory (per ending balance sheet)	$ 147,304	$ 208,948	$ 232,006	$ 111,904

presented in Exhibit 3.7, and details of the company's inventory costs appear in Exhibit 3.8.

FIFO-LIFO Switch. In 1981, Lakeside switched from FIFO inventory costing to unit LIFO inventory costing, and as Exhibit 3.5 details, this accounting change did not require a retroactive restatement of prior year results. Had the accounting method change been in the opposite direction (i.e., LIFO to FIFO), a retroactive adjustment for the cumulative effect of the change would have been required, and reported as a prior-period adjustment to Lakeside's retained earnings as of December 31, 1980.

Not surprisingly, the effect of the accounting change was to lower the level of reported 1981 profits by $7,365 before tax, and $4,714 after tax. (Note: These figures are restated to disguise the company's actual results.) Using the data in Exhibit 3.8, and assuming a periodic recordkeeping system,[10] these 1981 profit differences can be estimated as follows:

———————————————

[10] Lakeside did not in fact use a periodic system, and instead used the perpetual approach. Under the *periodic* approach, the cost of goods sold is determined at the end of each accounting period following a physical count of the inventory on hand. Under the *perpetual* approach, the cost of goods sold is determined for each and every sale based on the inventory available at that time. To simplify our illustration, however, we have adopted a periodic assumption.

Exhibit 3.8 ————————————————————————————————

LAKESIDE ENTERPRISES
INVENTORY COST AND UNIT SUMMARY

	No. of Units	Unit Cost	Total Cost
Beginning Inventory: 1981	60,000	$ 2.00	$ 120,000
Purchases in 1981: Lot #1	103,652	2.00	207,304
Lot #2	293,920	2.10	617,232
Total available	457,572		$ 944,536
Less: Sales in 1981	(383,920)		
Beginning Inventory: 1982	73,652		
Purchases in 1982: Lot #1	282,220	2.20	620,884
Lot #2	153,450	2.60	398,970
Total available	509,322		
Less: Sales in 1982	(407,650)		
Beginning Inventory: 1983	101,672		
Purchases in 1983: Lot #1	193,210	2.70	521,667
Lot #2	202,250	2.90	586,525
Total available	497,132		
Less: Sales in 1983	(386,920)		
Beginning Inventory: 1984	110,212		
Purchases in 1984: Lot #1	196,320	2.90	569,328
Lot #2	82,000	3.00	246,000
Total available	388,532		
Less: Sales in 1984	(332,580)		
Ending Inventory: 1984	55,952		

	LIFO Costing				FIFO Costing		
	Quantity	Unit Cost	Total Cost		Quantity	Unit Cost	Total Cost
				Beginning Inv.	60,000	@$2.00 =	$120,000
Lot #2	293,920	@$2.10 =	$617,232				
Lot #1	90,000	@ 2.00 =	180,000	Lot #1	103,652	@ 2.00 =	207,304
				Lot #2	220,268	@ 2.10 =	462,563
Cost of Goods Sold	383,920		$797,232		383,920		$789,867

1981 Difference = $7,365

	LIFO	FIFO
NIBT	$ 68,415	$ 75,780
NIAT (taxes @ 36%)	$ 43,785	$ 48,499

The difference of $7,365 between the LIFO and FIFO cost of goods sold is also manifested in the 1981 ending inventory reported on the balance sheet:

	LIFO	FIFO
Total cost of goods available for sale	$944,536	$944,536
Less: Cost of Goods Sold	(797,232)	(789,867)
Ending inventory	$147,304	$154,669

Difference=$7,365

These inventory costing differences affect not only the level of reported profits and the level of reported inventory values, but they also impact a number of significant financial ratios that investment and credit analysts frequently consider. For example, despite the fact that total sales ($1,053,422) are the same under either FIFO or LIFO, the return on sales ratio varies as a function of NIAT:

	LIFO	FIFO
	4.14%	4.58%

$$\text{Return on Sales} = \frac{\text{NIAT}}{\text{Net Revenues}}$$

The inventory turnover ratio will likewise vary, despite the fact that the actual inventory turnover was exactly the same under either inventory costing approach:

	LIFO	FIFO
	5.41 times	5.11 times

$$\text{Inventory Turnover} = \frac{\text{Cost of Goods Sold}}{\text{Ending Inventory}}$$

As a general observation, during a period of rising inventory prices, a company using FIFO inventory costing will result in: (1) higher net income, and consequently higher ratio values dependent on net income (e.g., return on sales, return of assets, return on equity, etc.); and (2) higher balance sheet inventory values, and consequently a higher working capital and higher ratio values dependent on inventory (e.g., current ratio), with one exception, the inventory turnover ratio. Thus, there is a tendency for financial statement analysts to prefer the investment and credit opportunities associated with FIFO-costed companies.

This preference would be wholly inappropriate if, as in the case of Lakeside Enterprise, the LIFO-costed company also used LIFO for tax purposes. In 1981, when Lakeside switched to LIFO costing for accounting purposes, it did so for tax purposes as well. Consequently, in 1981 alone, Lakeside saved $2,651 in taxes—cash that would now be available for debt repayment, dividends, or other corporate purposes. Thus, in spite of the apparent diminishment in Lakeside's financial condition in 1981, economically (i.e., from a cash flow perspective) the company was better off.

LIFO Reserve. Exhibit 3.6 reveals that the value of the LIFO reserve grew from $7,365 in 1981 to a high of $87,609 in 1983, reflecting the rather rapid increase in per unit inventory costs from $2.00 to $2.90 over this two year period. Since the LIFO reserve provides a good estimate of the pre-tax difference in net income resulting from using LIFO versus FIFO, we can estimate that the NIBT for Lakeside from year-end 1980 to year-end 1983 was approximately $87,609 less than it would have been had Lakeside continued using FIFO. However, while Lakeside's earnings were depressed by the inventory change, the company's actual cash flows for this same period were higher by $31,539 ($87,609 × .36, where Lakeside's effective tax rate is 36 percent).

In response to the loss of a major customer in 1984, Lakeside reduced the base level of its inventory. This was accomplished by cutting production and liquidating some of its previously existing inventory. According to note 1 in Exhibit 3.6, the effect of the LIFO inventory liquidation was to add $62,310 to NIBT. To see how this figure was arrived at, we again refer to Exhibits 3.7 and 3.8.

According to these exhibits, Lakeside began 1984 with 110,212 units on hand, valued at $232,006, with the following unit LIFO cost layers:

	Units		Unit Cost		Total Cost
1980 Layer	60,000	@	$2.00	=	$120,000
1981 Layer	13,652	@	2.00	=	27,304
1982 Layer	28,020	@	2.20	=	61,644
1983 Layer	8,540	@	2.70	=	23,058
	110,212				$232,006

By year-end, Lakeside reduced its base inventory from 110,212 units to only 55,952 units, a reduction of 54,260 units. Using the LIFO cost flow approach, the value of the liquidated units would have been:

8,540	@	$2.70	=	$ 23,058
28,020	@	2.20	=	61,644
13,652	@	2.00	=	27,304
4,048	@	2.00	=	8,096
54,260				$120,102

and the remaining 55,952 units valued at $111,904 ($232,006 – $120,102).

Relative to the current replacement cost of $3.00 per unit, the liquidation of the 54,260 units from beginning inventory added $42,678 to NIBT:

Replacement cost:	54,260	@	$3.00	=	$162,780
Less: actual LIFO cost					(120,102)
LIFO liquidation profit (1980-1983 layers)					$ 42,678

In addition, Lakeside assumed that a 1984 inventory layer had been created and liquidated:

Replacement cost:	196,320	@	$3.00	=	$588,960
Less: actual LIFO cost					(569,328)
LIFO liquidation profit (1984 layer)					$ 19,632

Thus, the aggregate increase in NIBT attributable to the LIFO liquidation was $62,310 ($42,678 + $19,632).

The analyst should note that while NIBT was increased by $62,310 as a result of the LIFO liquidation, the actual cash flows from operations did not experience a similar increase. In fact, the cash flows from operations were actually reduced by the additional income taxes due on the liquidation profits (i.e., $62,310 × .36 = $22,432). As a concluding observation, the analyst should note that in spite of the adverse cash flow effects associated with the LIFO liquidation profits, Lakeside remained in a superior cash flow position as a consequence of its FIFO-LIFO switch in 1981. Under FIFO, not only would Lakeside have encountered the $22,432 in additional taxes associated with the LIFO liquidation, but also the $31,539 in taxes effectively deferred by the LIFO methodology.

Conclusions

The accounting for cost of goods sold reveals that reported earnings, and ratios based thereon, can often be misleading. When inventory costs are rising, FIFO will yield higher reported earnings than will LIFO or the weighted-average method. From the lenders' or investors' perspective, however, higher earnings are not necessarily the most important performance criteria. Indeed, the level of cash flow is likely to be far more important to credit or investment analysts than are accrual earnings. Thus, when evaluating the financial health of a company, it is important to ascertain how the company is valuing its inventory for tax purposes, as well as financial statement purposes.

While it is always dangerous to make generalizations, particularly involving accounting methods, the following statement appears justified: during a period of rising prices, a company should utilize the LIFO inventory costing method for both taxes and financial statement purposes. Under these circumstances, not only will the cash flows of the company be preserved, but LIFO will also permit superior managerial decision making. In spite of these obvious advantages, some managers will nonetheless adopt the FIFO or weighted-average approach. Where this is the case, the analyst should investigate for any special circumstances (e.g., expiring tax credits) that might justify this inventory costing decision. Where no special circumstances exist, a lower quality of earnings may be implied.

Recall, however, that in regards to the balance sheet, FIFO will, in a period of rising prices, produce a more accurate valuation of ending inventory. LIFO, on the other hand, may yield a substantially understated inventory valuation. However, where LIFO is in use, the analyst should investigate the accompanying footnotes for the LIFO reserve, which will enable the analyst to obtain a truer picture of the current value of the ending inventory.

As a final issue, given that inventory prices may increase one year and decrease the next, the analyst may wonder about the ability of a company to periodically change its inventory costing method to obtain maximum benefits. From a financial reporting standpoint, the FASB and SEC place no constraints on accounting method changes by companies. So long as a company discloses the accounting method in use, and where appropriate, the effect of a method change on reported earning and assets, it is possible for a company to switch its method of inventory valuation every year. Naturally, the independent auditor will be required to so note these method changes in the auditor's report, but no other constraints exist. For tax purposes, however, before a company may change an accounting method, it must first apply and receive permission from the IRS; and in general, the IRS does not permit method changes on a frequent basis.

Depreciation and Amortization

Following the cost of goods sold and income taxes, the third largest deduction for operations is usually the depreciation and amortization expense.

Some manufacturing companies include depreciation and amortization in the cost of goods sold as a product cost. Where this practice is followed, the amount of depreciation and amortization will be separately revealed either in the footnotes or in the statement of cash flows.

Under accrual accounting, when a long-lived asset is purchased, its acquisition cost is prorated over its expected useful life. The purpose of the proration process is to match the cost of the asset with the revenues produced. In the case of fixed assets, such as property, plant, and equipment, the proration (or allocation) process is called *depreciation*. When the allocation process refers to intangible assets, such as patents, copyrights, or goodwill, the term *amortization* is used. When the allocation process refers to such natural resources as oil and gas, the term *depletion* is used. In spite of the variation in labels, the purpose of the allocation process is the same in each case: to match the acquisition cost of an asset with the revenues it produces.

Depreciation

When establishing a depreciation policy for an asset, a company must reach several decisions. First, it must select a depreciation method from the GAAP menu. Second, it must estimate the expected useful life of the asset. Third, it must estimate the expected residual value of the asset when it is retired from service with the company. Obviously, estimating the useful life of an asset and its expected future residual value is a difficult process, which consequently introduces some unintended (but inescapable) arbitrariness into the reported accounting results. Similarly, the decision to use one depreciation method over another is also an arbitrary decision, but one which has some fairly predictable accounting outcomes.

The most common GAAP depreciation methods include straight-line depreciation, accelerated depreciation, and production-based depreciation.

Straight-line depreciation assumes that the portion of the cost of an asset consumed in any period is constant. That is, independent of the quantity of units produced or the age of an asset, the depreciation deduction is fixed and is given by the following expression:[11]

Depreciation expense for a period = $1/n$ (Cost − Salvage Value), where

n = number of periods (usually months or years)
in the asset's expected useful life;

$1/n$ = depreciation rate per period;

Cost = acquisition value of the asset; and

Salvage value = value remaining at the end of
the asset's expected useful life.

Straight-line depreciation is clearly the method of preference for most companies. Relative to other depreciation methods, the straight-line approach yields a consistent, generally lower depreciation charge. Moreover, since the straight-line charge is constant over time, it facilitates the "smoothing" of reported earnings by those managers who believe that it is preferable to report stable earnings.

Accelerated depreciation, on the other hand, assumes that an asset is consumed faster in the early periods of its useful life than in the later periods. Presumably, an asset produces revenues more efficiently in these early periods, a view reinforced by the expectation that maintenance costs will be greater in the asset's later life. Consequently, under accelerated depreciation, large depreciation charges are deducted in the early periods, with relatively smaller deductions in later periods.

Two methods exemplify this approach: (1) the sum-of-the-years'-digits method, and (2) the declining balance method. The sum-of-the-years'-digits approach is calculated as follows:

Depreciation expense in a period = depreciation rate (Cost – Salvage Value), where

$$\text{depreciation rate} = n/s, n\text{-}1/s, n\text{-}2/s, \ldots, n\text{-}1/s;$$
$$n = \text{expected useful life; and}$$
$$s = \text{sum-of-the-years'-digits} = n(n+1)/2$$

Thus, for example, for an asset with a five year life, s = 15 and the depreciation rate would be 5/15, 4/15, 3/15, 2/15, 1/15, for years one through five, respectively.

For double-declining balance depreciation, the depreciation rate is twice the straight-line rate (i.e., $2 \times 1/n = 2/n$), and the depreciation expense is calculated as:

Depreciation expense in a period = 2/n (remaining asset book value).

Notice that in declining balance depreciation, the salvage value of the asset is ignored, and the rate of decline can be varied from a high of twice (or 200 percent) the straight-line rate to a low of one times (or 100 percent) the straight-line rate (i.e., $1/n$). Thus, for those firms preferring a less rapid write-off of an asset, a 150 percent declining balance (i.e., $1.5/n$) approach, for example, may be adopted.

Finally, production-based depreciation attempts to directly match the consumption of the asset with the units and revenues produced. This

---

[11] The accounting journal entry to record the depreciation expense under any GAAP method is:

    Debit: Depreciation expense $XX

      Credit: Accumulated Depreciation $XX

The "Accumulated Depreciation" account is an allowance (or reserve) account that is reported on the balance sheet as a deduction from the depreciable asset value. The cost of an asset less the accumulated depreciation balance is called the *book value* of the asset.

method cannot be used with all assets because of the difficulty of accurately estimating the total number of units to be produced over the expected useful life of an asset. Under this approach, the depreciation expense is calculated as:

Depreciation expense = R (Cost − Salvage Value), where R, the production ratio, is determined as follows:

$$R = \frac{\text{Units produced this period}}{\text{Total estimated lifetime production in units}}$$

In general, accelerated depreciation methods are considered to be more conservative than either straight-line depreciation or production-based depreciation. Consequently, in the eyes of many analysts, accelerated depreciation yields a higher quality of reported earnings and assets than either of the other methods.

Depreciation Policy Changes

As economic conditions change, companies frequently respond by changing their accounting policies. In the case of depreciation policy, such changes are typically manifested in either depreciation method changes or in depreciation estimate changes.

Consider, for example, the case of General Motors. In 1988, GM changed its estimate of the expected useful life of its production facilities, extending the life from 35 to 45 years. This estimate change added $790 million to GM's 1988 net income. In addition, GM revised the residual value assumption used for its leased cars, adding another $270 million to 1988 net income.

The use of accounting estimate changes to improve reported net income is not new to GM. In 1987, GM also revised (i.e., extended) the estimated lives of certain equipment and special tools, adding $2.55 to per share net income (out of $10.06 per share total).[12] In response to questioning by a *Wall Street Journal* writer in regard to GM's frequent use of accounting estimate changes to boost earnings, a GM spokesman replied that "each change has a rationale, many of which served to bring us more into line with the industry...we're not trying to hide anything at all."[13]

Consider also the case of Blockbuster Entertainment Corporation, the largest U.S. chain in video cassette rentals. During 1987, Blockbuster depreciated its rental videotapes on a straight-line basis over a nine month period.

---

[12] J. M. Schlesinger, "GM 3rd-Quarter Net Jumped as Change in Accounting Erased Operating Loss," *The Wall Street Journal* (October 25, 1987).

[13] J. M. Schlesinger, "GM Net Rose 18% in Quarter On Special Item," *The Wall Street Journal* (April 22, 1988).

Beginning in 1988, however, the company switched its videotape write-off policy to an accelerated method over 36 months. The net effect of these changes was to increase Blockbuster's 1988 earnings by approximately 20 percent.[14] Not surprisingly, in response to a Bear, Stearns & Co. report critical of the Blockbuster accounting, the company's stock price fell over 21 percent in just six days.

With respect to each of the above mentioned depreciation policy changes, the analyst should note that in spite of the increase in reported earnings, there was no parallel increase in operating cash flows. Further, since each of the changes resulted in an increase in net income, it is unlikely that any of the changes were also undertaken for tax purposes. Consequently, not only was there no increase in operating cash flows, the cash flows of each company were essentially unchanged. Thus, the effects of the accounting changes were limited to the accounting statements themselves. In effect, each change lowered the level of cost allocated to the current period, deferring those amounts to be deducted against future earnings. Thus, these policy changes constituted an implicit form of rear-end loading, to which we turn shortly.

Amortization

Amortization refers to the allocation of intangible asset costs against reported revenues. Unlike depreciation, there is one commonly utilized amortization approach—the straight-line method—although others are permitted.[15] In general, intangibles such as patents and copyrights are amortized over the lesser of their expected economic life or their legal life. Goodwill is an exception to this rule and may be amortized over periods not in excess of 40 years.[16]

If there is a quality-of-earnings concern with respect to amortization, it relates to the length of the amortization period. Given the uncertainty surrounding the useful life of an intangible, and the uncertainty associated with the revenue stream produced by intangible assets, most analysts prefer to see this asset category written off over a short period of time. An extreme view of this is found among lending institutions, which consider most intan-

---

[14] Bear, Stearns & Co., Inc., "Blockbuster: The Accountants Earn Their Pay," (May, 1989).

[15] Unlike depreciation, the accounting journal entry to record amortization expense does not involve the use of a reserve or allowance account:

| Debit: Amortization expense | $XX | |
| Credit: Intangible Asset | | $XX |

[16] Not all goodwill is subject to amortization. Under GAAP, goodwill acquired prior to 1971 is not subject to amortization; however, goodwill acquired in transactions after that date must be amortized against earnings.

gibles to be unacceptable collateral for loan commitments and explicitly exclude these assets in such covenant ratios as the debt-to-tangible net worth ratio. This view is justified on the grounds that the resale market for most intangible assets is limited or nonexistent.

Since the decision to amortize intangible assets over a short versus long period does not affect the operating cash flows of a company, the analyst can circumvent this issue by focusing on the cash flows from operations. This would be particularly important in those cases where the level of intangibles is large relative to total assets.

As a concluding observation, the IRS takes the position that only those intangibles (e.g., copyrights, patents, covenants-not-to-compete) with a defined legal life may be amortized for tax purposes. Thus, goodwill and other intangibles with indefinite lives (i.e., a franchise in perpetuity) are not tax-deductible.

Rear-end Loading

The principal accounting and reporting abuse associated with the expense-portion of the income statement involves the intentional understatement of current period expenses. A basic tenet of GAAP, commonly referred to as the *matching principle*, stipulates that when revenues are recognized on the income statement, all of the expenses associated with generating those revenues should also be recognized. Some companies, however, elect to postpone the recognition of some of these associated expenses through a process called *rear-end loading*.

Under rear-end loading, an expenditure (which may involve either an actual cash outflow or the incurrence of a liability for future cash outflows) is accounted for as an asset on the balance sheet rather than as an expense on the income statement.[17] As a consequence, current period expenses will be understated, causing net income and total assets to be overstated. Eventually, the deferred expenses will pass through to the income statement, and when that occurs, the future period expenses will be overstated, causing net income to be understated. Thus, rear-end loading effectively involves mortgaging future earnings for higher current period earnings. To illustrate this process, we consider several examples in the entertainment industry.

In the fourth quarter of 1980, the American Broadcasting Company changed its method of accounting for prime-time programming costs. Prior to this accounting change, as much as 75 to 80 percent of the costs associated with the production of a television show were expensed against advertising and sponsorship revenues when the show was originally broadcast,

---

[17] Definitionally, an *asset* is an expenditure having some future value to the operations of the company, whereas an *expense* is an expenditure whose value has been consumed.

leaving only 20 to 25 percent of the programming costs on the balance sheet to be matched with future re-run revenues. Faced with sluggish advertising sales, an erosion of network viewership, and a delayed Fall production schedule due to a Hollywood actors' strike, ABC decided to reduce the proportion of programming costs matched against revenues at the time of initial broadcast.[18]

ABC executives justified the change in accounting policy on grounds that there was a growing, and already significant, overseas market for American television programming, and on an expected significant growth in independent television stations (and thus a stronger domestic markct for re-run programming). The net effect of the decision, however, was to leave a greater proportion of programming costs on the balance sheet, presumably to be recovered through future foreign and domestic re-run revenues. Whether such revenues would be realized or not was a matter of speculation, with the final determination in the hands of ABC executives. Had the accounting policy change been made during a period of favorable rather than adverse conditions, it is unlikely that the motivation for the change would have been called into question.

Nonetheless, the decision to defer the recognition of these costs creates more, not less, uncertainty regarding the ability of ABC (and other similar companies) to generate future earnings. An analogy can be drawn between the deferral of these programming costs and the accounting treatment of research and development costs. In SFAS 2, the FASB took the position that, with few exceptions, R & D costs should be expensed during the period in which the costs are incurred because of the uncertainty as to whether and when such costs would be recovered by future revenues.[19] It seems (to us, at least) that an argument can be made that similar uncertainty exists with regard to ABC's deferred programming costs.

In another Hollywood case, the SEC charged that Cannon Group, Inc., an independent film production company, overstated its 1985 earnings by understating the amount of film production costs that were charged to expenses. In the movie industry, as in the television industry, revenues and expenses are recognized at the point of telecast. However, because a movie may have a first-run showing lasting several months, thereby spanning several accounting periods, the recognition of film production costs is based on the *individual film forecast* method. Under this method, the amount of film costs recognized in a given accounting period is based on the ratio of rev-

---

[18] J. E. Cooney, "ABC Acts to Enhance Earnings by Change in Its Accounting," *The Wall Street Journal* (November 17, 1980).

[19] In Chapter 7, the topic of interest capitalization is covered. Some financial writers have argued that interest capitalization is an FASB-approved form of rear-end loading. The principal thrust of this argument appears to center on cash flows: since the cash outflow for interest occurs currently, it is inappropriate to defer recognition of the expense.

enues earned during a period relative to total estimated film revenues (an allocation method not unlike the percentage of completion method).

According to the SEC, Cannon executives substantially overestimated the amount of future revenues that their films would earn during the first year of showing, thereby causing the ratio of actual film revenues to estimated film revenues to be understated. As a consequence, the amount of production costs charged against first year revenues was similarly understated. According to Cannon executives, the company amortized overall film costs at a rate of 64.7 percent of its film distribution revenues. Tri-Star Pictures, a Cannon competitor, however, amortized costs at a rate of 77.6 percent of film distribution revenues.

Although Cannon never issued restated financial statements, *The Wall Street Journal* (May 22, 1987) reported that Cannon adjusted downward its shareholders' equity as of December 28, 1985, by $32 million to make up for the previously overstated earnings. The securities market response to the Cannon case was substantial. Prior to the SEC's investigation of the company's accounting practices, Cannon shares traded as high as $34 3/4. Following the investigation, the shares traded at $3 5/8.[20]

Finally, consider the case of CUC International, a consumer-based "shop at home" company. Under GAAP, the costs of obtaining new CUC customers could be either expensed immediately when customers signed up, or deferred and amortized over the expected life of the new membership. CUC elected the later approach and amortized new membership costs over a three year period. By 1988, however, the level of deferred expenses exceeded the company's reported income, and in March of 1989, CUC took a $51 million write-off which eliminated not only its 1988 earnings, but those of the prior three years as well.[21]

Conclusions

This chapter focused on the quality of the reported cost of operations. Within this topic, we considered the two major expense items composing the cost of operations, namely the cost of goods sold and depreciation/amortization.

As noted earlier, it is difficult, if not inappropriate, to draw generalizations on the basis of accounting conventions; however, subject to that concern, the following inferences appear justified:

---

[20] For more information on the Cannon case, the interested reader is referred to K. R. Ferris, "Cannon Group, Inc.," *Issues in Accounting Education* (Spring, 1979).

[21] K. Bendis, "Cute Tricks on the Bottom Line," *Fortune* (April 24, 1989).

1. A higher quality of earnings and assets will generally exist where **LIFO** inventory costing and accelerated depreciation methods are in use.

2. The quality of earnings and assets is generally diminished in the presence of **LIFO** liquidation profits or depreciation/amortization policy changes which extend the useful life of assets or increase their expected residual value.

3. The quality of earnings and assets is diminished when costs that should be expensed are deferred and charged against future earnings.

For each of the above generalizations, the analyst is encouraged to carefully and thoroughly review the footnotes to the financial statements. Much of the needed information to evaluate these concerns will be contained therein.

CHAPTER FOUR

Income Taxes: Real and Deferred

The topic of income taxes can be distressing at almost any level, be it actually paying the taxes, trying to understand the provisions of the Internal Revenue Service Code, or merely trying to assess the relative impact of income taxes on the earnings, assets, and cash flows of a company. From an accounting perspective, income taxes are no less distressing, or complex. And, since they may represent a significant balance sheet and income statement item, as well as affect current and future cash flows, this entire chapter is devoted to the topic of understanding income taxes and their effect on reported financial statements.

From an analyst's perspective, the issues surrounding income taxes are both many and varied. For example: How much income tax was paid in the current year and how much will be paid in future years? What was the current tax rate and will it be different in the future? Are there any special items, such as tax-loss carryforwards, which will reduce current and future tax obligations? Also, how should the deferred income tax account be classified—as debt, equity, or as neither? These questions, and others, are the focus of this chapter.

As a point of departure in our discussion of income taxes, we begin by considering some of the institutional explanations for the differences that exist between GAAP and IRS regulations. Following this, we review the current reporting practices followed for income taxes, and then examine in detail the taxes reported and paid by one corporation. Finally, we examine the impact of deferred taxes on ratio analysis, and evaluate the effect of recent tax law changes involving investment tax credits.

Corporate Taxes

Although most corporations are subject to a variety of taxes (e.g., payroll taxes, property taxes, and franchise taxes), the financial effects of the income tax are so significant as to require that it be treated separately from the rest. Indeed, on most corporate earnings statements, while payroll, property and franchise taxes are normally lumped together as a single income statement item, the income tax account is given prominent disclosure as a separately reported deduction.

Income taxes are levied on corporate income by most states, as well as by foreign governments if the income is earned outside U. S. boundaries. By far the largest income tax, however, is levied by the U. S. government. Federal income taxes are enacted by the U.S. Congress, and are almost constantly undergoing change or revision. One major revision occurred in 1986, with the passage of the Tax Reform Act (TRA) of 1986. A principal element of the TRA was the reduction of the average corporate income tax rate from 46 to 34 percent. Unbeknownst to the U. S. Congress, this lowering of the corporate income tax rate would be a major catalyst for change in the generally accepted accounting for income taxes in corporate financial statements.

Much of the confusion and complexity surrounding income taxes derives from the fact that under existing GAAP, the amount of income tax expense reported on corporate income statements is rarely (if ever) equivalent to the amount of income taxes actually paid. This is not all that surprising when one considers that the tax laws enacted by Congress have substantially different goals than the accounting and measurement principles enacted by accounting standard-setters. The former are intended to assess the amount of taxes owed the government, and the latter to fairly assess a company's accrual net income. As a consequence of these fundamental differences, most companies maintain (at least) two sets of accounting records (or books)—one set prepared under GAAP and the other under the Internal Revenue Service Code.[1] A second consequence of these differences is that the

---

[1] While it is quite common for a company to maintain two sets of accounting data, some companies effectively maintain three or even four sets of financial data for: (1) the IRS, (2) GAAP reporting, (3) reporting to management, and (4) reporting to a regulatory agency if the company is subject to regulatory accounting principles (RAP).

level of income reported in corporate annual reports is seldom equivalent to that reported to the IRS.

As discussed in the Introduction to this book, the difference between accounting income and taxable income may be exacerbated by the actions of management. On the one hand, corporate management is quite likely to select those GAAP methods which maximize the level of reported accounting income, yet simultaneously adopt those tax regulations which legally enable the company to report the lowest level of currently taxable net income.[2] To curb the extreme case of this in which a company reports significant GAAP net income but pays no taxes to the IRS, the TRA of 1986 enacted an Alternative Minimum Tax (AMT) for corporations. Under the AMT provisions, if the AMT is closer to the level of income taxes reported under GAAP than the income taxes computed using existing IRS regulations, the company is required to pay the higher AMT. The AMT is a complex issue and is discussed further in Appendix 2.

GAAP versus IRS Accounting

Our discussion so far has highlighted several points. First, the regulations of the IRS and the measurement standards under GAAP differ, leading to the not unexpected result that net income before tax (NIBT) for accounting purposes will differ, and most probably exceed, the NIBT for IRS purposes. Second, even if the exact same income tax rates[3] are used for calculating accounting income taxes and IRS taxes, since the NIBT differs between the two sets of books, the income tax expense reported for accounting purposes will differ, and most probably exceed, the income taxes reported and actually paid to the IRS.

One approach to overcome these differences is to report the actual taxes paid to the IRS as the income tax expense on corporate income statements. This approach is known as the "flow-through" approach (i.e., the

---

[2] While income taxes on earned income may be temporarily postponed, such taxes will eventually become due. Nonetheless, because of the time value of money, the postponement of any tax is valuable to a firm, and so long as the tax statutes are not violated, it represents a fiscally sound, legal corporate strategy.

[3] Corporate tax rates are a function of the level of taxable income. In 1990, for example, the corporate income tax rates in effect were:

Income level		Tax rate
$ 0 – $ 50,000		15%
50,001 – 75,000		25
75,001 – 100,000		34
100,001 – 335,000		39
335,001 – above		34

Thus, given that the NIBT differs between the two sets of books, it is unlikely that the average tax rate used for GAAP purposes will equal that used for IRS purposes.

actual tax expense flows through to the accounting statements), but unfortunately is not permissible under existing GAAP. Current accounting standards require that the income tax expense reported on GAAP financial statements be a function of GAAP net income.

The differences between GAAP and IRS net income may be divided into two groups: permanent and temporary. *Permanent* differences result because some items of revenue and expense reported for financial accounting purposes are never reported for income tax purposes under the provisions of the Internal Revenue Service Code. One example is goodwill, which must be amortized against earnings under GAAP, but which may not be deducted in the determination of IRS taxable net income. A second example is municipal bond income, which is includable in accounting net income, but is (in reality) tax free and thus excludable from IRS taxable net income.

Temporary differences, on the other hand, are those revenue and expense items which are reported in one period for accounting purposes but are reported in an earlier or later period for income tax purposes. One example is installment sale income, which is usually recognized in full for accounting purposes when the sale occurs, but which may be deferred until received in cash for tax purposes. A second example is depreciation on short-lived equipment. The IRS requires that such assets be depreciated under a three year write-off period using the Modified Accelerated Cost Recovery System (MACRS),[4] whereas for accounting purposes the asset may be depreciated, say, over a four year period using straight-line depreciation.

By definition, temporary differences are just that—temporary; and, in the long run, they balance or reverse themselves out. Thus, these differences will, after one or more periods, be eliminated. For this reason, temporary differences are often called *timing* differences. The distinction between permanent and temporary differences, however, is an important one—permanent differences can never be reconciled, whereas temporary ones can.

Accounting for Temporary Differences

A long-standing position taken by accounting standard-setters is that the temporary differences between accounting and taxable income should be

---

[4] For tax purposes, the depreciation deduction for equipment (and other depreciable assets) is determined by the year in which an asset is placed in service. Assets acquired prior to 1981 may be depreciated using any of the traditional methods, such as straight-line, declining balance, or sum-of-the-years-digits. Assets placed in service between 1981 and 1986 must be depreciated using the Accelerated Cost Recovery System (ACRS). And, assets placed in service after 1986 must be depreciated using the MACRS. Under ACRS or MACRS, depreciable assets are classified into various age categories. Once so classified, the depreciation deduction in any period is determined by pre-established percentages. For example, an asset (e.g., a car) classified as a 3-year asset is depreciated using the following percentages for years 1, 2, and 3, respectively: 25, 38, and 37 percent.

accounted for using a process known as *interperiod tax allocation*. Under this process, the total taxes to be paid by a corporation are allocated over the various periods in which revenues (expenses) are earned (incurred), independent of when the revenues (expenses) are actually subject to taxation. Because the amount of taxes allocated to a given accounting period might differ from the amount of taxes actually paid, it becomes necessary to reflect this discrepancy in the financial statements (principally because the debits don't equal the credits).[5] Thus arises the Deferred Income Tax account.

In 1987, the FASB adopted Statement of Financial Accounting Standard No. 96, which mandated a new approach to the measurement of deferred income taxes. Previously, interperiod tax allocation was achieved using the *deferred method*, as required under Accounting Principles Board (APB) Opinion No. 11. Under SFAS 96, interperiod tax allocation is accomplished using the *liability method*, although it is uncertain when this new method will be required. Due to the many complexities in the implementation of SFAS 96, the adoption date originally scheduled for fiscal years beginning after December 1989, has been extended to fiscal years beginning after December 15, 1992 (i.e., effectively 1993 for calendar year companies). Nonetheless, some companies have elected to adopt SFAS 96 before its required adoption date, and thus the analyst must be familiar with both measurement approaches in order to effectively analyze all financial statements.

Under the deferred method of APB 11, the amount of income taxes deferred for any period is essentially a plug figure, representing the difference between the amount of income taxes recorded for accounting purposes and those actually paid or payable to the IRS. Since NIBT for GAAP purposes exceeds (in most cases) the NIBT for tax purposes, the balancing plug figure involves a credit to the balance sheet account "Deferred Income Taxes." For a growing, or even stable company, the credit balance in the deferred tax account would appear to increase indefinitely, unless liquidation occurred first. In effect, instead of being paid, deferred taxes were simply rolled forward, over and over again. The underlying nature of this account was thus called into question.[6] Was it really a liability account? And, if so, when would it be paid off?

---

[5] The journal entry to record income taxes on the GAAP financial statements is:

Debit: Income Tax Expense	$XXX	
Credit: Income Tax Payable		$XX
Credit: Deferred Income Taxes		X

This entry assumes that NIBT for accounting purposes exceeds NIBT for tax purposes. As a consequence, the taxes actually payable are less than those reported, resulting in a balancing credit to Deferred Income Taxes.

[6] According to H. D. Moskowitz, a national partner with Seidman and Seidman: "The deferred taxes on the balance sheet bear almost no relationship to what is actually going to be owed. So, the current [deferred] method of income tax accounting makes it almost impossible for an investor to evaluate a company's liquidity, solvency, or cash flows." See R. Green, "Rollover," *Forbes* (January 18, 1982).

The repayment of this "liability" became so long-term in nature for most companies that some financial institutions stopped considering the account as part of a company's debt structure, and instead treated it as equity (i.e., an interest-free investment from the U.S. government), or as neither debt nor equity (e.g., similar to the minority interest in a consolidated subsidiary). Many corporations publicly acknowledge the very long-term nature of this account by classifying the deferred income tax account not as debt, but rather under the rubric "Deferred Credits" on the credit side of the balance sheet (i.e., between the debt and equity sections).

Concerned over the declining informational content of the deferred income tax account, the FASB was forced into action by the TRA of 1986. Since the TRA lowered the effective statutory corporate income tax rate from 46 to 34 percent, and since the deferred method provided no effective means of immediately recognizing this tax rate change, the FASB adopted the liability method. Under the liability method, the tax rates used are those expected to be in effect when the temporary differences reverse. Under the deferred method, the deferred tax liability is calculated using the tax rate in effect as of the balance sheet date, with no subsequent adjustment if tax rates change. Thus, when tax rates fall, as they did under the TRA, the deferred method creates a permanent balance in the deferred income tax account. The permanent balance is based upon the difference between the old and new tax rates.

Under SFAS 96, however, deferred tax liabilities are accounted for at the new lower rates, thereby decreasing the total balance sheet liability for future taxes. Similarly, on the income statement the current income tax expense will also be lower (than under the deferred method), reflecting the lower statutory rates under the TRA of 1986.

The Transition Period

When a company adopts SFAS 96, the transition from the deferred method to the liability method may be handled in one of two ways: (1) retroactive restatement, or (2) cumulative effect. Under the *retroactive restatement method*, which is preferred by the FASB, the deferred tax account is adjusted as if the liability method had been utilized in prior periods. (The company itself may determine the number of periods of data that it wishes to restate.) If the earliest restated year is presented in the company's comparative financial statements, the effect of the restatement is reported as a change in accounting principle, and the cumulative adjustment is reported on the income statement, usually prominently highlighted near the extraordinary items. If, on the other hand, the earliest restated year precedes the years reported in the comparative financial statements (e.g., the restatement year is 1988 while comparative data is presented for 1989 and 1990), the effect of the restatement is made to the beginning balance of retained earnings (i.e., 1989 in our example).

The retroactive restatement approach is likely to be preferred by late-adopters or by firms reporting a large negative adjustment and who do not want the negative adjustment to flow through to the current income statement. A large negative adjustment may arise from the exclusion of tax-loss carryforwards netting out deferred tax liabilities, a procedure permitted under the deferred method but not under the liability method.

Under the *cumulative effect method*, the effect of adopting SFAS 96 on the deferred tax account is reported as a change in accounting principle in the current income statement. This method is likely to be preferred by companies reporting a positive cumulative adjustment (similar to that of a gain) arising from the fact that the liability method uses lower tax rates for purposes of calculating income taxes than does the deferred method. For example, in 1989, Exxon Corporation implemented SFAS 96 and reported a gain of $535 million on its income statement, representing the cumulative effect of the accounting change on prior years (for approximately an 18 percent increase in earnings exclusive of the accounting change).

The financial statement disclosure under the cumulative effect method would appear as shown in Exhibit 4.1, the comparative income statements for Centex Corporation for 1987-1988. Centex adopted SFAS 96 for the fiscal year ended March 31, 1988. A $50.1 million cumulative adjustment associated with the adoption of the liability method led to the reporting of $74.163 million in total net earnings on only $24.063 million of after-tax operating income. This illustrates the type of effect that can be expected for many companies utilizing the cumulative effect method. The positive change in net income reported by Centex reflects the reduction in the statutory tax rates under TRA. A search of various financial data bases (i.e., Compustat and Disclosure) for 1988 revealed that for those companies adopting SFAS 96 early, only the cumulative effect method was used. And, in each case, a positive adjustment to earnings was reported.[7]

Thus, when SFAS 96 is adopted, analysts should typically expect to observe a large positive cumulative adjustment. If, in the future, tax rates are revised upward, a cumulative negative adjustment to deferred taxes will result. How these adjustments relate to cash flows are discussed shortly.

Deferred Taxes on the Balance Sheet

Another change brought about under SFAS 96 involves the interpretation of the balance sheet accounts. Under APB 11, the balance sheet accounts for

---

[7] As a counter illustration, Maxus Energy Corporation adopted SFAS 96 effective January 1, 1988; and while the effect of adopting SFAS 96 was to increase the 1988 tax benefit by $7.7 million, or $.09 per share, the company also recorded a negative $70 million adjustment (or $.78 per share) for the cummulative effect of the method change relating to years prior to 1988. Maxus explained the negative adjustment, noting that, under SFAS 96, the calculation of deferred taxes "includes items on which deferred taxes had not previously been provided."

Exhibit 4.1 ────────────────────────────────

CENTEX CORPORATION
COMPARATIVE INCOME STATEMENTS
(in thousands of dollars)

	For the Year Ended 1988	For the Year Ended 1987
Total Revenues	$ 1,460,061	$ 1,303,897
Costs and Expenses	1,423,890	1,226,645
Earnings Before Income Taxes and 1988 Accounting Change	36,171	77,252
Provision for Income Taxes	12,108	33,048
Earnings Before 1988 Accounting Change	24,063	44,204
Cumulative Effect of Change in Accounting for Income Taxes	50,100	—
Net Earnings	$ 74,163	$ 44,204

deferred income taxes were labeled "current" and "noncurrent." Typical accounting usage of the terms current and noncurrent relates to the timing of obligation repayment. This, however, was not the case under APB 11. The titles current and noncurrent were associated with the deferred income tax account based on whether the deferred income tax was associated with a current or noncurrent asset or liability, and not whether the obligation was due within the current period. Under SFAS 96, however, the titles current and noncurrent are associated with the timing of the payment of the obligation. Thus, under SFAS 96, this dichotomization should improve the analysts' ability to predict the real future tax obligations of a company.

─────── Interpreting Deferred Tax Numbers: ─────── Centex Corporation

One of the critical aspects of financial analysis involves the prediction of future cash flows. In the normal operating environment, taxes must be paid and the analyst must consider such questions as: How much tax was paid in the current year and how much will be paid in future years? What was the current tax rate and will it be different for the future? Are there any special circumstances such as tax-loss carryforwards which will reduce current and future tax obligations? To answer these questions, the analyst must develop a methodology for interpreting the financial statements and related footnotes under SFAS 96.

Exhibit 4.2 _____

CENTEX CORPORATION
COMPARATIVE BALANCE SHEETS
(in thousands of dollars)

	March 31, 1988	March 31, 1987
Total Assets	$1,038,552	$ 993,722
Liabilities Except Deferred Taxes	533,939	402,761
Deferred Income Taxes	139,767	227,947
Shareholders' Equity	364,846	363,014
Total Liabilities and Equity	$1,038,552	$ 993,722

Exhibit 4.3 _____

CENTEX CORPORATION
NOTES TO THE FINANCIAL STATEMENTS - 1988
(in thousands of dollars)

During fiscal 1988, the company adopted Statement of Financial Accounting Standards No. 96 (SFAS No. 96), "Accounting for Income Taxes," which, among other things, requires companies to currently recognize the effects of changes in statutory tax rates on temporary differences for which deferred income taxes were previously provided. Accordingly, the company recognized a gain in fiscal 1988 of $50.1 million as the cumulative effect of this change in accounting for income taxes, representing the reduction in the deferred tax liability at April 1, 1987, resulting from the statutory decrease in corporate tax rates from 46% to 34%. Prior to the adoption of SFAS No. 96, the provisions for more tax were based on transactions included in the determination of pretax accounting income, with appropriate provisions for deferred income taxes based on the statutory rates in effect at the time the temporary differences arose. Under SFAS No. 96, deferred tax liabilities and related expense accounts will be adjusted each year for changes in statutory rates. The effect of this change in accounting principle for the year ended March 31, 1988, was not significant.

To demonstrate how deferred income tax measures can be interpreted, we examine financial statement data from Centex Corporation for fiscal years 1987 through 1989. Exhibit 4.1 contains comparative income statement data, and Exhibit 4.2 contains comparative balance sheet data for fiscal years 1987 and 1988. Exhibit 4.3 contains the notes to the financial statements pertaining to income taxes from the 1988 financial statements, and Exhibit 4.4 displays a statement of cash flows for fiscal year 1988.

Although income tripled in 1988 after the adoption of SFAS 96, the analyst should note that the cash flows from operations for Centex were

Exhibit 4.3 (continued) ────────────────────────────────

Section One

The provision for income taxes includes the following components:

	1988	1987
Current Provision		
Federal	$ 44,621	$ 11,626
State	2,030	1,764
	46,651	13,390
Deferred Provision		
Federal	(33,471)	20,232
State	(1,040)	(148)
	(34,511)	20,084
Deferred provision related to minority interest	(32)	(426)
Provision for Income Taxes	$ 12,108	$ 33,048

Section Two

The effective tax rate is less than the federal statutory rate of 37% in 1988 and 46% in 1987 and 1986 due to the following items:

	1988	1987
Financial Income Before Taxes	$ 36,171	$ 77,252
Income Taxes at Statutory Rate	13,384	35,536
Changes in tax resulting from:		
State Income Taxes, Net	595	834
Investment Tax Credit	—	(468)
Statutory Depletion in Excess of Cost	(426)	(596)
Tax Exempt Interest	(1,005)	(670)
Other	(440)	(1,588)
Provision for Income Taxes	$ 12,108	$ 33,048
Effective Tax Rate	33%	43%

Exhibit 4.3 (continued) ————————————————————————————

Section Three

The deferred provision for income taxes results from the following timing differences in the recognition of revenues and expenses for tax and financial reporting purposes:

	1988	1987
Sales reported on the installment method	$ (29,734)	$ 18,656
Net operating loss and investment tax credit	—	13,559
Expenses capitalized for tax purposes	(3,361)	(2,760)
Construction contracts reported on completed basis	4,207	(7,636)
Tax depreciation less than book	(520)	(3,321)
Expenses deferred under consolidated return reg.	4,602	3,027
Interest and real estate taxes expensed	(4,546)	(4,037)
Hedging losses expensed as incurred	(911)	(532)
Other	(4,248)	3,128
	$ (34,511)	$ 20,084

Section Four

In 1987 the company utilized its tax and net operating loss and investment tax credit carry-forwards of $24.5 million and $2.3 million, respectively. In prior years, the carryforwards were recognized for financial reporting purposes as reductions of deferred income taxes.

———

unaffected by this method adoption. The adoption of SFAS 96 simply produced a reduction of $50.1 million in the long-term deferred income tax account and a corresponding credit to income. This cumulative change should not be misinterpreted as having any short-term economic effect on the company. The $50.1 million cumulative effect represents the summation of the reduction in future taxes attributable to the lower corporate tax rates. The analyst, for example, who is interested in the payment of interest and principal on debt, cannot look to this cumulative effect as a source of cash for these loans. The cumulative effect arises from a reduction in the deferred income tax account attributable to the new tax rate. The absence of supporting cash flow, for example, is well illustrated in the cash flow statement (Exhibit 4.4) as a reduction of net earnings. A partial cash flow statement is replicated here:

Net Earnings	$ 74,163
Cumulative Effect	(50,100)
Cash Flow Before Change and other Non-Cash Items	$ 24,063

Exhibit 4.4 ————————————————————————————

CENTEX CORPORATION
STATEMENT OF CASH FLOWS
(in thousands of dollars)

	For the Year Ended 1988
Cash Flows - Operations	
Net Earnings	$ 74,163
Adjustments:	
Cumulative effect of change in accounting	(50,100)
Depreciation, depletion and amortization	11,765
Deferred income taxes	(34,543)
Equity in earnings of joint ventures	7,075
Minority stockholders' interest	486
Increase in payables and accruals	42,952
Increase in receivables	(8,884)
Increase in inventories	(74,399)
Other, net	(10,947)
Total cash flow from operations	$ (42,432)
Net cash flow from investing activities	19,638
Net cash flow from financing activities	15,907
Net decrease in cash for the year	$ (6,887)

The "Real" Effects

The analyst, however, should not be interested in the cosmetic effects associated with the adoption of SFAS 96, but rather in predicting the impact of taxes on future cash flows. To gain such information, the analyst must come to understand the relationship among the income statement, balance sheet, and footnotes to the financial reports, to which we now turn.

The first obvious change to the Centex balance sheet is in the Deferred Income Taxes account. Between March 31, 1987 and March 31, 1988, this account decreased by $88.18 million. The cumulative change accounts for $50.1 million of this decrease; but what of the other $38.08 million? How much did Centex really pay in taxes in 1988? What will the company pay in 1989? What is Centex's effective tax rate in those years?

The first income tax account to be considered is the Provision for Income Taxes (i.e., Income Tax Expense). Under SFAS 96, this account is the sum of taxes currently payable and the change in Deferred Income Taxes

Payable. For Centex, this information is presented in Exhibit 4.3, section one. The Provision for Income Taxes for 1988 was $12.108 million. The two components are: current—$46.651 million, and deferred—($34.511 million). Centex therefore owed and paid (since no current tax payable exists as of March 31, 1988) $46.651 million. The deferred part of the provision represents the income taxes owed due to the reversals of various temporary differences.

This picture is very different from the one represented by the single number Provision for Income Taxes. If one calculated the tax rate represented on the income statement by the Provision for Income Taxes, a rate of 33 percent would result ($12.108/$36.171). This rate closely corresponds to the federal statutory rate of 37 percent in 1988. The difference between the effective rate of 33 percent and the statutory rate of 37 percent shown in Exhibit 4.3, section two, is attributable to various permanent differences. If, however, one considers the tax rate for just the current provision, a rate of 129 percent is observed ($46.651/$36.171).

Where the analyst is interested in predicting the future cash flows due to taxes, the relevant rate to consider is represented by the current portion of the Provision for Income Taxes. However, to fully understand the current portion of the Provision, the analyst must understand the likely change that will occur in the deferred part of the Provision. In 1988, for example, the deferred part of the Provision for Centex involved a $34.511 million decrease, which led to taxes paid of that amount in excess of the total Provision shown on the income statement. The reasons for this decrease in the deferred part of the Provision are analyzed in the footnotes and reported in Exhibit 4.3, section three. The major component of the change in Deferred Income Taxes resulting from timing differences was the reporting of sales for tax purposes which were reported earlier for accounting purposes (i.e., the installment method—$29.734 million of additional taxes). If Centex experiences the same level of reversals in 1989 that occurred in 1988, one would expect the effective tax rate on the current part of the Provision to be in excess of 100 percent, as it was in 1988. As a consequence, Centex might experience a severe cash shortage in 1989, calling into question the company's ability to service debt or pay dividends.

Centex has elected to use an unclassified balance sheet, thereby circumventing the need of SFAS 96 to separate the balance sheet deferred income tax account into its current and noncurrent components. If this had been done, the analyst would have a better perspective of the effect of the reversals in 1989.

The final tax issues that may affect actual taxes paid are net operating loss carryforwards and investment tax credits. This information is provided by Exhibit 4.3, section four. In 1987 Centex used these items to reduce actual taxes paid by $13.599 million. This computation was derived by adding the effect of the investment tax credit of $2.3 million and the tax effect of loss carryforwards of $24.5 million. A rate of 46 percent was applied to the $24.5 million; hence, the total of $13.599 million is obtained by adding $2.3 million and $11.259 million.

Carryforwards under SFAS 96 are only recognized in periods where they can be applied. For the analyst, a knowledge of the amount of loss carryforward is important in predicting future tax payments. This information is part of the income tax footnote and is not incorporated in the financial statements themselves. In the case of Centex, no loss carryforwards other than the ones utilized in 1987 appear to exist, and Centex cannot expect to reduce its tax payments for 1988 by these means.

Unfulfilled Expectations

Centex's comparative balance sheet data, comparative income statement data, notes to the financial statements pertaining to income taxes, and the cash flow statement for 1989 are shown in Exhibits 4.5, 4.6, 4.7, and 4.8, respectively. Given Centex's lack of cash flows from operations in 1988 (shown by the negative amounts in Exhibit 4.4), the analyst would have expected a continued depressed cash flow in 1989. The depressed cash flow in 1988 centered on two major problems—the noncash nature of the cumulative change of $50.1 million and the reversal of $34.543 million of deferred taxes. The reversal of the deferred taxes was caused by the recognition of installment sales for tax purposes. When predicting cash flows from operations in 1989, the analyst would normally expect a like reversal and a large cash outflow for current taxes due. Yet, Exhibit 4.8 reveals a net positive $29.439 million cash flows from operations. How could our expectations have been so wrong?

Centex did not anticipate a change in tax rates in 1989. If the company had, an adjustment would have been made to income for the effect of this change. Hence, a change in tax rates was not the cause of the failure in expectations.

Unlike 1988, the "real" tax rate did not exceed 100 percent in 1989. The "real" tax rate was 66 percent ($26.373 million of the current Provision for Income Taxes/$40.02 million of earnings). This tax rate, however, does not correspond to our expectations given the anticipated reversal of installment sales. In Exhibit 4.7, section three, one does find a significant reversal of $46.544 million as expected. This major reversal, however, was offset by two components—the net operating loss carryforward of $38.091 million and tax depreciation in excess of book depreciation of $12.447 million. Neither of these two components could have been predicted from the financial statements of 1988.

The loss carryforward came to Centex from its acquisition in late 1988 of a savings and loan trust (See Exhibit 4.9), which merged four insolvent Texas S&Ls. The tax depreciation in excess of book depreciation arose from

Exhibit 4.5 ──

CENTEX CORPORATION
COMPARATIVE INCOME STATEMENTS
(in thousand of dollars)

	For the Year Ended 1989	For the Year Ended 1988
Total Revenues	$ 1,845,484	$ 1,485,068
Costs and Expenses	1,786,737	1,448,897
Earnings Before Income Taxes and 1988 Accounting Change	58,747	36,171
Provision for Income Taxes	18,727	12,108
Earnings Before 1988 Accounting Change	40,020	24,063
Cumulative Effect of Change in Accounting for Income Taxes	—	50,100
Net Earnings	$ 40,020	$ 74,163

Exhibit 4.6 ──

CENTEX CORPORATION
COMPARATIVE BALANCE SHEETS
(in thousands of dollars)

	March 31, 1989	March 31, 1988
Total Assets	$ 1,096,228	$ 1,038,552
Liabilities except deferred taxes	637,567	533,939
Deferred Income Taxes	74,487	139,767
Shareholders' Equity	384,174	364,846
Total Liabilities and Equity	$ 1,096,228	$ 1,038,552

Centex's expansion in its general construction division in 1989, as shown in the increase in construction revenues for that year. The tax-loss carry-forward was a phenomenon of 1989, something that could not have been predicted in 1988. It does not appear from Exhibit 4.7, section four, that any further net operating loss carryforwards are available from the acquisition of the S&Ls, but with the current operating performance of Texas S&Ls, Centex may have available operating loss carryforwards for years to come. Without the loss carryforwards, the amount of the taxes due would have

Exhibit 4.7 ————————————————————————————

CENTEX CORPORATION
NOTES TO THE FINANCIAL STATEMENTS - 1989
(in thousands of dollars)

Section One

The provision for income taxes includes the following components:

	1989	1988
Current Provision		
Federal	$ 25,192	$ 44,621
State	1,181	2,030
	26,373	46,651
Deferred Provision		
Federal	(7,900)	(33,503)
State	254	(1,040)
	(7,646)	(34,543)
Provision for Income Taxes	$ 18,727	$ 12,108

Section Two

The effective tax rate is less than the statutory rate of 34% in 1989, 37% in 1988 due to the following items:

	1989	1988
Financial Income Before Taxes	$ 58,747	$ 36,171
Income Taxes at Statutory Rate	19,974	13,384
Changes in tax resulting from:		
State income taxes, net	863	595
Statutory depletion in excess of cost	(467)	(426)
Tax exempt interest	(214)	(1,005)
Tax exempt FSLIC assistance	(1,453)	—
Other	24	(440)
Provision for Income Taxes	$ 18,727	$ 12,108
Effective Tax Rate	32%	33%

Exhibit 4.7 (continued) ————————————————————————————

Section Three

The deferred provision for income taxes results from the following temporary differences in the recognition of revenues and expenses for tax and financial reporting purposes:

	1989	1988
Sales reported on the installment method	$ (56,544)	$ (29,734)
Net operating loss and investment tax credit	38,091	—
Expenses capitalized for tax purposes	(1,786)	(3,361)
Construction contracts reported on completed basis	(3,051)	4,207
Tax depreciation in excess (less than) book	12,447	(520)
Expenses deferred under consolidated return reg.	(1,280)	4,602
Interest and real estate taxes expensed	5,499	(4,546)
Hedging losses expensed as incurred	(2,778)	(911)
Other	1,756	(4,280)
	$ (7,646)	$ (34,543)

Section Four

The net operating loss and investment tax credit carryforwards utilized in 1989 were those of the savings and loan group existing at the acquisition date. In 1987, the company utilized its tax and net operating loss and investment tax credit carryforwards of $24.5 million and $2.3 million, respectively.

———

been $64.464 million ($26.373 + $38.091), or a "real" tax rate of 161 percent ($64.464/$40.02). This latter tax rate is in line with the expectations developed from the 1988 financial data.

For an investment of $26.3 million (see Exhibit 4.9) in the S&L trust, Centex obtained tax benefits of $38.091 million in loss carryforwards, which were included in the amount Centex recognized in negative goodwill of $38.981 million. Given this type of transaction, it is very difficult for the analyst to predict the taxes to be paid from the published financial statements and the related footnotes.

——————————— **Deferred Taxes and Ratio Analysis** ———————————

As a consequence of the uncertainty associated with the timing of payment of deferred taxes, there exists considerable disagreement regarding the classification of this account for ratio analysis purposes. Should the analyst, for example, treat a credit balance in deferred taxes as long-term debt, equity, or

Exhibit 4.8

CENTEX CORPORATION
STATEMENT OF CASH FLOWS
(in thousands of dollars)

	For the Year Ended 1989
Cash Flows-Operations	
Net earnings	$ 40,020
Adjustments:	
Depreciation, depletion and amortization	11,273
Deferred income taxes	(7,646)
Equity in earnings of joint ventures	5,087
Increase in payables and accruals	42,890
Increase in receivables	(19,383)
Increase in inventories	(37,321)
Other, net	(5,481)
Total cash flow from operations	29,439
Net cash flow from investing activities	(10,796)
Net cash flow from financing activities	(9,029)
Net increase in cash for the year	$ 9,614

as neither? Our experience has been that, even among relatively similar financial institutions, there is considerable diversity of opinion and practice.

Under existing GAAP (i.e., APB 11), a credit balance in deferred taxes may persist for substantial periods of time, certainly for the full duration of, say, a ten-year credit arrangement. Thus, given that payment is unlikely for the foreseeable future, it is quite reasonable to consider this account to represent a form of equity (e.g., a long-term, interest-free investment by the U.S. government). Alternatively, since reversal, and hence payment, of the credit is expected at some point in the future (albeit when is uncertain), the account does retain characteristics of debt and thus classification as a long-term liability also has merit.[8] However, if the analyst anticipates that a

---

[8] An interesting controversy associated with the treatment of deferred taxes as long-term debt concerns discounting of the future obligation. GAAP requires that long-term debt be carried on the balance sheet at the discounted value of the future cash flows required to satisfy the obligation. This general valuation rule is not followed, however, with respect to deferred taxes, in part because of the uncertainty regarding the timing of payments and the appropriate discount rate to be used. Moreover, it can be argued that since the tax payments will not occur for many periods, the discounted value at any legitimate interest rate would be very low.

Exhibit 4.9 _____

CENTEX CORPORATION
PARTIAL NOTES TO THE FINANCIAL STATEMENTS - 1989
CONCERNING S&L ACQUISITION

ACQUSITION

On December 29, 1988, the company purchased certain assets and assumed certain liabilities of four central Texas savings and loan associations under the FSLIC's Southwest Plan. The acquisitions were made by Texas Trust, a newly formed federal stock savings bank which is a subsidiary of CTX Holding, a wholly-owned subsidiary of the company. CTX Holding contributed a total of $26.3 million in exchange for 1,600,000 shares of common stock and $10.3 million of 10% cumulative, redeemable preferred stock. The FSLIC received a warrant to purchase (for $400,000) a 20% interest in Texas Trust. The warrant is exercisable for a 10-year period beginning December 29, 1993.

The acquisition was made pursuant to acquisition agreements and an assistance agreement with the FSLIC. Under the terms of these agreements, the FSLIC provided assistance to Texas Trust in the form of a note representing the aggregate negative capital (as defined) of the insolvent associations as of December 29, 1988. This note is due in full on December 29, 1998.

Following is a summary of the condensed consolidated financial position as of March 31, 1989 of CTX Holding and its subsidiary, Texas Trust (dollars in thousands):

Assets

Cash and amounts due from banks	$ 10,636
Loans and receivables, primarily residential mortgage loans	35,620
Assets covered by FSLIC assistance	336,099
Notes and receivables from FSLIC	217,595
Other assets, including $68 million from affiliate	70,067
	$ 670,017

Liabilities and Stockholder's Equity

Deposits	$ 452,135
FHLB advances	135,970
Other liabilities	15,051
Negative goodwill	38,981
Stockholder's equity	27,880
	$ 670,017

company will continue to roll forward an existing balance in deferred taxes, effectively postponing payment indefinitely, a third alternative involves treating the account as neither debt nor equity (e.g., as a minority interest in a consolidated subsidiary), and thus ignoring it in any analysis whatsoever.

Regardless of which viewpoint is adopted, for many companies the balance in deferred taxes is sufficiently large that many traditional ratios will be affected by this decision. Consider, for example, the debt-to-equity ratio. Using the Centex Corporation data for 1987 (Exhibit 4.2), when deferred taxes are classified as debt, the ratio is 1.74; when classified as equity, the ratio is 0.68; and, when disregarded altogether, the ratio is 1.11. In each case, the apparent debt capacity of Centex is altered.[9]

While each of these three views has merit under current GAAP, much of this controversy may be eliminated with the implementation of SFAS 96. One important consequence of SFAS 96 is the clarification of the deferred income tax account. Under the liability method, a credit balance in deferred taxes should be a more reliable estimate of the expected future cash outflows for corporate income taxes that are deferred from current periods. Thus, under SFAS 96, there appears to be solid ground for treatment of deferred taxes as debt (assuming a credit balance), and not equity.

Tax Credits

Tax credits have historically provided significant tax relief for most corporations, and by far the most important tax credit was the investment tax credit (ITC). Prior to 1986, an ITC could be earned by any company by merely buying a depreciable asset. The TRA of 1986, however, eliminated the ITC (effective January 1, 1986) for most companies, while permitting a phased-down ITC for others.

For IRS purposes, tax credits earned in a particular year are used to reduce a company's actual tax liability in that year. Unused credits may be carried forward up to fifteen years or backward up to three years. For

---

9 Another more extreme illustration is the General Electric Credit Corporation. The following figures illustrate the effect of deferred taxes on GECC's debt-to-equity ratio:

	Deferred Taxes as debt	Deferred Taxes as equity
1983	9.14	3.00
1982	8.99	3.23
1981	10.00	4.12

For more information on GECC, the interested reader is referred to L. Hoshower and W. Ferrara, "Deferred Taxes and Consolidations—A Case of Change," *Management Accounting* (December, 1985).

accounting purposes, however, tax credits can be accounted for using either a "flow-through" approach (i.e., credits are taken in the year earned, consistent with the IRS approach) or a deferral approach.

Under the deferral approach, a tax credit is amortized against accounting taxes over the life of the related asset whose purchase created the tax credit. And, the portion of the ITC not yet amortized is carried on the balance sheet as a long-term liability, a deferred credit (i.e., between the debt and equity sections), or as an "other liability."

Because of its positive impact on reported net income, most companies utilize the flow-through approach to account for the ITC in their published financial statements. According to a survey by the AICPA, over 90 percent of the companies surveyed who disclosed an ITC used the flow-through method.[10] In recent years, moreover, there has been an increasing trend of companies using the deferral approach switching to the flow-through method.

One such company was the Union Carbide Corporation. In 1980, UCC switched from the deferral approach to the flow-through method, increasing its 1980 earnings per share by $3.64, an increase of over 37 percent:

Earnings per share (EPS), excluding ITC method change	$ 9.72
Increase in EPS for 1980 due to ITC method change	.36
Cumulative effect of ITC change through December 31, 1979	3.28
EPS, including ITC method change	$ 13.36

In addition to realizing a $0.36 per share increase in 1980 EPS, UCC also realized a one-time cumulative adjustment to earnings for the $217 million in deferred ITCs that had accumulated on its balance sheet through December 31, 1979.[11] The analyst should note that in spite of the very positive impact on accrual net income, the switch from deferral to flow-through accounting had no parallel effect on UCC's operating cash flows. Further, when analyzing the various financial ratios for a company experiencing this type of cumulative accounting change, it is necessary to exclude the current period adjustment in order to avoid unwanted ratio distortions.

---

[10] AICPA, *Accounting Trends & Techniques* (AICPA, 1987).

[11] The accounting journal entry to transfer deferred ITCs from the balance sheet to the income statement would appear as:

Debit: Deferred Investment Tax Credits	$217 million
Credit: Cumulative Effect of Change in Accounting Principle	$217 million

Conclusions

This chapter focused on the question of income taxes. It was noted that the accounting income tax expense and the actual income taxes paid are rarely, if ever, equivalent. The principal explanation for the differences between accounting income taxes and real income taxes relates to the use of different revenue and expense recognition methods for financial reporting purposes versus income tax purposes. As observed in Chapter 1, many corporations attempt to maximize the level of reported accounting net income, while simultaneously minimizing the level of taxable net income, subject to the constraints imposed by the AMT. Analytical issues relating to income taxes are two-fold: (1) how should deferred taxes be treated—as debt, equity, or neither; and (2) assessing the actual cash outflow for income taxes. As the Centex Corporation data revealed, predicting the actual cash outflow for income taxes is difficult at best, but can be substantially enhanced by available footnote information.

PART III

The Balance Sheet

The balance sheet has been compared by one financial wag to the bikini bathing suit: what it reveals is interesting, but what it conceals is critical. Although seemingly humorous, the sarcasm is truer than most accountants are normally willing to admit. Perhaps the greatest shortcoming of the balance sheet today concerns the issue of off-balance sheet debt—or debt that should be reported on the balance sheet but is not. A primary agenda item for the FASB during the decade of the 1990s will be attempting to overcome this shortcoming. The adoption of SFAS 105, "Disclosure of Information about Financial Instruments with Off-Balance-Sheet Risk . . . ," in 1990 was an important step in that direction.

A second important balance sheet concern focuses on the conditions surrounding, and the timing of, long-term asset write-downs. It is not particularly surprising that the managers of most corporations are reluctant to write down the value of their company's long-term, revenue-producing assets. Not only do these write-downs produce income statement losses, but the net worth, book value, and total asset position of a company is also correspondingly impaired. Thus, the prevalent practice in industry appears to be to delay such write-downs until a company is in an optimal position to absorb the anticipated losses, and then to

81

take the asset write-downs en masse. This practice has become euphemistically labelled the "Big Bath," and in recent years the financial press has reported many examples of this practice in the banking and thrift industries, the oil and gas industry, and the real estate industry.

In this section, we explore both what is revealed, but also what is concealed on the balance sheet. Most of our attention will be devoted to questions concerning the valuation of assets (Chapters 5, 6, and 7) and liabilities (Chapters 8 and 9). Only one chapter (Chapter 10) is devoted to owners' equity because, by definition, it is a derivative measure, largely determined by the valuation approaches adopted to measure the assets and liabilities of a company.

CHAPTER FIVE

Working Capital: Current Assets and Current Liabilities

Most financial analysts agree that the balance sheet, or statement of financial position, is indispensible because it describes the composition of, and value of, a company's individual resources (i.e., its assets), obligations (i.e., its liabilities), and net worth or book value (i.e., its owners' equity). Some balance sheets, however, may be more informative than others because they present a company's assets and liabilities classified according to whether they are current or noncurrent in nature.[1] Knowing the dollar value of a company's current assets and current liabilities may be critical to accurately assessing the dividend or debt-paying ability of a company. Thus, this chapter focuses on the analytical and valuation issues associated with those current accounts, which are frequently called the *working capital* accounts.

To begin, let us establish some commonly accepted definitions of the working capital accounts:

---

[1] Classified balance sheets are not required for all companies. Real estate development companies and financial institutions, for example, whose operating cycles naturally exceed a calendar year in duration usually present unclassified balance sheets.

Current assets include cash and any other assets that are reasonably expected to be converted into cash, sold, or consumed by a company as part of its normal operations, within one operating cycle or one year, whichever is longer.[2] Examples of current assets include cash, short-term marketable securities, accounts and notes receivable, inventory (including raw materials and finished goods), and in some cases, certain prepaid expenses such as insurance, rent, and taxes.

Current liabilities, on the other hand, are those obligations whose liquidation is reasonably expected to require the use of existing current resources, or the creation of other current liabilities (e.g., a debt rollover), within one operating cycle or one year, whichever is longer. Examples of current liabilities include accounts payable, short-term notes payable, accrued expenses (such as income taxes), unearned revenues, dividends payable, and any portion of long-term debt that is due for payment in the current accounting period.

Finally, *working capital* is defined as a company's current assets less its current liabilities. This measure can be particularly important to financial statement users in that it provides an indication of the *liquidity* of a company. Liquidity, or short-term solvency, refers to the ability of a company to pay its short-term obligations and continue operating at current levels. Obviously, if a company's working capital is insufficient, it may be unable, at the extreme, to maintain adequate inventory levels to support the necessary sales volume to keep it operating profitably.

In the remainder of this chapter, we focus on the analytical and valuation issues relating to current assets and current liabilities, before returning to the concept of working capital.

Current Assets

The valuation of current assets is essentially driven by the role that they play relative to a company's current liabilities. Since current liabilities are expected to be satisfied in the short run, an assumption normally made is that the resources to satisfy those current obligations will come from a company's current assets. Thus, to enable financial statement users to accurately assess the debt-paying ability of the current assets, they are valued at their *net realizable value.*

The concept of net realizable value is similar to what some analysts call "cash liquidation value." It is essentially the level of reasonably expected

---

[2] An *operating cycle* is the length of time that it takes a company to acquire inventory for cash, process or manufacture the inventory into a final product, sell the product, and then convert the account (or note) receivable from the sale back into cash.

future cash flows to be derived from an asset. Net realizable value, however, is subject to a ceiling value, namely the original cost of the asset, such that if the net realizable value of a current asset exceeds its historical cost, it will be valued on the balance sheet at its original cost. On the other hand, if an asset's net realizable value is below its original cost, its balance sheet value will be written down to the lower value to reflect the diminished expected future cash flows. Thus, the concept of net realizable value, as applied to current assets, ensures that the balance sheet value closely approximates an asset's expected future cash value, unless that value exceeds the asset's original cost. As a consequence, analysts can be certain that when assessing the debt-paying (or dividend-paying) ability of a company's current assets, the current asset values will never be overstated, but indeed may be understated.

As we shall see when the concept of net realizable value is applied to inventories, marketable securities, and receivables, various "allowance" accounts are created as contra-asset accounts. These allowance accounts reflect the expected diminishment in future cash flows from a given asset; in essence, they reflect the degree of riskiness associated with the cash flows from the asset account, and form a reserve against such future cash losses.

Cash. A long-standing accounting convention is to present the various current assets on the balance sheet in the order of their apparent liquidity, or expected conversion to cash. Thus, since cash is, by definition, the most liquid current asset, it is traditionally listed first amongst the current assets on the balance sheet.

Most analysts assume that cash is comprised only of currency and demand deposits; however, under GAAP, the definition of cash is expanded to include items that are also "cash equivalents," for example savings accounts, negotiable checks, bank drafts, and securities with a maturity of ninety days or less (e.g., certificates of deposit, commercial paper, and U.S. Treasury bills). Other securities are not considered to be cash equivalents and are usually classified as marketable securities.

Certain items are restricted from being classified as cash or as a cash equivalent. Examples of these include compensating balances, postdated checks, and bank overdrafts. *Compensating balances* are any (or any portion of any) demand deposit maintained by a company as support for, and as required by, an existing borrowing arrangement with a lending institution. Compensating account balances are usually separately disclosed, either parenthetically on the balance sheet or in the notes to the financial statements (unless immaterial in amount) and represent a restricted resource of the company. Postdated checks, on the other hand, are excludable from cash because they are not readily convertible to cash. Bank overdrafts are excludable because they represent an overdrawn demand deposit, and hence should be classified as a current liability rather than as a current asset.

Marketable Securities. If a company's business is cyclical, it may find itself with excess quantities of cash (and hence working capital) during the relatively low activity periods. Effective asset management will ensure that any surplus cash is productively used during these interim periods, possibly invested in short-term marketable securities.

Marketable securities represent investments in any security for which a quotation is readily available from a national, international, or over-the-counter market. Although these investments may be in foreign currency, futures, options, or warrants, they are most commonly made in dividend-paying equity securities and interest-bearing debt securities. In all cases, however, it is assumed that the investment is highly liquid and that it is management's intention to convert the securities to cash in the near-term.

Like all assets, marketable securities are initially recorded on the balance sheet at their historical cost (i.e., the market price of a security plus any brokerage fees or transaction costs). Subsequent to acquisition, the valuation on the balance sheet will depend upon the type of security (i.e., debt or equity) involved. Under GAAP, the valuation of marketable equity securities is based on the *lower-of-cost-or-market* method (L.C.M.), whereas the valuation of marketable debt securities will most commonly continue under the cost method. Under L.C.M., the balance sheet value of an equity investment is the lower of the end-of-period market value (as revealed, for example, by the *Wall Street Journal*) or its accounting book value. Unlike inventories, L.C.M. may only be applied on a portfolio basis for marketable securities, with the aggregate portfolio market value compared to the aggregate portfolio cost.

In the event that the aggregate market value of a company's portfolio of short-term equity securities is less than its aggregate cost basis, the balance sheet value of the portfolio will be written down to avoid overstating the net realizable value of the securities.[3] In this case, an unrealized loss is reported on the income statement and deducted against current earnings in anticipation of a realized loss when the securities are actually sold at a subsequent date. (This reflects the old conservatism adage—recognize losses immediately, even if currently unrealized, but defer the recognition of any gains

---

[3] The accounting journal entry to record the end-of-period L.C.M. adjustment is:

Debit: Unrealized loss in market value
    of short-term portfolio $XXX

Credit: Allowance for temporary decline
    in market value of short-term portfolio $XXX

The "unrealized loss" account is treated as a deduction against earnings on the income statement, while the allowance account is treated as a contra-asset account on the balance sheet, deducted from the marketable securities account carried at its original historical cost. L.C.M. applies only to temporary fluctuations in securities prices. If a given security experiences a permanent impairment in value (perhaps due, for example, to a bankruptcy declaration), L.C.M. is not used and instead a write-down of the cost basis of the security is made.

until fully realized.) If, in a later period, the market value of the portfolio recovers its prior losses, the balance sheet value of the portfolio can be written back up, but not above the original acquisition cost of the portfolio. In this case, an unrealized gain will be recorded on the income statement and added to current earnings.

The analyst should note that these unrealized gains and unrealized losses are just that—unrealized. Since no exchange transaction has occurred, there are no corresponding cash inflows or outflows; and, of course, the IRS recognizes neither the taxability of the unrealized gains nor the tax-deductibility of the unrealized losses. In short, these are merely accounting valuation adjustments undertaken to avoid overstating the net realizable value of a company's portfolio of marketable securities.

The analyst should further note that while the use of L.C.M. prevents the overstatement of a portfolio's net realizable value, it does not prevent an understatement in value of such assets. Thus, if an understatement in value is thought to exist (as evidenced by the absence of an allowance account) the analyst should use whatever information is available to assess the true value of the portfolio of marketable securities. Unfortunately, unless a company holds five or more percent of the voting shares of another entity, it is not required to disclose, in either its annual report or its 10-K filings, the number or percentage shares held in the other company. Thus, it is frequently quite difficult to determine the current value of a company's portfolio of marketable securities when this value exceeds its cost basis.

As a final point, it is noteworthy that a company may disclose both unrealized gains (or losses) and realized gains (or losses) on its income statement. Realized gains and losses are recognized when individual securities are sold from a company's portfolio. These transactions produce actual cash flows and real tax effects. Thus, when analyzing the recurring earnings and cash flows of an entity, the unrealized gains and losses may be largely ignored, unless expected to recur.

To illustrate these points, consider Exhibit 5.1, which presents the footnote disclosure regarding the marketable securities held by Winnebago Industries, Inc., in 1986. According to this footnote, Winnebago is following established GAAP for the valuation of its current marketable securities. Its equity investments are valued using L.C.M. on a portfolio basis, and its nonequity investments are valued at cost.[4] Exhibit 5.1 reveals that, in 1986, Winnebago experienced a net unrealized loss of $488,000 on its portfolio of marketable equity securities. Note that while the portfolio's net realizable value of $18.898 million is $552,000 less than its aggregate cost of $19.45 million, only $488,000 of this loss is recognized in 1986, with $64,000 being

---

[4] Under GAAP, marketable debt securities may be valued using either L.C.M. or the cost method, with the latter method most common since it avoids recognizing the value fluctuations associated with interest rate movements.

Exhibit 5.1 _____

WINNEBAGO INDUSTRIES, INC
FOOTNOTE DATA FROM THE 1986 ANNUAL REPORT

Marketable Securities

Marketable equity securities are carried at the lower-of-cost-or-market and marketable nonequity securities are carried at cost. Net realized gains and losses on security transactions are determined on the specific identification basis.

Included in marketable securities at August 30, 1986, and August 31, 1985, were equity securities having an aggregate cost of $19,450,000 and $6,595,000, respectively, and an aggregate market value of $18,898,000 and $6,531,000 respectively. Marketable securities also include nonequity securities at an aggregate cost of $32,603,000 and $22,460,000 (which approximates market) at August 30, 1986, and August 31, 1985, respectively.

At August 30, 1986, and August 31, 1985, unrealized gains totaled $336,000 and $204,000 and unrealized losses totaled $888,000 and $268,000, respectively.

_____

previously recognized in 1985. Winnebago discloses no information in regards to realized gains or losses, and thus it is reasonable to assume that either no securities were actually sold or, if sold, the gains and losses were immaterial in amount. (If immaterial in amount, the realized gains or losses are frequently aggregated with other immaterial items under the account title "Other income/loss.")

Accounts and Notes Receivables. When revenue has been recognized in the income statement, but no cash has been received, an account or note receivable equivalent to the outstanding cash is created. Frequently, the full cash value of these credit sales will be realized, but all too often customers will fail to make all (or any) of the expected payments. Hence, one of the more delicate trade-offs that management must assess is whether the additional returns generated from extending credit to customers adequately exceeds the inherent risk of nonpayment.

Most managers conclude that, with the availability of personal and corporate credit information from various credit rating agencies, it is possible to minimize the degree of customer default risk. Nonetheless, some level of default is expected in almost all business settings, and from an accounting perspective, it is necessary to estimate these potential losses and to recognize them for income statement purposes (under the matching concept) in the period when sale occurs.

There are two widely utilized approaches to estimating the extent of expected bad debts, or alternatively, default risk: (1) the percentage of credit sales method, and (2) the percent of receivables method (also known as

Exhibit 5.2 ——————————————————————————————————————

ESTIMATING BAD DEBTS: THE AGING METHOD

Classification	Amount	Estimated Percent Uncollectible	Allowance Amount
Currently due	$ 7,000,000	0.5	$ 35,000
1-30 days overdue	2,000,000	1.5	30,000
31-60 days overdue	750,000	3.0	22,500
over 61 days overdue	250,000	7.5	18,750
	$ 10,000,000		$ 106,250

the aging method).[5] Under the *percentage of credit sales* method, a company determines the percentage relationship between recent historical credit sales and credit losses, and then multiplies this percentage by current period credit sales to arrive at an estimate of expected uncollectible accounts. Under the *percentage of receivables* method, a company determines the percentage relationship between credit losses and the level of outstanding receivables. To increase the accuracy of this estimate, most companies group their outstanding receivables into categories based upon their age, or time unpaid. It is widely accepted that the older a receivable becomes, the lower the probability that it will ultimately be paid. Exhibit 5.2 presents an aging schedule for illustration purposes.

Under either method, once the expected loss is determined, it is then recognized in the income statement as an expense and on the balance sheet as a contra-asset account.[6] The allowance account, or contra-asset account, is deducted from gross accounts receivable to arrive at the net expected cash flow from the outstanding receivables. Because of the greater accuracy provided by the aging method, it has become the method of preference for most companies and most lenders.

To illustrate the role and the importance of this loss estimation process, consider the case of Urcarco. Urcarco was incorporated in 1989 and

——————————————

[5] Some companies, usually privately owned, do not estimate the extent of expected bad debts, but rather record the expense (and the account write-off) only after a particular receivable has proven to be uncollectible.

[6] The accounting entry to record the bad debts expense would appear as:

Debit: Bad debts expense	$XXX	
Credit: Allowance for uncollectible accounts		$XXX

operates the first chain of used car lots in the U.S. As the company's prospectus for its initial public stock offering readily revealed, it "finances customer purchases of used cars in a relatively high-risk market, and some number of repossessions and related losses are anticipated." According to the prospectus, for the fiscal years ended June 30, 1988 and 1989, respectively, 510 (or 22.7 percent) and 1,329 (or 18.4 percent) of the cars sold in those years were repossessed—quite high percentages when compared to the typical retail setting. In dollar-terms, Urcarco's bad debts expense equalled 18 and 15 percent, respectively, of 1988 and 1989 gross sales. As a percentage of the outstanding receivable balance, the "allowance for losses" was 6.9 and 8.9 percent, respectively, for 1988 and 1989. Given the nature of this company's business, investors and analysts will be wise to closely follow this company's experience with actual repossessions and debt write-offs. Indeed, the accuracy of this company's current and recurring earnings will be largely tied to the reasonableness of its default estimation efforts.[7]

One of the best analytical tools for evaluating the quality of a company's receivables, and also the adequacy of its reserves for default risk, is the receivable collection period ratio. To illustrate the value of this tool, consider the case of Cardillo Travel Systems, Inc., a receivable-intensive travel-service company. As of September, 1985, Cardillo's receivables accounted for over 40 percent of the company's total assets. According to an SEC complaint issued on July 27, 1987, the company had experienced serious liquidity problems which had not been publicly disclosed. To the careful analyst, however, Cardillo's liquidity problems could have been identified in 1985 by examining the receivable collection period ratio, which had escalated to over 563 days. (The average collection period for most companies ranges between 30 and 90 days.)

While there is rarely good news associated with the estimation of customer default risk, very infrequently a silver lining may appear. Consider, for example, the Longhorn Real Estate Group, a Texas-based real estate conglomerate whose name is intentionally disguised. After several years of significant income deductions for bad debts expense, reflecting the downturn in the commercial real estate market in the Southwest U.S., this company reported a bad debts expense reversal of over $9 million, increasing 1987 pre-tax earnings by over 70 percent. According to the company's footnotes:

---

[7] In July, 1990, two lawsuits were filed against Urcarco, one alleging that the company concealed a "serious liquidity crisis" from shareholders, and the other charging that the company's financial statements were not prepared in conformity with GAAP. The suits also challenge the company's revenue recognition policy and the adequacy of its allowance for loan losses. In the three months prior to the lawsuits, Urcarco's stock tumbled from $25.50 per share to approximately $11 per share (adjusted for a 3-for-2 stock split).

During 1985, market conditions in the areas where certain of the Group's partnerships are located became severely depressed. Some of these partnerships lacked adequate cash flows to meet their obligations, and hence the Group loaned substantial amounts to them during 1985. The recovery of these advances was determined to be questionable, and as a result, a provision for bad debts was provided.

In 1987, management updated the valuation analysis of the partnership loans as a result of the completion of certain loan renegotiations. As a consequence of the renegotiations, and improved operations in certain markets, the computation of the allowance for doubtful receivables resulted in a reduction in the allowance of $9.2 million in 1987.

The analyst should note, however, that while the Group's 1987 income was significantly enhanced by the bad debts reversal, current cash flows were unaffected. Clearly, though, the longer-term prognosis for the Longhorn Group (and its cash flows) was on the up-turn. The Group's cash infusions in 1985 and 1986, designed to buy time, had apparently worked.

As a final consideration in our discussion of receivables, it is noteworthy that some companies also adjust the ending balance in receivables to reflect their estimate of expected sales returns (i.e., the "allowance for sales returns"). This accounting reflects the common business practice that when customers become dissatisfied with a purchased item, the seller often permits the customer to return the good for a cash refund or a credit to his or her account. Given the dominance of credit transactions, it is most often the latter, and hence the need to reflect this potential reduction in the net realizable value of the receivable balance.

Both the allowance for uncollectible accounts and the allowance for sales returns represent loss reserves which attempt to reflect the relative risk associated with the future cash flows from a company's outstanding receivables. The analytical concern that is inherent in both of these allowance accounts is that they may be underestimated, thereby overstating the net realizable value of the receivable balance and similarly overstating the level of current earnings. A recent example of this involved the Regina Company, a manufacturer of consumer vacuum cleaners. In 1986, Regina introduced a new product line without adequate testing. By early 1987, some retail outlets were experiencing customers returns on the new product line as high as 40 percent; and, to avoid adversely affecting earnings, Regina chose not to recognize the product returns in its financial statements. Following an SEC complaint, Regina restated its previously reported positive 1988 earnings to reflect a $16.8 million loss. The restated loss was largely attributable to the recognition of $13 million in unrecorded product returns.

Inventories. Inventory refers to those tangible current assets which are held for sale in the ordinary course of business, are in the process of production for sale, or are to be consumed in the production of goods or services for sale. Inventories are frequently the largest current asset account on the balance sheet. In 1988, for example, inventories represented an average of 61 percent of the total assets for variety stores, 40 percent for manufacturers of lawn and garden equipment, and 35 percent for sporting goods producers. Not only is this asset category important because of its size (and hence the inherent cash investment), but also because of its relationship to future earnings and cash flow (i.e., inventory represents "unrecognized profits" carried on the balance sheet). Moreover, it is an important source of collateral for lenders.

For financial statement purposes, a major objective of the accounting for inventories is the proper matching of product costs against the revenues generated from the sale of inventory in order to insure a correct determination of earned income. To accomplish this matching, inventories and the cost of goods sold are generally measured on the basis of historical cost, where historical cost is defined as the purchase price of the inventory (or raw material) plus any other expenditures (e.g., for labor, manufacturing overhead, etc.) incurred to bring the inventory to its saleable condition.[8] Once the cost of the available inventory is known, management must then determine how these cost values will be assigned to the income statement. That is, management must choose one of several popular cost flow assumptions: LIFO, FIFO, or some form of average cost.

As we saw in Chapter 3, which method is selected can have a material effect on the cost of goods sold (and hence, reported net income), as well as the value assigned to ending inventory on the balance sheet. For example, assuming that inventory quantities remain constant but costs rise from year-to-year, companies using FIFO will show an unchanged physical inventory valued at an increasing dollar value. During periods characterized by rising prices, the LIFO method is usually preferred, despite the fact that the ending inventory may be relatively understated in value as compared to current market value. As noted in Chapter 3, however, an understatement in inventory value attributable to the LIFO method can be compensated for by adjusting the ending balance with the LIFO inventory reserve, as reported in a company's footnotes.

For companies with large quantities of different inventory items, it is frequently beneficial to use the *dollar-value LIFO* method. Dollar-value LIFO

---

[8] In Chapter 3, we discussed two alternative approaches to the accounting for fixed overhead costs—the absorption costing and variable costing methods. Under the former, fixed overhead costs are considered part of the cost of producing inventory, and thus are added to the balance sheet value of ending inventory and the cost of goods sold on the income statement. Under variable costing, these costs are simply deducted on the income statement as a period expense. Note that if the quantity of overhead costs is high, there can be a significant discrepancy in the value of ending inventory on the balance sheet between the two methods. In effect, the variable cost method understates the value of inventory relative to the absorption cost method. GAAP-prepared financial statements require the use of absorption costing. When analyzing unaudited statements, the analyst should be certain to determine which method is in use.

is applied to "inventory pools" rather than to individual inventory items, thereby reducing the recordkeeping costs associated with the LIFO method. For a merchandising company, for example, inventories are often accumulated into pools by major product lines, classes, or even departments (e.g., the hardware department versus the clothing department). By creating such pools, not only are administration costs reduced, but the potentially adverse effects of a LIFO-liquidation are also minimized (because the price gains of one product in a pool may be used to offset the price declines of another). In short, dollar-value LIFO is generally thought to be superior to regular LIFO, which in turn is generally thought to be superior to other inventory costing methods, at least during periods of rising prices which characterize most companies.

As a final point, recall that the ending balance sheet value of inventory is also subject to a final valuation check to ensure that its net realizable value is not overstated; and this is accomplished by applying the L.C.M. method. In the case of inventories, L.C.M. may be applied in a variety of ways—using the portfolio basis, the individual item basis, or the pool (or puddle) basis. Analysts should also recall that the "M" in L.C.M. refers to the inventory's input (or replacement) market price, and not its output (or selling) price. Thus, the L.C.M. comparison for inventories is whether the calculated cost, via LIFO, FIFO, or average, is below its current replacement (by repurchase or reproduction) cost.

Prepaid Expenses. Assets are often defined as the probable future economic benefit to be received by a business entity as a result of past transactions or events. A good example of this involves such items as rent or insurance, which are usually paid in advance of the benefits to be received or consumed. These prepaid expenses are valued at their historical cost, and as the benefit is received, the portion of the asset which has been received (or consumed) is transferred to the income statement as an expense.

Prepaid expenses are typically the smallest current asset account on the balance sheet. Moreover, rarely, if ever, can a cash refund or rebate be obtained on these assets, and they are seldom saleable (i.e., they lack "pounce" value). Thus, in the absence of a readily determinable or recoverable cash value, most financial institutions do not consider prepaid expenses to be a liquid current asset, and instead reclassify them as an intangible asset, or alternatively write them off the balance sheet entirely. Thus, for purposes of calculating the level of working capital (i.e., current assets less current liabilities) or the current ratio (i.e., current assets divided by current liabilities), most lenders ignore any balance in prepaid expenses. Similarly, when calculating the tangible net worth of a company, lenders subtract not only the intangible assets, but also any prepaid expenses as well. In the case of a lender, whose perspective might be defined relative to a five year loan agreement, this treatment of prepaid expenses is probably well justified. However, for analytical purposes involving long-term investment or acquisition, the treatment appears overly conservative.

Current Liabilities

Liabilities are the probable future sacrifices of economic benefits by a company, arising from present obligations to transfer assets or provide services. *Current liabilities* are those obligations expected to come due within one operating cycle or one year, whichever is longer. The current liabilities consist principally of accounts and notes payable, accrued expenses payable (such as taxes), and the currently due portion of long-term debt. The listing of current liabilities on the balance sheet typically reflects both the expected sequence of payment (i.e., obligations due in 30 days or less are listed first) and the seniority of the various creditors (i.e., notes due in 30 days or less are usually listed before accounts due in 30 days).

Accounts payable (or trade payables) arise from the purchase of inventory, supplies, or other materials on credit. Sometimes, as in the case of accounts receivable, a discount will be offered by a creditor to ensure timely account payment. Accordingly, accounts payable are normally recorded net of any available discount (e.g., 2/10, net/30) in that proper cash management requires that any discounts be taken.[9]

Accounts payable, and effectively all current liabilities, are recorded at the expected amount of cash required to satisfy the obligation at its maturity. As we shall see in Chapter 8, long-term liabilities, on the other hand, are recorded at the *present value* of the expected cash amount needed to satisfy the obligation. As a consequence, the only exception to the valuation rule for short-term liabilities involves the currently due portion of long-term debt, which is valued at its present value rather than maturity value.

Notes payable typically arise from short-term bank financing, usually due in 90 to 180 days, and are frequently secured by inventories or receivables. Trade notes, on the other hand, represent amounts owed to suppliers

---

[9] While cash discounts of 2 percent may appear immaterial, and can easily be ignored in the desire to delay payment on outstanding payables, failure to take advantage of the typical discount can result in an annualized opportunity cost of as much as 36 percent (assuming that all goods are purchased on credit and that full payment occurs on the 30th day following billing). One method to check whether a company is taking advantage of available discounts is by calculating the *average payable period*:

Average payable period =

$$\frac{\text{Average balance in Accounts Payable}}{\text{Cost of Goods Sold}} \times 365 \text{ days}$$

This ratio gives an approximation of the average number of days that a payable is outstanding before it is paid.

for goods or services purchased on credit. Trade notes payable usually represent a longer-term form of trade accounts payable, or for amounts in excess of the credit limits associated with an account payable.

Accrued expenses payable represent those obligations arising from expenses that have already been incurred, but have not yet been paid. Examples include salaries earned but unpaid, utilities billed but unpaid, and income taxes due but unpaid. Under the matching concept, these expenses must be recorded even though unpaid in order to properly determine the level of income earned for the period.

Sometimes a company will receive advance payments for services to be performed in the future. Under GAAP, when cash is received under these circumstances, a liability account called *unearned* or *deferred revenue* is created for the amount of cash received. This process recognizes that the acceptance of a cash advance creates an implicit future obligation to perform. Later, as services are performed or work is completed, the unearned revenue will be transferred from the balance sheet to the income statement as earned revenue. This latter treatment also reflects the matching concept.

A final current liability is the *currently maturing portion of long-term debt*, which represents the portion of long-term bank debt or other borrowings which are due to be paid within the next operating cycle. For example, the portion of a long-term serial debenture due to be paid in the next twelve months should be classified as a current liability on the balance sheet. In some instances, the currently-due portion of long-term debt will *not* be reclassified as current, for example when a company has made firm arrangements to refinance or roll-over the maturing debt. PepsiCo, Inc., for example, classified $3.5 billion of short-term borrowings as long-term at the end of 1990; this classification approach reflected PepsiCo's intent and ability to refinance these borrowings on a long-term basis, either through long-term debt issuance or a rollover of existing short-term borrowings. Under regulatory accounting principles (RAP), a regulated company may not be required to reclassify its currently maturing long-term debt *even if* no refinancing arrangements are in place. Where this occurs, the company will disclose the portion of its long-term debt that is effectively current in its footnotes. Thus, as always, the onus falls on the analyst to carefully review the footnotes for such information.

An Illustration

To illustrate the balance sheet disclosures for current liabilities, Exhibit 5.3 presents the current liability section of the Valhi, Inc. 1989 consolidated balance sheet. Valhi's footnotes reveal that of the total $628.1 million in notes and current maturities as of year-end 1989, $550.7 million are short-term borrowings and $77.4 million are current maturities. The footnotes to Valhi's 10-K filing reveal even greater detail on the short-term borrowing,

Exhibit 5.3 _____

VALHI, INC.
CONSOLIDATED BALANCE SHEET
(in thousands)

	as of December 31	
	1989	1988
Current Liabilities		
Notes payable and current maturities of long-term debt	$ 628,149	$ 295,261
Accounts payable and accrued liabilities	523,888	530,333
Income taxes	26,466	47,177
Deferred income taxes	6,400	6,308
Total current liabilities	$ 1,184,903	$ 879,079

identifying which subsidiary undertook the borrowing, the nature of the borrowing agreement (e.g., bank debt or commercial paper), and the amounts involved.

Note also that in addition to the $26.4 million in income taxes incurred in 1989 that has not yet been paid, Valhi expects to pay an additional $6.4 million in previously deferred taxes. Thus, the total cash outflow to satisfy the company's tax liabilities in 1990 will equal the sum of the 1989 taxes paid in 1990, the deferred tax reversal of $6.4 million (and any reversal in 1990), plus any income taxes incurred and paid in 1990.

Working Capital

As noted earlier, working capital is the excess of current assets over current liabilities. And, since creditors and investors alike are concerned about a company's ability to satisfy its maturing obligations (particularly those maturing in the short-run) and its ability to leverage its operations effectively, the concept of working capital takes on particular importance.

While most analysts prefer, and often expect, working capital to be positive, this will not always be the case, particularly for some well-managed organizations. Sybra Inc., for example, perpetually maintains a negative working capital position. This is possible for several reasons. First, Sybra owns and operates a chain of fast-food restaurants, providing it with a significant, recurring cash flow from sales, and virtually no cash investment in accounts receivable. Second, the turnover of inventory is naturally quite fast, particularly relative to the account payable terms on its inventory purchases. Thus, rather than maintaining (or needing) a large quantity of current assets to satisfy both its operating needs and its current obligations, Sybra is effectively able to finance operations through its current liabilities (specifically its accounts payable). Consequently, a greater portion of the company's current resources can be invested in long-term revenue-producing assets.

Companies with a slow inventory turnover and/or predominantly credit-based sales will obviously require a greater proportionate investment in their current assets and working capital. However, even for these companies, the level of working capital can be minimized (or even be negative) through the use of effective inventory and receivable management techniques. The use of "just-in-time" inventory management systems, for example, allows many manufacturers to minimize both the level of inventory on hand and the level of accounts payable. Similarly, the selective extension of credit and the judicious use of trade discounts for timely receivable payment enables many companies to minimize the level of, and the cash invested in, accounts and notes receivable. Thus, when analyzing the working capital of a company, it is not sufficient to conclude that a positive working capital position is "good" and a negative one is "bad." Indeed, a positive working capital position for a company operating in the fast-food industry may be indicative of weak current asset management. A good strategy is to compare the working capital practices of a company against those utilized by the leader of its industry.

Alternative Indicators

In addition to examining the actual *level* of working capital some analysts also find it valuable to consider various ratios constructed from the working capital accounts. For example, the *current ratio* or the *working-capital ratio* is given by:

$$\text{Current ratio} = \frac{\text{Current assets}}{\text{Current liabilities}}$$

Although a current ratio in excess of one, or 100 percent, may be quite comforting to a credit or investment analyst, it may also reflect excessive liquid assets not optimally invested. Recall also the discussion in Chapter 3 concerning the effect of alternative inventory valuation approaches on financial ratios. It was noted that the FIFO method will consistently yield the highest current ratio and LIFO method the lowest, potentially erroneously suggesting the conclusion that a FIFO-based company is more liquid (i.e., has more working capital) than a LIFO-based company.

To avoid these concerns, we prefer a refinement of the current ratio commonly known as the *quick ratio* or the *acid-test ratio*. This ratio omits both inventories (and the attendant information miscues often associated with LIFO versus FIFO) and prepaid expenses from the current assets due to their illiquidity:

$$\text{Quick ratio} = \frac{\text{(Current assets - Inventory - Prepaid expenses)}}{\text{Current liabilities}}$$

Finally, a very useful measure of the long-term earnings-generating capacity of a company, which incorporates the concept of working capital, is the *working capital from operations,* calculated as:[10]

Net income after taxes
+ depreciation, depletion, and amortization expense
+/- increase/decrease in deferred income taxes
-/+ nonrecurring gains/losses
_____
Working capital from operations

Many financial institutions utilize this measure as an indicator of a company's future recurring earnings capacity, or "earnings power." The measure approximates operating earnings by deleting nonrecurring items, and focuses on a company's ability to generate working capital (including cash) from its operations by deleting such non-working capital (and non-cash) items as depreciation, depletion, amortization, and deferred income taxes. This measure appears to be quite useful for evaluating long-term lending opportunities, particularly in combination with the level of existing debt, for example in the following ratio:

$$\text{Recurring earnings coverage} = \frac{\text{Working capital from operations}}{\text{Debt due next year}}$$

Conclusions

This chapter focused on the working capital accounts. Since the current assets of most companies tend to be dominated by inventories and receivables, it is in the analyst's best interests to focus his or her attention on these accounts in particular. In addition, the current liability classification tends to be dominated by the accounts (and notes) payable and by accrued expenses payable. Since there are few valuation issues related to current liabilities, the analysis of these accounts is often more clear cut and reliable.

---

[10] Depending upon the specific circumstances, it may be useful to adjust this measure for capitalized interest, the equity in unconsolidated subsidiary earnings or losses, and for minority shareholder earnings or losses.

'The analyst's key concerns, however, should revolve around the following questions:

1. Is the level of default risk inherent in the company's operations adequately reflected on the balance sheet (via the allowance for uncollectible accounts and the allowance for sales returns) and on the income statement (via the bad debts expense and the sales returns and allowances)?

2. Is the balance sheet value of ending inventory fairly stated? Should the LIFO reserve be used to obtain an estimation of the current value of ending inventory?

3. Is the value of the portfolio of short-term equity securities understated, and if so, by how much? Is the value of the portfolio of short-term debt securities potentially overstated?

4. Should the value of any prepaid expenses be excluded from the analysis of working capital and liquidity?

5. Are all currently due obligations correctly classified as current? And, are all currently due obligations being paid in a timely manner to take advantage of any discounts?

CHAPTER SIX

Intercorporate Investments

A major problem in analyzing financial statements is the lack of clear boundaries between economic entities. While the basic accounting model assumes that well-defined boundaries exist between economic entities, nothing can be further from the truth when a company engages in intercorporate investments. Thus, this chapter focuses on the reporting and analytical issues encountered when entities undertake intercorporate investments.

Business Combinations

Under the laws of the United States, a corporation is given certain rights which include the ability to make investments in the financial securities or financial resources of other entities. These investments may include debt securities (bonds), equity securities (common and preferred stock), as well as the assets and liabilities of other economic entities. As noted in the previous chapter, an investment in the debt securities of another entity is usually valued at its historical cost, whereas temporary investments in equity securities are valued using the lower-of-cost-or-market method. Thus, this chapter focuses on those long-term investments by a corporation in the equity securities and/or assets and liabilities of another legal entity. These transactions fall into the general category called *business combinations*.

Three basic forms of business combinations are recognized from an accounting and legal perspective. They are:

1. Merger
2. Consolidation, and
3. Acquisition

In reality, the acquisition constitutes the majority of business combinations occurring in the U.S., and thus will be the principal focus of this chapter. The analyst will often be correct in assuming that a given business combination is an acquisition, even if the popular media uses the term "merger" or "merged." The principle concern of the analyst in understanding intercorporate investments centers on valuation and reporting issues; however, these are intertwined with accounting rules, and consequently we explore the accounting for intercorporate investments first.

———— Accounting for Intercorporate Investments: ———— Cost Versus Equity

Two basic methods have been devised for accounting for intercorporate investments: the cost method and the equity method. A knowledge of the two methods is best gained through an example.

Assume that Company P was formed for the sole purpose of making long-term investments in the common stock of other companies. Starting with an original investment of $1 million, P purchased a 20 percent interest in Company S for $100,000. On the date of purchase the two companies' balance sheets were as follows:

Company P

Assets = Liabilities + Owners' Equity
$1,000,000 = $0 + $1,000,000

Company S

Assets = Liabilities + Owners' Equity
$700,000 = $200,000 + $500,000

Company P made no other investments during the year, and Company S produced net income of $25,000 and paid cash dividends of $10,000.

Under either the cost or equity method, Company P would record its initial investment in the stock of Company S at its purchase price of

$100,000. The balance sheet of Company P would remain relatively unchanged as the transaction involves simply an exchange of one asset (cash) for another (an investment in Company S). Company S's financial statements would also remain unaffected as the purchase of the shares of stock would have been from the shareholders of Company S, and not directly from the company.

Under the cost method, as the name implies, P's investment in S remains recorded at the historical cost of the investment unless an impairment in value is determined to have occurred. If the impairment is judged to be permanent, the investment account would be reduced accordingly and a loss reported on the current income statement. If, on the other hand, the impairment is judged to be only temporary, the investment account would be reduced by an allowance account, but no loss is recorded on the income statement. Instead, a reduction in owners' equity is recorded via a contra-account.[1] The only other information that would be reflected in Company P's financial statements would be the dividends received from S. Hence, the income statement of Company P would only reflect income if Company S paid dividends. This gives rise to the main problem associated with the cost method—if Company P desires to increase its reported income, it must only have Company S pay more in dividends in any one period.

Obviously, to force S to pay more in dividends would require P to have the ability to exert control over Company S's dividend policies. GAAP identifies, however arbitrary, a 20 percent ownership interest as indicative of an ability by one company to exercise operating influence over another. And, if 20 or more percent of the voting common stock is owned as an investment (or control can be shown for smaller investment percentages) the investor, in this case Company P, would be required to use the equity method instead of the cost method.

The 20 percent rule is, realistically, only a guideline, and exceptions may be found. For example, the well-publicized investment by T. Boone Pickens in Koito, Ltd., a Japanese manufacturer of automobile parts, would be accounted for using the cost method. In spite of Mr. Pickens' 26 percent shareholding in Koito, he was unable to gain election to the company's board of directors, thereby providing evidence that he was unable to influence Koito's operating policies. Similarly, in a reversal of relationships, Leasco, Inc., a computer leasing company previously spun-off by Reliance Corporation, purchased a 3 percent shareholding in Reliance.

---

[1] For example, on December 31, 1990, Valhi, Inc held approximately 12.5 million shares (or 19.8 percent) of Lockheed Corporation common stock. These noncurrent marketable equity securities had been purchased at an average cost of $42.85 per share, and had a year-end market value of $33.63 per share. Valhi reported a contra-owners' equity account of $73.5 million, reflecting the temporary unrealized loss of approximately $115 million on the Lockheed investment, offset by temporary unrealized gains of $41.5 million on other equity securities held by the company on a long-term basis.

Since Leasco's president and other key executives were on the board of directors of Reliance, Leasco accounted for its investment using the equity method—a decision that was questioned by many financial analysts as well as accountants.

To understand the equity method, the analyst must recognize the meaning of the transactions of Company S that are summarized by its net income and dividend results. When a company produces income, it is indicative of two facts. First, that the revenues exceeded expenses. And second, that not only did owners' equity increase, but so too did the company's assets. Thus, in the case of Company S, net income of $25,000 implies that both S's assets and owners' equity increased by $25,000:

$$\text{Assets} = \text{Liabilities} + \text{Owners' Equity}$$
$$\$700,000 = \$200,000 + \$500,000$$
$$+25,000 = + +25,000$$

From the perspective of Company P, this increase in assets would imply that the underlying book value of P's investment similarly increased. To reflect this increase in underlying asset value, the following information would be entered on P's financial statements:

Dr. Investment in Company S	$5,000	
Cr. Equity in S's Earnings		$5,000

Notice that the investment account is increased to reflect the equity change that occurred in Company S, and that P's income will be correspondingly increased by its proportionate ownership interest in S's earnings. The dividend transaction can also be analyzed with respect to its effect on S's balance sheet:

Company S
$$\text{Assets} = \text{Liabilities} + \text{Owners' Equity}$$
$$\$700,000 = \$200,000 + \$500,000$$
$$-10,000 = + -10,000$$

The use of cash to pay dividends produces a reduction in the underlying book value of Company S, and thus to P's investment in S. If Company P reflects this reduction in its investment account, the following information would be recorded:

Dr. Cash	$2,000	
Cr. Investment in Company S		$2,000

Notice that while P's cash increased by the dividends received, the investment account declined by an equivalent amount reflecting the implicit liquidation of S's net book value. This entry completes the accounting for an intercorporate investment under the equity method. Note that Company P would be unable to manipulate its own earnings under the equity method since a dividend payment has no effect on its reported income. Company P's reported income from its investment in Company S is limited to its proportionate share of the earnings (or losses) generated by Company S.

The equity method has certain drawbacks, however. For example, a company using the cost method to account for an intercorporate investment may manipulate its earnings stream, but the analyst can be certain that a related cash inflow has occurred. Under the equity method, a manipulation of earnings may not take place but the recognized income in the form of the "Equity in Subsidiary's Earnings" account may have no supporting cash inflows. As with all accounting choices, neither method is without fault and the analyst must consider the problems inherent in both methods.

Reporting For Intercorporate Investments

Without the benefit of specific disclosures in a company's footnotes, an analyst will never really know how an intercorporate investment is being accounted for, but can usually assume that the reporting procedures follow certain conventions. If the ownership interest in the common stock of an investment is between 0 and 20 percent, the investment is usually reported as a one-line consolidation using the cost method. If the ownership interest falls between 20 and 50 percent of the common stock outstanding, the investment is usually reported as a one-line consolidation using the equity method. Finally, if an investment of 50 percent or more of the common stock is acquired, the parent will report the investment by incorporating the assets and liabilities of the subsidiary together with the parent's assets and liabilities in what is known as consolidated financial statements, to which we now turn.

The Acquisition

An *acquisition* involves a long-term investment in a majority (i.e., over 50 percent) of the common stock of another company. The stock is usually obtained through a solicitation of current stockholders called a *tender offer*. It is important to note that no transaction is made directly with the company itself, but rather with the company's shareholders.

The acquisition of 100 percent of the outstanding common stock of a company is equivalent (except on some legal grounds) to the purchase of all of the net assets of a company—a transaction that is called a merger. Whether a company invests in the net assets or in the common stock of another company is not important economically. Both types of investments give the acquiring company the exclusive use of the acquired resources.

An acquisition is ⟨handwritten⟩ ng equation:

Thus, both companies r ⟨handwritten overwrite⟩ ...urate legal identities following this form of business combination.

To understand how an acquisition is accounted for, it is first necessary to identify the various transfers that occur between the two parties (i.e., between X and Y). As shown above, Y as an entity experiences no directly measurable economic effect as a consequence of the acquisition of its common stock by X. X, however, transfers consideration (e.g., cash, debt, or shares of its own stock) to the shareholders of Y.

The question that must be answered before an accounting for the transaction can take place is: At what value will the stock of Y be recorded on the accounting records of X? In an exchange between X and the shareholders of Y, this question can best be answered by identifying the flow which is most easily valued—the flow of stock from Y's shareholders or the flow of consideration from X. Whichever flow is most easily (and correctly) valued will normally be the one used to value the transaction.

The stock of Y, for example, typically has two inherent values at the time of acquisition. The first is its market value as defined by the consideration given by X, and the other is the underlying book value of Y. It is unlikely that the book value of Y's net assets will be equivalent to the current fair market value of the stock of Y, except by chance. On the other hand, if X exchanges cash for the shares of stock, it can be assumed that the cash price represents the fair market value of the net assets acquired through the stock rights. The cash price, then, is typically used by accountants to value the stock of Y obtained in an acquisition. Likewise, if debt is issued to the shareholders of Y in exchange for their stock, the discounted value of the debt is assumed to represent the fair market value of the stock.

The value of the consideration paid by X is used in both the case of cash and debt to record the stock of Y on X's financial statements. Whenever the consideration value is used to measure an acquisition, a so-called *purchase* has taken place. And, any difference between the fair market value of Y's net assets and the consideration given by X in the form of cash or debt will be recorded as *goodwill*. Thus, goodwill is the excess of the purchase price over the fair market value of the acquired net assets.[2] Stated alternatively, accounting goodwill is the difference between (1) the value of the consider-

---

[2] In the rare event that the consideration given by X to Y's shareholders is less than the book value of Y's net assets, *negative goodwill* is said to occur. By convention, negative goodwill is seldom disclosed in financial statements. Instead, the negative goodwill is eliminated by reducing the value of Y's tangible fixed assets (if any) when transferred to the consolidated financial statements.

ation paid and (2) the sum of the market values of identifiable assets less the sum of the market values of identifiable liabilities.

A third form of consideration to transact the acquisition involves the issuance of stock by X. If the stock of X is exchanged for the stock of Y, the acquisition may be more difficult to value. While the transaction could take on a variety of values, under GAAP only two are generally accepted. The first valuation alternative uses the market value of the stock of X to assign a value to the stock of Y. This is exactly the situation discussed above and is identified as the purchase method. Second, the market values of both stock X and stock Y are ignored and instead the value assigned to the acquisition is the book value of Y's net assets. Whenever common stock is exchanged and the book value of the acquired net assets is used in the valuation process, the *pooling-of-interests* method is being used. Thus, the stock issued by X in the exchange is valued at the book value of the net assets acquired, and hence no goodwill can ever exist under this approach.

To help illustrate these issues, let us consider a simple acquisition between two independent companies. Assume Marmee Company and Small Enterprise have the following balance sheets:

	Marmee Company	Small Enterprise
Assets	$ 700,000	$ 312,000
Liabilities	$ 150,000	$ 100,000
Common Stock($1 par)	160,000	64,000
Additional Paid In Capital	120,000	34,000
Retained Earnings	270,000	114,000
Total Equities	$ 700,000	$ 312,000

Further assume that the following is true for Small Enterprise:

	Book Value	Fair Market Value
Assets	$ 312,000	$ 362,000
Liabilities	100,000	95,000
Net Worth	$ 212,000	$ 267,000
	$ 55,000	

The increase of $55,000 in the value of Small's net worth may be assumed to be caused by an increase in the market value of the company's assets and by a decrease in liability value caused by an increase in interest rates since certain debt was issued.

Assume further that Marmee purchased 90 percent of the common stock of Small Enterprise in the secondary stock market for $243,000.

Marmee would record the investment in Small Enterprise stock using the equity method as follows:

Dr. Investment in Small Enterprise	$243,000	
Cr. Cash		$243,000

The balance sheets of Marmee would be relatively unaffected by this purchase. Marmee would simply have exchanged one asset (cash) for another (an investment in Small). Hence, if Marmee were to prepare a balance sheet on the date of acquisition, it would appear as follows:

Marmee Company
Balance Sheet

Assets other than investment	$ 457,000
Investment in Small Enterprise	243,000
Total Assets	$ 700,000
Liabilities	$ 150,000
Common Stock ($1 par)	160,000
Additional Paid In Capital	120,000
Retained Earnings	270,000
Total Equities	$ 700,000

Marmee, however, owns more than 50 percent of Small and therefore must report the subsidiary via consolidated financial statements. Consolidation involves simply replacing the "Investment in Small Enterprise" with the assets and liabilities that it represents. The excess of the acquisition cost over the fair market value of the acquired net assets is of course goodwill. And, the consolidated balance sheet would appear as follows:

Marmee Company
Consolidated Balance Sheet

Assets:		Liabilities & Equities:	
Marmee Assets	$ 457,000	Marmee Liabilities	$ 150,000
Small Assets	312,000	Small Liabilities	100,000
Parent's Share of		Parent's Share of	
Fair Market Value	45,000*	Fair Market Value	(4,500)*
Goodwill	2,700+	Minority Interest	21,200
Total Assets	$ 816,700	Common Stock	160,000
		Additional Paid In Capital	120,000
		Retained Earnings	270,000
			$ 816,700

* .90($50,000) + .90($5,000) = $49,500. This represents, respectively, the parent's share of the change in the fair market value of Small's assets and liabilities.

+ $243,000 − .90($267,000) = $2,700.

Note the presence of a "minority interest" in the net assets of Small, calculated by multiplying the ownership interest of the minority stockholders by the book value of Small Enterprise (.10 × $212,000). Also note that only the parent's share of the increased value of Small's assets and liabilities is reflected in the consolidated balance sheet, and the minority interest in the increase is not.

If for this same example, Marmee had issued 81,000 shares of its own stock in exchange for 90 percent (i.e., 57,600 shares) of Small's stock, a new valuation question arises: What value do we place on the shares issued, and subsequently on Small Enterprises' assets and liabilities? The two possible values are (1) the market value of Marmee's shares (i.e. the purchase method), or (2) the book value of Small's assets and liabilities (i.e., the pooling-of-interests method).

Assume that each share of Marmee's stock is selling for $3. Under the purchase method, Marmee would record the acquisition as follows:

Dr. Investment in Small Enterprise	$243,000	
Cr. Common Stock		81,000
Cr. Additional Paid In Capital		162,000

And, the unconsolidated balance sheet for Marmee would appear as follows:

Marmee Company
Unconsolidated Balance Sheet

Assets:

Assets Other Than Investment	$	700,000
Investment in Small Enterprise		243,000
	$	943,000

Liabilities and Equities:

Liabilities	$	150,000
Common Stock		241,000
Additional Paid In Capital		282,000
Retained Earnings		270,000
	$	943,000

If Marmee Company were to present a consolidated balance sheet, it would appear as:

Marmee Company
Consolidated Balance Sheet

Assets:		Liabilities & Equities:	
Marmee Assets	$ 700,000	Marmee Liabilities	150,000
Small Assets	312,000	Small Liabilities	100,000
Parents' share in		Parent's share in	
Fair Market Value	45,000	Fair Market Value	(4,500)
Goodwill	2,700	Minority Interest	21,200
Total Assets	1,059,700	Common Stock	241,000
		Additional Paid In Capital	282,000
		Retained Earnings	270,000
			1,059,700

If, on the other hand, the book value of Small's assets and liabilities were used to value the investment, thereby indicating that a pooling approach should be adopted, Marmee would make the following entry:

Dr. Investment in Small Enterprise	190,800	
Cr. Common Stock		81,000
Cr. Additional Paid In Capital		7,200
Cr. Retained Earnings		102,600

And, Marmee's unconsolidated balance sheet would appear as:

Marmee Company
Unconsolidated Balance Sheet

Assets:	
Assets Other Than Investment	$ 700,000
Investment in Small Enterprise	190,800
	$ 890,800
Liabilities and Equities:	
Liabilities	$ 150,000
Common Stock	241,000
Additional Paid In Capital	127,200
Retained Earnings	372,600
	$ 890,800

In consolidating Marmee and Small, the $190,800 investment account would be replaced by the assets and liabilities of Small Enterprise. Under the pooling-of-interests method, the investment account equals the book value of the assets and liabilities that it is being replaced with, and hence goodwill will not be recorded. The consolidated balance sheet would appear as follows:

Marmee Company
Consolidated Balance Sheet

Assets:		Liabilities & Equities:	
Marmee Assets	$ 700,000	Marmee Liabilities	150,000
Small Assets	312,000	Small Liabilities	100,000
Total	$ 1,012,000	Minority Interest	21,200
		Common Stock	241,000
		Additional Paid In Capital	127,200
		Retained Earnings	372,600
		Total	$ 1,012,000

Consolidated versus Unconsolidated Subsidiaries

The issue of when consolidation is appropriate is not always as clear as the previous discussion may lead one to believe. Before the adoption of SFAS 94 in 1987, the authoritative accounting literature recognized that certain types of subsidiaries might appropriately remain unconsolidated because of their "nonhomogeneous" nature. For example, Sears, Inc., a large retail chain, wholly owned the Allstate Insurance Company, but did not consolidate the subsidiary's financial results until required to do so by SFAS 94. Were the operations of these two companies so different that consolidation was inappropriate? Probably not, but the "nonhomogenity" of certain subsidiaries was used by some parent companies as a vehicle to avoid consolidating the large debt positions held by certain subsidiaries. As more and more companies acquired diverse subsidiaries, it became obvious that the nonhomogenity issue no longer applied and that the true financial position of an entity might be more fairly presented by viewing all subsidiaries in the context of consolidated financial statements. To this end, SFAS 94 now requires the consolidation of essentially all subsidiaries where more than 50 percent of the common stock is owned. This accounting requirement has brought about higher debt-to-equity ratios for many entities which had previously not consolidated debt-laden subsidiaries.

Consider, for example, the case of General Motors and its wholly-owned financing subsidiary, General Motors Acceptance Corporation. Prior to 1988, GM accounted for GMAC on an unconsolidated basis using the equity method (because the parent could exercise significant operating influence over the subsidiary). Beginning in that year, GM consolidated the operations of GMAC, and the effect of this accounting change can best be illustrated by comparing the total debt-to-equity ratio for GM in 1988 both with and without the operations of GMAC:

	1988
Total debt-to-equity: without consolidation	1.54
Total debt-to-equity: with consolidation	3.56
Percent change	131

Although one might infer that SFAS 94 has brought about the end to this form of off-balance sheet financing, this is not the case. SFAS 94 fails to specify the accounting to be used for joint ventures and limited partnerships that are owned in the majority, but for which some question exists regarding control. And, as a general convention, joint ventures involving minority ownership are equity accounted. Thus, joint ventures and limited partnerships remain a vehicle for parent companies to keep debt off the consolidated balance sheet. To the extent that such debt is guaranteed by the parent, it should probably be directly reflected in any long-term debt analysis of the parent.

Analytical Concerns

The pooling-of-interests method in the Marmee-Small acquisition illustrates one of the classic analytical concerns associated with the pooling approach—it often leads to a current (and future) understatement of net assets, and corresponding overstatement of earnings. The overstatement of future earnings results because the increase in the fair market value of Small's net assets is not recognized in the consolidated financial statements under the pooling method; thus, that increase is neither amortized nor depreciated against earnings, as it would be under the purchase approach, which does record the higher net asset values (and hence higher depreciation) in the consolidated statements.

In addition to the advantage of higher reported earnings due to reduced depreciation and amortization charges, another reason that the pooling approach is preferred by some companies is that the acquisition is assumed to have occurred at the beginning of the accounting period, regardless of when the transaction actually took place. The effect of this is to raise reported earnings for the current year above that which would be otherwise reported under the purchase method. Under purchase accounting, only the earnings since the date of acquisition may be consolidated. Thus, the analyst should note that under pooling, the balance sheet accounts may be understated and the earnings overstated, relative to purchase accounting.

A final analytical concern relates to goodwill. As noted above, goodwill will frequently arise under a purchase, but never occurs under a pooling. Unfortunately, while GAAP requires the amortization of goodwill against accounting earnings over a period not to exceed 40 years, current IRS regulations do not permit goodwill to be deducted against taxable earnings. Thus, goodwill effectively represents a non-tax deductible investment; it also represents an asset with potentially little or no resale or recovery value. Thus, it is not surprising that most analysts ignore goodwill when making credit and investment evaluations (i.e., by reducing the level of total assets and owners' equity by the amount of goodwill).

Because of these notable financial statement effects, accounting standard-setters have established rigid guidelines that must be met before the pooling method may be used. For example, at least 90 percent of the voting shares of the acquiree must be obtained in the exchange, and voting shares of the acquiror must be exchanged for voting stock of the acquiree. Preferred stock is assumed to have the characteristics of debt, and therefore is not amenable to the pooling method.

Chili's, Inc.: An Illustration

To illustrate the various reporting and valuation issues associated with a pooling transaction and a purchase, we refer to the Chili's, Inc., 1989 financial statements. Other than a general increase in the reported assets and liabilities of the acquiring company, little economic information is presented directly on the face of the financial statements following an acquisition. To understand the economic substance of such a transaction, a careful reading of the footnotes and prior financial statements is required.

A Pooling-of-Interests

Exhibit 6.1 presents Chili's footnote disclosure for its business combinations through 1989. On February 29, 1989, Chili's acquired Grady's, Inc. in an exchange of 772,500 newly-issued shares of Chili's stock for all of the outstanding shares of Grady, Inc. Since the transaction met all necessary criteria for a pooling-of-interests, Chili's was permitted to restate its financial statements to include the results of Grady for all prior periods reported.

Exhibit 6.1 ————————————————————————————————

CHILI'S, INC.
FOOTNOTE DISCLOSURE: BUSINESS COMBINATIONS

Effective February 28, 1989, the Company exchanged 772,500 newly issued shares of its common stock for all of the outstanding shares of Grady's, Inc. ("Grady's"), an operator of six casual dining restaurants in the southern United States. The acquisition was accounted for as a pooling of interests and, accordingly, the Company's consolidated financial statements have been restated to include the accounts and operations of Grady's for all periods presented. Grady's fiscal year end and reported financial results have been adjusted to conform to the financial presentation of the Company. These adjustments were not significant and, accordingly, are not reflected below. Revenues, Net Income and Primary and Fully Diluted Net Income Per Share combined for the eight months ended February 28, 1989 and the years ended June 30, 1988 and 1987 are as follows:

	EIGHT MONTHS ENDED FEBRUARY 28, 1989	YEAR ENDED JUNE 30	
	(UNAUDITED)	1988	1987
Revenues:			
Chili's	$ 170,217	$ 218,298	$ 177,236
Grady's	12,012	14,047	10,077
Combined	$ 182,229	$ 232,345	$ 187,313
Net Income:			
Chili's	$ 7,505	$ 8,734	$ 6,486
Grady's	292	518	220
Combined	$ 7,797	$ 9,252	$ 6,706
Primary Net Income Per Share:			
Chili's	$ 0.81	$ 0.97	$ 0.74
Grady's	$ —	$ —	$ —
Combined	$ 0.77	$ 0.94	$ 0.70
Fully Diluted Net Income Per Share:			
Chili's	$ 0.79	$ 0.96	$ 0.74
Grady's	$ —	$ —	$ —
Combined	$ 0.76	$ 0.94	$ 0.70

As a result of the acquisition, Stockholders' Equity at June 30,1986 has been increased by $322,000. Income taxes on income for the period Grady's was taxed as a Subchapter S corporation has been provided at statutory corporate rates as a pro forma provision for income taxes.

Exhibit 6.1 (continued) ————————————————————————————————

In July, 1987, CBS Development Company ("CBS"), a wholly-owned subsidiary of the Company, acquired Border Stop-Lemmon, Ltd., the trademark "Border Stop," (the "Mark"), the system for operating Mexican style, fast food restaurants under the Mark, an existing restaurant located in Dallas, Texas and certain other real and personal property (together "Border Stop"). The transaction was accounted for as a purchase, and the consolidated statement of income for the year ended June 30, 1988 includes the results of operations from the purchase date. All of these assets were acquired in exchange for 106,761 newly issued shares of the Company's Common Stock and $200,000 in cash. The assets acquired were included in the consolidated financial statements at a cost of $2,700,000, allocated on the basis of fair values at the acquisition date. (See Note 10 for discussion of the subsequent disposition of certain assets.)

The consolidated results of operations on a pro forma basis as though Border Stop had been acquired on July 1, 1986 are not presented as the results do not differ materially from the results as presented.

The Mark acquired in the purchase is recorded as a deferred cost and is being amortized on a straight-line basis over an estimated useful life of 30 years.

——

A comparison of Chili's original 1988 financial results with those restated in the 1989 report reveals the following:

	Results originally reported in 1988	1988 Results restated in 1989	Change
Total Assets	$ 127,303,000	$ 130,819,000	$ 3,516,000
Total Debt	67,006,000	69,558,000	2,552,000
Shareholder Equity	60,297,000	61,261,000	964,000

Thus, it can be seen that Chili's acquired $964,000 in new net assets in exchange for 772,500 shares of stock. At the time of the transaction, Chili's shares were trading at approximately $20 per share, giving the newly-issued shares a market value of over $15 million. Consequently, the true cost of the Grady acquisition is not reflected in Chili's financial statements, enabling the company to show higher current and future earnings, as well as a higher return on the acquired net assets than realistically will occur.

A Purchase

Exhibit 6.1 also reveals that during 1987, CBS Development, a wholly owned subsidiary, acquired Border Stop-Lemmon, Ltd. in exchange for $200,000 and 106,761 newly issued Chili's shares. Based on Chili's share price at the time of the acquisition, the transaction had an aggregate value of $2.7 million, and was accounted for as a purchase.

A comparison of Chili's 1987 and 1988 financial statements reveals that the company's assets and shareholder equity increased by approximately $2.5 million (i.e., $2.7 million – $200,000), and that the principal asset involved was the "Border Stop" trademark, valued in excess of $2 million. Of considerable interest is the fact that Chili's management decided to amortize the trademark over a period of 30 years, a seemingly excessive period for a restaurant trademark. At the current rate of amortization, only $66,666 is charged against income annually (i.e., $2 million/30 years), whereas if a five year amortization period were adopted, $400,000 would be charged against earnings. Thus, it appears as if Chili's may be rear-end loading much of the cost of the Border Stop acquisition.

As these examples from Chili's reveal, how an acquisition is accounted for may dramatically affect both the balance sheet and the income statement. In both instances, however, the positive financial statement effects were obtained by "managing" the reported cost of the acquisition. Fortunately, the statement of cash flows, and particularly the cash flows from operations, remain unaffected (except in the year of acquisition) by the various accounting policies adopted by management. Thus, a careful review of a company's recurring cash flows from operations will reveal exactly how much new cash flow the acquired assets are producing.

Conclusions

The use of consolidated financial statements to make credit and investment decisions concerning subsidiaries is, at best, questionable. Even for the parent entity, however, statements constructed using current GAAP may be misleading. This is especially true in those situations involving pooling-of-interests, but may also be true under purchase accounting when the purchase price is below the fair market value of the assets and liabilities of the acquired company (i.e., negative goodwill). In that case, the long-term fixed assets are arbitrarily reduced, causing a reduction in the recognized depreciation expense and potentially making the consolidated financial statements appear as if operating efficiencies have occurred when in fact they have not.

CHAPTER SEVEN

Noncurrent Operating Assets

This chapter focuses on the long-lived, revenue-generating assets of a company, namely the *noncurrent operating assets*. For most companies, these assets constitute the largest capital investment, and as such, deserve appropriate consideration by the analyst. Moreover, for lenders, noncurrent operating assets constitute an important source of debt collateral, and for investors, an important source of cash flow production.

Noncurrent operating assets may be either tangible or intangible, and are generally grouped into four categories: fixed assets, natural resources, intangible assets, and other noncurrent assets. Two fundamental accounting issues characterize this category of assets: (1) the cost or asset value that should be *capitalized* (or reported) on the balance sheet; and, (2) the portion of the capitalized cost that should be *allocated* to the income statement as the asset is consumed. In Chapter 3 we considered the allocation issue; thus, the principal focus of this chapter is the capitalization issue.

Both the capitalization and the allocation processes require corporate management to exercise considerable accounting policy discretion, often with incomplete information. Consequently, as we saw in Chapter 3 and will see again shortly, this causes the valuation of noncurrent assets for financial statement purposes to become somewhat subjective. Thus, considerable variance may arise in the valuation of substantially identical assets, both between and within companies. Hence, with respect to assessing the quality of earnings and assets, the analyst will need to consider such issues as the extent to which the capitalized asset values are over or understated, and the extent to which the periodic charge to earnings (i.e., depreciation, amortization, or depletion) is adequate.

Valuation Overview

In general, all noncurrent assets are initially recorded at their acquisition cost, or fair market value as of the date of acquisition. With the exception of land, goodwill acquired prior to 1971, and certain miscellaneous noncurrent assets, these assets are assumed to be "wasting assets" in that a portion of their initial cost is assumed to expire or be consumed each accounting period, regardless of the level of their usage. Noncurrent assets are consumed as part of a company's revenue-generating activities and a portion of their value is assumed to deteriorate through obsolescence or wear and tear even if no revenues are produced.

In order to accurately match a company's expenses with its revenues, the portion of the asset cost which has expired or been consumed is recognized as an expense, and its balance sheet valuation reduced accordingly. This systematic allocation of asset cost against revenues is called *depreciation* when it relates to fixed assets, *amortization* when it relates to intangible assets, and *depletion* when it relates to natural resources. Although the labels differ and the specific allocation methods may vary, the purpose of the allocation process is the same in each case: to match the historical (rather than economic) cost of an asset with the revenues produced by the asset over its economic life.

At any point in time subsequent to acquisition, noncurrent assets are valued on the balance sheet at their original cost less the portion of this cost which has expired or been consumed. This net value (e.g., cost less depreciation taken to date) is often referred to as the asset's *book value* or *carrying value*. In some cases, the future revenue-generating ability of these assets will become impaired. Where such impairments are judged to be permanent, the carrying value of the impaired asset should be reduced to reflect the diminished expected future revenues and cash flows. Consistent with the GAAP concept of conservatism, these expected future losses should be recognized immediately for income statement purposes. However, in the event that the value of a noncurrent asset appreciates above its carrying value, no gain should be recognized, unless or until the asset is sold.

Fixed Assets

Fixed assets, or property, plant and equipment, generally includes such assets as factories, building and equipment, and land. Like all noncurrent assets, the future service potential of fixed assets is consumed over many periods, and the process of accounting for this is called depreciation.[1] Only land is not assumed to be consumed with use; historically, most commercial land has maintained or increased in value.

Fixed assets are originally recorded on the balance sheet at their initial acquisition cost: the amount of cash and cash equivalents exchanged for the asset. The "initial acquisition cost" includes all costs incurred to acquire the asset and to prepare it for its intended use. Moreover, where a company constructs its own assets, all costs associated with the development of an asset and to bring the asset to a functioning condition (i.e., revenue-producing state) should be capitalized.[2] For example, interest on borrowed funds used for the construction of an asset should be capitalized into the asset's cost basis; however, once the asset is in a revenue-producing state, all further interest costs should be expensed as incurred.

After an asset has been placed in service, many costs are incurred related to its continued use. In most cases, these costs involve maintenance or repairs and are expensed as incurred. In some cases, however, the incurred costs will actually increase the future service potential of the asset by extending its expected economic life or increasing the volume of expected service during its original economic life. In these cases, the additional costs are considered to be betterment expenditures and are capitalized to the asset's book value.

Analytical Concerns

The principal concerns that exist for the analyst with respect to these assets involve the capitalization of costs that would otherwise be expensed and the failure to adequately reduce asset values to reflect the consumption or impairment of an asset. To illustrate the first concern, we focus on the

---

[1] The analyst should note that depreciation, amortization, and depletion are all cost allocation processes. And as such, the initial cash outlay for an asset is not deducted against revenues in the period of initial acquisition, but rather is prorated over the revenue-producing life of the asset. Thus, the periodic depreciation (amortization and depletion) charge has no effect on the current cash flows of a company. For this reason, when calculating the cash flows from operations, the depreciation charge is added back to net income in order to correctly assess the level of cash generated from operations. We will return to this issue in Chapter 11.

[2] If, for example, an existing structure must first be demolished before a new asset can be built on the same site, the demolition costs are capitalized into the cost basis of the new facility.

capitalization of interest, and to illustrate the second, we examine the asset impairment question.

Capitalization of Interest. As noted above, GAAP requires that all costs incurred in the acquisition of an asset and its preparation for use be capitalized into the asset's balance sheet valuation. An extreme case of this arises when assets are internally developed or constructed. Under SFAS 34, any financing costs incurred during the developmental stage of an asset are appropriately capitalized to the asset's cost basis. This accounting standard stipulates that the amount of interest to be capitalized be based on the interest charges actually incurred for a specific project, or if unknown, the firm's weighted average cost of capital and the average dollar amount of construction in process.

While it is true that interest that is currently capitalized to a fixed asset under construction will ultimately be written off in the form of higher future depreciation charges, of concern to the analyst is that current earnings will appear to be higher than anticipated because borrowing costs are being capitalized rather than expensed. Similarly, while earnings will appear to be currently improved, actual cash flows are reduced by the current payments for debt service charges. Thus, under capitalization of interest, current earnings and cash flows are moving in an opposite, rather than parallel, direction.

Consider, for example, the Union Carbide Corporation. In 1980, UCC adopted SFAS 34 and capitalized $45 million of interest costs attributable to major capital construction projects. The effect of this accounting change was to increase 1980 net income by approximately $24 million, or $0.36 per share; but not one cent of this earnings increase carried through to operating cash flows. From a cash flow perspective, the interest costs were reflected as an increase in cash invested in noncurrent operating assets.[3]

Since many companies, like UCC, engage in ongoing asset construction projects, the capitalization of interest may be a recurring accounting phenomenon. As a consequence, the FASB requires that companies capitalizing interest disclose annually in the footnotes to the financial statements the total interest charges for the period and the portion of those charges capitalized to the balance sheet. With this information, the analyst can restate both the current income statement and the balance sheet value of the capitalized asset, if so desired.

An extreme form of interest capitalization is found among public utilities. Consider, for example, electric utilities throughout the U.S. which are

---

[3] The accounting journal entry to record the capitalization of interest is

    Debit: Asset under construction $XX
        Credit: Cash $XX

Note that instead of debiting "interest expense," the cash outlay for debt service is added to the "asset under construction" account.

subject to the directives of the Federal Energy Regulatory Commission (FERC), formerly the Federal Power Commission. The FERC, as well as other regulatory agencies, are empowered to establish operating and reporting procedures for those companies under the agency's authority. In some instances, the regulatory accounting principles (RAP) prescribed by such agencies deviate from GAAP for nonregulated companies, and where this occurs, the public utility may utilize RAP for purposes of preparing publicly disseminated financial statements.

One such example involves the capitalization of interest. Under FERC-RAP, an electric utility must capitalize its cost of borrowing on self-constructed assets, consistent with SFAS 34. However, unlike SFAS 34, not only must actual interest costs be capitalized, but where no funds have been borrowed, an implicit cost of capital on equity funds used for construction must also be capitalized. These amounts are called the "allowance for funds used during construction" (AFUDC).

Under RAP, the AFUDC on borrowed funds (AFUDC-B) is the actual interest cost on borrowed funds used for asset construction during a given period. The AFUDC on equity funds (AFUDC-E) is, on the other hand, a weighted average cost of capital imputed on the outstanding shareholder equity. Thus, the AFUDC-B involves an actual cash outflow, while the AFUDC-E may not (e.g., if dividends are not paid). Nonetheless, both the AFUDC-B and the AFUDC-E are capitalized to the balance sheet as part of long-term fixed assets, and are added to the utility's income statement under "Other Income."[4] In essence, while the AFUDC-B offsets actual interest charges on the income statement (i.e., a "wash"), the AFUDC-E represents a source of "income," involving no actual cash flows either into or out of the company.

As a consequence of the AFUDC-E, many utilities are able to report positive accrual net income and pay significant dividends in the face of negative operating cash flows. Take, for instance, Ohio-based Centerior Energy Corporation. In 1987, Centerior reported $2.82 in per share earnings and paid shareholders a dividend of $2.56 per share, most of which was nontaxable. Without the AFUDC-E, Centerior would actually have reported a loss, and did so for tax purposes, enabling the dividend to be treated as a liquidating dividend (i.e., a nontaxable return of capital).

The analyst should note that while the AFUDC-E is an interesting economic concept, its value as a source of income is highly questionable, and thus has little or no credit or investment value. Thus, like an unusual or

---

[4] The accounting journal entry to record either the AFUDC-B or AFUDC-E is:

Debit: Construction in progress	$XX
Credit: Allowance for Funds Used During Construction	$XX

The construction in progress is reported on the balance sheet as an asset and the AFUDC appears on the income statement as "Other Income."

Exhibit 7.1

LONE STAR REAL ESTATE CORPORATION
CONSOLIDATED BALANCE SHEET

	June 30, 1987	December 31, 1986
Assets		
Cash and investments	$ 14,313	$ 29,877
Accounts and notes receivable	30,852	21,659
Inventories of land	519,197	500,115
Rental real estate	13,244	13,438
Property and equipment	2,812	3,127
Other assets	4,421	3,811
Total	$ 584,839	$ 572,027
Liabilities and Shareholder Equity		
Accounts payable and accrued liabilities	$ 20,908	$ 23,817
Notes payable	420,047	410,455
Total liabilities	$ 440,955	$ 434,272
Common stock	100	100
Additional paid-in capital	30,475	30,475
Retained earnings	113,309	107,180
Total shareholder equity	143,884	137,755
Total	$ 584,839	$ 572,027

extraordinary item, the analyst would be wise to exclude this account from the income statement and balance sheet for analytical purposes. On the statement of cash flows, the noncash nature of the AFUDC will be readily apparent—it will be subtracted from net income to arrive at the real cash flows from operations.

A final example of interest capitalization, and its associated analytical problems, is found in the real estate industry. Consider, for example, the financial statements of the Lone Star Real Estate Corporation, a Texas-based land development and sales company, presented in Exhibits 7.1 and 7.2. (Note that while the corporate name has been changed and the figures scaled to hide the identity of the company, the facts are true.)

A review of Exhibits 7.1 and 7.2 reveals that not only is the company profitable, it has a net worth in excess of $140,000 and cash or cash equivalents in excess of $14,000. Yet, in mid-1987, the president of Lone Star

Exhibit 7.2 ———————————————————————————————

LONE STAR REAL ESTATE CORPORATION
CONSOLIDATED STATEMENT OF INCOME

	For the Six Months Ended June 30	
	1987	1986
Total revenues	$ 19,538	$ 18,072
Cost and expenses		
Cost of land sold	5,592	3,325
Development services expense	3,712	9,145
Interest expense	22,707	19,569
Interest capitalized	(22,707)	(19,569)
Selling, general, and administrative expenses	4,104	3,216
Total	13,408	15,686
Income before taxes	6,130	2,386
Income taxes	2,820	1,098
Adjustment from parent company	(2,820)	(1,098)
Net Income	$ 6,130	$ 2,386

approached its primary lender, a Dallas savings and loan association, requesting a renegotiation of its existing bank debt terms. If the debt was not favorably restructured, the president indicated that the real estate company would be forced to file for voluntary bankruptcy.

If the company was profitable, had a growing asset base, and cash on hand, how could it be on the verge of bankruptcy? Unfortunately, as Exhibit 7.2 reveals, the GAAP accounting used by the company hid the fact that without the capitalization of interest of $22,707, Lone Star would have reported a pre-tax net loss of $16,577, instead of a net gain. Apparently, Lone Star was carrying so much debt that the current debt service charges exceeded its total level of revenues, as well as its existing balance in cash or cash equivalents. Obviously, a cash flow analysis would reveal that in spite of the positive accrual net earnings, the cash flows from operations was significantly negative.

A second important distortion caused by the capitalization of interest by Lone Star involves its balance sheet valuation of "inventories of land." During the period 1986-1987, land values in Texas were substantially depressed, and falling. Note, however, that as a consequence of the capitalization of interest to this account, the value of the land appears to be rising, contrary to reality.[5] In fact, Lone Star probably should have written down the value of its real estate holdings, but had not done so as of the date of the financial statements. Why the asset write-down (and the associated loss) had not yet been taken is a topic to which we now turn.

Permanent Impairment. GAAP requires that if the future economic value of an asset has been permanently impaired, the value of the asset should be currently written down by a charge against earnings to reflect the expected diminishment in future earnings and cash flows.[6] Just when an asset is "permanently" impaired, however, is a matter of professional judgment. And, in most cases, corporate management is reluctant to adjust the value of its corporate assets downward, hoping that the observed decline in value is only temporary. From an accounting standpoint, an asset write-down is unpopular for two reasons—not only are total assets and net worth reduced, but current earnings are similarly reduced.

Because of the general reluctance on the part of most managers to write-down asset values, a phenomenon known as the "Big Bath" has been observed with some frequency. A "bath" occurs when management accumulates a material amount of asset write-offs and takes these write-offs in a single period. In so doing, all of the bad news is effectively isolated into a single accounting period; and, following this one-time adjustment, the company is normally well positioned to return to a profitable accounting posture.

Consider, for example, Honeywell. Even though its computer-related business had been deteriorating over several years, Honeywell took a $400 million "bath" in 1986 when it wrote off its computer business. According to *Fortune* magazine, Honeywell was "back in the tub again" in 1989, taking a $480 million charge for the discontinuation of its solid-state electronics product line.[7]

Consider also the case of Squibb Corporation. In 1986, Squibb concluded that the economic and political conditions in South America and Asia had deteriorated sufficiently to place in jeopardy the recoverability of certain of the company's investments located in those regions. As a consequence, Squibb took a write-down of $68 million on pharmaceutical operations in those geographical areas, declaring the assets to be "permanently impaired."[8]

---

[5] One financial wag refers to this as an example of "accrual and unusual punishment."

[6] The accounting journal entry to record an asset write-down or write-off is:

    Debit: Loss on asset value impairment $XX
        Credit: Asset $XX

[7] "Cute Tricks on the Bottom Line," *Fortune* (April 24, 1989).

[8] P. Wang, "You Know It When You See It," *Forbes* (July 25, 1988).

Finally, consider the case of Southland Corporation, the struggling owner of the 7-Eleven convenience store chain. In 1987, Southland had been taken private in a $4.9 billion leveraged buyout. Unfortunately, intense competition from convenience store operators put severe pressure on Southland's earnings, which were insufficient to meet the substantial interest payments resulting from the huge buyout debt. To reflect this diminished earnings power of its assets, Southland took a one-time writedown of $947 million in the fourth quarter of 1989. In addition, the company began negotiations with the Seven-Eleven Japan Co. in an effort to generate a new cash infusion for the ailing U.S. company.[9]

Of concern to the analyst in regard to the question of permanent impairment is the vagueness inherent in existing accounting standards which effectively provides corporate management with considerable leeway in the timing and amount of asset write-downs. These issues are also of concern to the FASB, which is attempting to construct guidelines that would delineate when, and by what amount, asset write-downs should occur. Some steps have already been taken in this direction. For example, SFAS 90 requires that electric utilities that have abandoned nuclear facilities write-off any construction costs that cannot be recovered through expected rate increases. Similarly, in recent years, the FASB and SEC have acted to clarify exactly when banks and other financial institutions must increase their loan-loss reserves for expected troubled-debt.

Intangible Assets

Intangible assets refer to those long-lived, revenue-producing assets which lack a tangible, physical presence. Examples of these include copyrights, franchise agreements, patents, research and development costs, and goodwill. Most intangible assets convey a monopolistic right to a future earnings stream. In the case of a patent, the monopolistic right might involve the earnings stream associated with an innovative product, and in the case of a franchise agreement, it might be the earnings stream associated with an exclusive territorial sales agreement.

Intangible assets may be segmented into those that are internally-generated and those that are externally-generated. For externally-developed intangible assets, the asset is initially recorded at its acquisition cost. For internally-developed intangibles, however, valuation may be problematic.

Under SFAS 2, all research and development costs are required to be expensed in the period in which they are incurred, subject to only a few exceptions which we will discuss shortly. As a consequence, most (if not all) of the costs associated with internally-developed intangibles are written-off

---

9 K. Blanton, "Red Ink Flows at 7-Eleven," *Dallas Times Herald* (April 3, 1990).

as incurred, leaving little or no value to be capitalized to the balance sheet. This produces two significant analytical problems. First, for a company actively involved in a research and development program, little (if any) of this investment will ever appear on its balance sheet. Consequently, these companies may have significant unreported intangible asset values. Second, since little of the initial development cost is ever capitalized to the balance sheet, current earnings may be relatively understated due to R & D write-offs, with future earnings relatively overstated due to the absence of any expenses to be matched with future revenues.

Several industries have been exempted from this general treatment of R & D. Computer software development companies, for example, are permitted to capitalize R&D costs once a commercially viable prototype has been developed; however, all original or new product development costs must be expensed as they are incurred. Similarly, the natural resource industry is permitted to capitalize all R & D costs under the full cost method, but only some costs under the successful efforts method. (These two methods of accounting for exploration and development costs are discussed shortly.)

Regardless of whether an intangible asset is internally or externally developed, its carrying cost must be amortized against earnings over its expected economic or legal life, whichever is shorter. One exception to this rule is goodwill. Goodwill acquired prior to 1971 need not be amortized at all, whereas goodwill acquired after 1971 may be amortized over any period not in excess of 40 years.

Analytical Concerns

The analytical concerns relating to intangible assets fall into three categories. First, as noted above, due to the required accounting for R & D, some quite valuable intangible assets may not appear on the financial statements of companies actively involved in research and development programs. Hence, for these companies, there may be significant "hidden" intangible asset values. Second, for those intangibles which do appear on the balance sheet, the potential resale or liquidation value of these assets may be substantially limited. For example, a patent on an innovative manufacturing system may have little or no transferability to other industries or markets. Consequently, it is unclear whether these assets have any investment or credit value in a worst-case scenario involving a company's liquidation. Finally, for many intangibles, it is unclear exactly how long an asset can be expected to produce revenues. In the case of a computer software copyright, for example, the competitive marketplace faced by these products clearly suggests a very short half-life.

To illustrate this latter concern, consider the case of Roadway Express, a trucking industry leader. Prior to 1980, this industry had been subject to governmental regulation by the Interstate Commerce Commission. Under the Motor Carrier Act of 1935, the ICC issued "certificates of public convenience and necessity" to common carriers which conveyed an exclusive right to haul freight of a particular class between various points. To facilitate growth, many carriers, like Roadway, purchased these rights-of-way from the original recipients. And by 1980, trucking companies had accumulated significant investments in these intangible assets.

On July 1, 1980, however, Congress passed the Motor Carrier Act of 1980, which effectively deregulated the transportation industry. As a consequence, in September of 1980, Roadway Express wrote off all $27 million in operating rights that it had previously carried on its financial statements. The write-off constituted 5 percent of Roadway's total assets and over 8 percent of its net worth. While Roadway's relative market position was essentially unchanged as a consequence of the deregulation, its future competitiveness and earnings were clearly adversely affected. From an analyst's perspective, the message is quite clear—be wary of intangible assets resulting from governmental regulation or legislation: what is here today may be gone tomorrow.

Natural Resources

Natural resources refer to those non-renewable, in-ground assets such as oil and gas, coal, iron ore, and uranium. Like intangible assets, a useful delineation of these assets involves internally versus externally developed. When natural resources are externally developed, they are reported on the balance sheet at their acquisition cost, less any depletion recognized subsequent to acquisition. Alternatively, when natural resources are internally developed, several valuation approaches may be followed.

To begin, the process of internal resource development is typically segmented into four phases, and hence cost categories: (1) *acquisition* costs, or the cost of the right to explore for natural resources (e.g., mineral leases); (2) *exploration* costs, or the cost to determine if a particular lease contains an economically viable quantity of recoverable resource reserves; (3) *development* costs, or the cost of putting a lease on full production; and (4) *production* costs, or the day-to-day costs of maintaining the extraction operation.

As noted earlier, all costs incurred in the acquisition of an asset and its preparation for use should be capitalized. In the case of internally developed natural resources, this implies that all costs associated with the first three phases of development (i.e., acquisition, exploration, and development) should be capitalized, whereas the costs associated with the fourth phase (production) should be expensed as incurred. While this accounting process appears relatively straightforward, there is considerable controversy surrounding just how it should be implemented when a property or lease fails to indicate the existence of a commercially viable quantity of recoverable reserves.

One view holds that the process of finding, for example oil and gas reserves, is a highly speculative and uncertain process in which many "dry" wells may first be drilled before a successful "wet" well is found. In essence, some level of failure is a natural part of the development process. This view is reflected in the *full cost method* in which the cost of all exploratory activities for a given property or lease, whether successful or not, are capitalized to the balance sheet as part of the natural resource asset account. Once a successful well is found and placed into production, the capitalized costs are then matched with revenues through the depletion process.

The analyst should note that the full cost method suffers from the limitation that some nonrevenue-producing costs are capitalized to the balance sheet, and subsequently inappropriately matched against future revenues generated from a company's successful exploration activities. A fundamental construct of accrual accounting violated by this approach is that only those assets that can reasonably be expected to contribute to the future revenues of a company should be capitalized to the balance sheet. In essence, current earnings are overstated at the expense of future earnings, which will be understated. (The method is implicitly a form of rear-end loading.) The full cost method tends to be preferred by smaller companies, which characteristically do not have significant income from existing producing reserves to offset current unsuccessful exploration costs.

An alternative view, known as the *successful efforts* method, holds that only the costs associated with successful exploration activities should be capitalized to the balance sheet. The costs associated with unsuccessful exploration activities are expensed when it becomes known that further exploration or development is unwarranted. This method is the method of preference by large integrated companies with substantial existing production and sufficient revenue streams to cover the cost of unsuccessful exploration.[10]

For a company actively involved in the exploration for, or internal development of, natural resources, the use of the full cost method versus the successful efforts method can produce radically divergent results. Consider, for example, the case of Conquest Exploration Company, which in 1986 switched from the full cost method to the successful efforts methods. As a

---

[10] In 1977, the FASB issued SFAS 19 which required oil and gas producing companies to utilize the successful efforts method. In 1978, however, the SEC ruled that either method was acceptable, necessitating the issuance of SFAS 25, which suspended SFAS 19 and permitted companies to utilize either approach. The SEC argued that under successful efforts, small exploration and production companies would be placed at a disadvantage when attempting to raise capital in the capital markets due to the accounting losses that could be expected under the successful efforts method. The analyst should note that in an efficient capital market, the SEC's argument is not well grounded.

consequence of the accounting method change, Conquest lowered its previously reported earnings as follows:

	Earnings under Full Cost (original)*	Earnings under Successful Efforts (restated)*
1985	$ 3,719	$ (17,035)
1984	4,274	(15,304)
1983	3,449	(5,530)

(*figures in millions of dollars)

Note that there is a profit differential of over $20 million in 1985 alone between the two methods. As part of the restatement process, Conquest also wrote down its oil and gas properties by $66.7 million as of December 31, 1985.

The Conquest case is unusual in that it represents a company moving from a liberal reporting approach (full cost) to a more conservative one. An obvious question is why would Conquest undertake such a change? One likely explanation involves the fact that in late January, 1986, the price of oil fell below $10 per barrel; and, under the full cost method, Conquest would have been required to take an estimated $73 million write-down ($66.7 million as of 12/31/1985) during 1986. Hence, rather than suffer a major write-off in 1986, the company chose to switch to the successful efforts method, which allowed Conquest to effectively spread the large write-down over a three-year period. According to the company's annual report, if Conquest had remained on the full cost method it would have reported an $83 million after tax loss for 1986, instead of the $10.3 million loss it actually reported under successful efforts. For tax purposes, most natural resource companies adopt a successful efforts-type approach. Thus, on a cash flow basis the full cost and the successful efforts methods produce identical results. The apparent differences are just that—differences in accounting appearances only.

From a quality of earnings perspective, the successful efforts method is clearly the method of preference. Under the full cost method, not only are current earnings relatively overstated, but so too is the natural resource asset account balance on the balance sheet. Even for successful efforts-accounted companies, however, analysts tend to discount the accrual-based financial statements, and instead base credit and investment decisions on the discounted cash value of a company's natural resource reserves.[11]

---

[11] For lending purposes, for example, while most financial institutions evaluate a company's current income statement to assess the quality of ongoing operations and the balance sheet to assess debt capacity and repayment capability, the amount of any loan will be tied to the discounted cash value of recoverable reserves. Note that a lender can substantially impact the discounted value of such reserves by lowering or raising the discount rate used in such calculations.

Exhibit 7.3 _____

CAPITALIZATION OF INTEREST: OIL INDUSTRY SURVEY

Company	1981 Pre-tax Earnings*	Percent of 1981 Pre-tax Earnings	1982 Pre-tax Earnings*	Percent of 1982 Pre-tax Earnings
Exxon	$174	2%	$207	2%
Mobil	134	3	240	7
Standard Oil of California	30	1	104	4
Standard Oil of Indiana	51	1	94	3
Gulf	103	5	139	8
Shell	462	15	384	14
Atlanta Richfield	90	5	141	8
Sun	87	5	105	11
Tenneco	210	14	190	13
Amerada Hess	84	22	98	33
Diamond Shamrock	24	11	33	10

*Figures are in millions of dollars.

Source: K.R. Ferris and M.E. Barrett, "Assessing the Quality of Reported Earnings in the Oil and Gas Industry: Some Guidance for Credit Analysts, "*The Journal of Commercial Bank Lending* (February, 1984).

Analytical Concerns

In addition to the overstatement of earnings and assets present under the full cost method, the analyst should be concerned about two additional issues: (1) the capitalization of interest, and (2) the depletion of resource values.

As noted earlier, the interest on funds borrowed for purposes of self-constructing assets must be capitalized to the balance sheet value of such assets. Whether or not this practice has a material effect upon the financial statements is substantially dependent upon the extent to which a company (a) self-constructs assets and (b) borrows funds for that purpose.

The oil and gas industry provides an example of an industry that is substantially dependent upon the self-construction of new assets. Moreover, because of the significant cost of finding new reserves, considerable sums are often borrowed for this purpose. Exhibit 7.3 presents survey data from the oil industry for the period 1981-1982 illustrating the relative impact of interest capitalization on pre-tax earnings for those years. The data reveals that in many cases the impact of interest capitalization on corporate earnings was negligible; however, in some cases, such as Amerada Hess, interest capitalization added as much as 22 and 33 percent, respectively, to 1981 and 1982 pre-tax earnings. The analyst should recall that in spite of the apparent increase in earnings, the level of cash flows is actually diminished by the payment of this debt servicing.

A second analytical concern involves the depletion of natural resources and the organizational structure of natural resource companies. For all natural resource companies, depletion is calculated using the unit-of-production approach:

$$\text{Depletion expense} = \text{R (Cost-Salvage value),}$$

where

$$\text{R} = \text{production ratio} = \frac{\text{Production this period}}{\text{Total Estimated Lifetime Production}}$$

Consider now the question of just how a natural resource company should be organizationally structured. Should, for example, a company be highly centralized, with few cost or profit centers, or highly decentralized, with many cost or profit centers? Unfortunately, the question of organizational design in conjunction with the unit-of-production depletion approach can produce some unintended distortions in the reported earnings and assets of natural resource companies.

To illustrate this problem, consider the data presented in Exhibit 7.4. This exhibit details the cost data for two hypothetical companies that are identical in every economic respect—they have the same quantity of recoverable reserves (i.e., 21 million barrels), the same total cost basis for the reserves (i.e., $30 million), and the same total annual production (i.e., three million barrels). The only differentiating factor between the two companies is that Company A is decentralized with three cost (or profit) centers, and Company B is centralized with only one overall cost center.

Most analysts assume that the organizational design of a company would not, and indeed should not, impact the reported accounting results. Unfortunately, if the production ratio (see step 5 in Exhibit 7.4) differs between the various cost centers, the sum of the depletion charges for the parts (i.e., the three cost centers of Company A) will not equal that for the total company (i.e., Company B). In Exhibit 7.4, Company A discloses depletion charges of $12 million, while Company B reports depletion of only $4.286 million. And, as a consequence, the pre-tax earnings of Company B exceed those of A by the difference in the depletion charges (or $7.714 million). Not surprisingly, the financial ratios for Company B will also be superior to

Exhibit 7.4 ————————————————————————————————————

DEPLETION AND ORGANIZATIONAL DESIGN

	Company A				Company B
	1	2	3	Total	1
1. Number of cost or profit centers	1	2	3	Total	1
2. Economically recoverables reserves in barrels (000's)	1,000	10,000	10,000	21,000	21,000
3. Production costs to be depleted (000's)	$10,000	$10,000	$10,000	$30,000	$30,000
4. Annual total production in barrels (000's)	1,000	1,000	1,000	3,000	3,000
5. Production ratio (4÷2)	1.0	0.1	0.1		0.143
6. Depletion charge (5x3)	$10,000	$ 1,000	$ 1,000	$12,000	$ 4,286
7. Operating income before depletion (000's)	$10,000	$10,000	$10,000	$30,000	$30,000
8. NIBT after depletion (7–6)	-0-	$ 9,000	$ 9,000	$18,000	$25,714

those for Company A. However, unless these same differences exist for tax purposes as well, the two companies are, in reality, economically identical.

Exhibit 7.4 appears to suggest that having more cost (or profit) centers is a disadvantage in that it leads to a higher level of total depletion. This inference is incorrect, however, in that the "problem" is not the number of centers, but rather a variance in the production ratio between the centers. Thus, it is conceivable that even with a large number of cost (profit) centers (i.e., Company A), the actual depletion charge will be less.

This possibility is depicted in Exhibit 7.5. Again, Company A and Company B are identical in all respects except for their organizational structure. In this example, however, Company A has chosen to shut in production center No. 1, causing its entire production of three million barrels to come from the remaining two cost centers. Exhibit 7.5 reveals that the total depletion charge for A is reduced to only $3 million, while B remains at $4.286 million. Under these circumstances, Company A reports a higher NIBT after depletion (by $1.286 million) than does Company B. Again, however, unless these differences exist for tax purposes, the underlying cash flows of the two companies will be identical.

It should be noted that the analytical conundrum revealed by Exhibits 7.4 and 7.5 is not restricted to natural resource companies, and may be observed in the financial statements of any company using production-based depletion or depreciation methods. What these exhibits also reveal is that reported accounting data may be unintentionally influenced by such inno-

Exhibit 7.5

DEPLETION AND ORGANIZATIONAL DESIGN

	Company A				Company B
	1	2	3	Total	1
1. Number of cost or profit centers	1	2	3	Total	1
2. Economically recoverables reserves in barrels (000's)	1,000	10,000	10,000	21,000	21,000
3. Production costs to be depleted (000's)	$10,000	$10,000	$10,000	$30,000	$30,000
4. Annual total production in barrels (000's)	-0-	1,000	2,000	3,000	3,000
5. Production ratio (4÷2)	-0-	0.1	0.2		0.143
6. Depletion charge (5×3)	-0-	$ 1,000	$ 2,000	$ 3,000	$ 4,286
7. Operating income before depletion (000's)	-0-	$10,000	$20,000	$30,000	$30,000
8. NIBT after depletion (7-6)	-0-	$ 9,000	$18,000	$27,000	$25,714

cent externalities as the organizational design of a company. The exhibits also emphasize why it is essential for the analyst to consider a multiplicity of factors beyond accrual net income when assessing the performance of a company.

Conclusions

The noncurrent operating assets are, for most companies, the largest single asset category on the balance sheet. They represent a principal source of earnings generation and cash flows. They also constitute an important source of collateral for lenders.

The analysis of this asset category should focus on several key issues: (1) the asset values capitalized to the balance sheet, and whether those values are over or understated; and, (2) how the assets are being depreciated, amortized, or depleted, and whether this allocation approach is reasonable given the business climate faced by the company. The key analytical concerns involve the rear-end loading of costs, the capitalization of interest, and the timing and amount of asset write-downs when asset impairment occurs.

Because all of these quality issues arise from the somewhat arbitrary cost allocations that are necessary under the accrual system of accounting, the analyst should examine a company's operations independent of the effects of these cost allocation decisions. The best way to do that is by examining the cash flows from operations (CFFO). As noted earlier, and will be discussed in Chapter 11, the CFFO reflects the actual cash flows of a company from its principal operations. To arrive at this figure, net income is adjusted for the level of depreciation, depletion, and amortization. And, while SFAS 95 requires that a company disclose its CFFO, the analyst will (depending upon the particular viewpoint taken) still need to adjust the reported CFFO for any capitalized costs (e.g., interest, unsuccessful exploration, etc.) that would otherwise be expensed.

CHAPTER EIGHT

Long-term Debt

One widely held view in the investment industry is that when valuing a company or an individual asset for acquisition purposes, the price to be paid should be based upon the company's (or asset's) future net cash flows discounted to the present at an interest rate (or hurdle rate) reflecting the riskiness of the future cash flows. In essence, an investor should be willing to pay an amount equal to the discounted future cash flows associated with the given investment. This same concept is also used in the valuation of long-term debt instruments for purposes of financial statement preparation.

Long-term debt refers to those existing obligations which are not expected to be repaid within the next year or operating cycle. Examples include bonds and debentures, mortgages, long-term bank debt, lease obligations, pension obligations, and deferred income taxes.[1] As noted above,

---

[1] The topic of deferred income taxes was covered in Chapter 4 and will not be readdressed here.

the principal method of valuing these obligations is at the present value of the future cash flows needed to satisfy the debt.

In this chapter, we briefly overview the valuation of long-term liabilities and investigate the analytical concerns associated with early debt retirement and troubled-debt restructuring.

Liability Valuation: An Overview

To illustrate the accounting and valuation of long-term obligations, consider the issuance and amortization of a typical interest-bearing debenture. Bonds of this type are usually issued in denominations of $1,000, carry a stated rate of interest payment (usually payable semiannually) called the coupon rate, and may be of any term, but usually range from 10 to 20 years.

Once the debentures are approved for sale by the SEC, they are usually acquired in total by one or more brokerage houses for sale into the marketplace. It is usually quite inefficient for a corporation to itself undertake the sale of a bond offering, and hence for a fee, it can be efficiently handled by a bond placement specialist. Unless otherwise negotiated, bond sales by a brokerage house are undertaken on a "best efforts" basis, in which any unsold bonds may be returned to the issuing corporation.

The proceeds actually received by an issuing corporation are largely determined by the market rate of interest on the day (or days) immediately preceding the bond sale. Normally, the issuing corporation and the offering manager (i.e., a brokerage house) meet approximately one week prior to the scheduled offering date to agree upon the coupon rate that the bonds will carry—a rate normally projected to be the market rate of interest on the date the bonds are offered for sale to the public (unless the bonds are zero-coupon debentures).

Not surprisingly, it is quite difficult to exactly peg the expected market rate of interest as much as one week prior to offering; hence, there will often be a discrepancy between the coupon rate of interest and the market rate of interest on the date of offering. This discrepancy will cause the bonds to be sold for either a premium or a discount from their face value. And, the actual proceeds received by the issuing company will equal the market price of the bonds, less a selling fee and a management fee paid to the firm handling the offering.

To illustrate, consider the case of IBM. In 1979, IBM undertook its first ever debt offering for the substantial amount of $1 billion. IBM's offering was to consist of $500 million in 7-year, 9.5 percent coupon notes, and $500 million in 25-year, 9.375 percent coupon debentures. The offering was sufficiently large that an underwriting syndicate of 225 firms was organized, under the lead of Merrill Lynch and Salomon Brothers. Under the placement agreement, each of the lead firms would receive $1.25 per note ($2.50

in total for managing the issue), with the actual seller of a note receiving a commission of $3.75, for a total of $6.25 per note in fees.

On Wednesday, October 3, 1979, IBM met with representatives of the syndicate to arrive at a final price for the bonds which would be offered for sale the following day. It was agreed, for example, that on the basis of current market rates, the 7-year notes would be sold to yield 9.62 percent (or 4.81 percent semiannually), and thus would be sold at a price of $994 per $1,000 note. Of the $994, IBM would receive $987.75, with the remaining $6.25 going to the underwriting syndicate. Thus, on IBM's financial statements, the $500 million in 7-year notes would be reported at a value of only $497 million. A review of IBM's footnotes would reveal that the notes were sold at a discount of $3 million.[2]

To summarize, IBM received a total of $493.875 million in cash on the sale of the 7-year notes, but was obligated to repay a full $500 million in 7 years. The additional payment of $6.125 million can be broken down as follows: (1) $3.125 million in bond issuance costs, which were initially paid out of the proceeds of the bond sale; and (2) $3 million in additional interest payments representing the difference between the coupon rate of 9.5 percent and the effective yield of 9.62 percent. Note that the degree of error in predicting the market rate of interest on the offering date was only 12 basis points (or 12/100's of one percent), which equated to a discount of $6 per $1,000 bond.

Just as IBM's notes were sold at a discount because market rates of interest moved upward between the coupon-setting date and the October 3 pricing date, the notes could just have easily been sold at a premium if market rates had moved downward during that same period. In general, when setting coupon rates, most firms prefer to err on the low side of market rates in that, psychologically, it is far easier to sell debt at a discount than it is at a premium. The analyst should note, however, that buying debt at a discount does not imply that it is a "better deal" than buying debt a premium. At any given time, unless unexplained market inefficiencies exist, the market price of all debt in a given risk category should be comparably priced in terms of yield.

---

[2] The accounting entry to record IBM's sale of the 7-year notes would appear as follows:

Debit: Cash	$493,875,000	
Debit: Bond discount	3,000,000	
Debit: Bond issuance costs	3,125,000	
Credit: Bonds Payable		$500,000,000

The "bond issuance costs" represent a long-term deferred charge (an asset), and the "bond discount" represents a contra-liability account which is reported as a deduction from the "bonds payable" account to arrive at the bond carrying value (initially $497 million in this case). Each period, as the semiannual cash payment of $23,750,000 (i.e., .0475 X $500 million) is recorded, a charge to "interest expense" is made, reflecting not only the cash payment, but also the amortization of the bond discount using the effective interest method. Bond issuance costs are typically amortized on a straight-line basis.

Accounting Yields Versus Market Yields

It should be apparent that what drives the current market value of any debt instrument is the current market rate of interest for a comparable risk instrument. Thus, when a company issues debt, the proceeds it receives are a function of the prevailing market rate on the date of (or shortly preceding) offering, and of course, the perceived riskiness of the borrower itself. If the coupon rate is set, either accidentally or intentionally, below the prevailing market rate, the debt will (of necessity, if it is to be sold at all) be sold at a discount. By requiring buyers to invest only a lesser amount, investors will be able to earn a higher yield equivalent to the existing market rate. If, on the other hand, the coupon rate is set above the prevailing market rate, the debt will command a higher price and consequently be sold at a premium. By paying a premium for the bond, buyers actually lower their effective return from the higher coupon rate to the lower prevailing market yield. In essence, since the bond market involves securities which carry a fixed coupon rate, a fixed maturity value, and a fixed term, the only factor that can vary to compensate investors for changes in prevailing market interest rates is the selling price of the bond instrument.

It is important for the analyst to note one key accounting convention for all long-term debt instruments: debt is recorded on a company's financial statements at the date of issuance, to reflect the market rate of interest prevailing at that time; however, if market interest rates subsequently change, causing the market value of a debt instrument to fluctuate, those fluctuations are never recognized in the financial statements. Stated alternatively, for accounting purposes, the effective rate prevailing at the time of issuance is assumed to prevail throughout the entire term of the debt instrument. A consequence of this is that the current value of a company's debt may be greater or less than its recorded accounting value. This, however, is generally not regarded as a serious concern unless early retirement of the debt is anticipated—a topic which we consider shortly.

Zero Coupon Debentures

A special form of the corporate debenture is the zero-coupon bond. Under the terms of the indenture agreement, zero-coupon debentures carry no stated coupon rate. Thus, a purchaser of a zero-coupon bond receives no periodic interest payments; instead, the implied interest is retained by the issuer to accumulate and becomes payable in full at maturity.

Although available in the United Kingdom since the early 1960s, zero-coupon bonds were first issued by U.S. corporations in the early 1980s. Since 1986, however, the availability of corporate zeros has fallen substantially, largely in response to limitations placed on the availability of individual retirement accounts. Zero-coupon debentures have unique tax features which make them principally attractive to tax-free or tax-deferred purchasers, such as pension funds and other retirement accounts. Under existing tax laws, the issuer of a zero-coupon debenture is entitled to currently deduct the implied but unpaid interest, and the bondholder (unless subject to tax-free or tax-deferred status) is required to report the corresponding accretion of interest as income, even though unpaid.

From an analyst's perspective, zero-coupon debentures have a significant impact on a company's cash flows, particularly its cash flows from operations (CFFO). Under GAAP, the accrued but unpaid interest on a zero-coupon bond is deducted as an expense in arriving at net income.[3] Thus, when calculating the CFFO, the analyst must remember to add back the amount of accrued interest previously deducted, since it does not represent a cash outflow of the company.

Consider, for example, McDonald's Corporation, which issued $160 million (maturity value) of zero-coupon debentures in 1982. This offering was comprised of $40 million in six-year notes, yielding 12.3 percent, and $120 million in 12-year notes, yielding 12.6 percent. The six-year notes yielded proceeds of $20 million, and the 12-year notes proceeds of $30 million, or an aggregate of $50 million. Thus, McDonald's effectively sold for $50 million, notes maturing to $160 million, inclusive of interest. (Note: $50 million is the present value of $160 million at the stated effective interest rates.)

The value of the notes on McDonald's financial statements were initially recorded at $50 million. Subsequently, each period, the value of the debt increased by the amount of interest earned but unpaid, until in the final period the notes would be valued at their maturity value. The accretion of interest on the 12-year notes alone could be as high as $12 million per period, and it is this amount which the analyst would need to add back in order to arrive at a proper assessment of McDonald's CFFO.

Unless dealing with zero-coupon debentures, however, the analyst need not normally worry about adjusting the CFFO for the amortization of bond premiums or discounts, in that the effect on the CFFO in any given period is likely to be minimal. But, where zeros are involved, the adjustment to arrive at the CFFO may be material, as in the case of McDonald's.

---

[3] The accounting entry to record the interest expense on a zero-coupon debenture would appear as:

Debit: Interest expense	$XXX
Credit: Amortization of Bond Discount	$XXX

Note that even though an expense is recorded, no cash flow is currently paid from the company's cash reserves. Full payment of the interest only occurs when the zero-coupon debenture matures.

——————— Early Debt Retirement and Paper Profits ———————

One of the unfortunate outcomes of the attempt to legislate appropriate accounting principles, is the concommitant exploitation of weaknesses in established GAAP. Consider, for example, the prescribed accounting treatment for the early retirement of long-term debt. Under existing GAAP, in the event of an early retirement, the difference between the redemption price of debt and its accounting book value is accounted for as an extraordinary gain or loss in the year of retirement.[4]

Since the 1960s, when many companies issued low costing debt as a means to finance the merger and acquisition binge of that decade, market interest rates have increased, reaching as high as 20 percent in the early 1980s. As a consequence of these significant interest rate movements, bond market prices correspondingly declined. And, since financial statement values are not adjusted to reflect these market changes, accounting debt values have tended to (substantially) exceed the related market values.

Not surprisingly, many companies choose to exploit this situation by retiring, in whole or in part, their outstanding debt issuances. A survey of over 200 debt retirements from 1980 to 1982, for example, revealed that every one of the transactions resulted in a substantial gain being reported on the earnings statement of the retiring company. (See Exhibit 8.1 for a sampling of these transactions and their effect on the financial statements.) The analyst should note the transparent and economically questionable logic of an early retirement under the then-prevailing conditions (i.e., companies were retiring low costing debt at a time when the cost of funds was twice, and even three times, the cost of the retired debt). In effect, many companies borrowed at a substantially higher interest rate just to effect the retirement transaction and to produce a gain for accounting purposes.

From a cash flow perspective, the early retirement is also misleading. The presence of a gain on retirement implies that a current cash inflow occurred as a consequence of the transaction. Not only is there no cash inflow, but there may be a cash outflow for the amount needed to retire the outstanding debt. And, in most cases, there is a tax effect—the gain on the early retirement is a taxable event (unless accomplished via a defeasance). While there are no current cash inflows associated with an early debt retirement, the gain on retirement does represent a future cash savings. In essence, the gain is the future cash payments which will not be required for interest on

---

[4] The accounting entry for an early retirement would appear as:

Debit: Bonds Payable	$XXX	
Credit: Cash		$XXX
Credit: Gain on early retirement		XXX

This entry assumes that the cost of retirement was less than the debt's book value. Any outstanding discount or premium would also be written off when the debt is retired.

Exhibit 8.1

A SAMPLE OF 1982 EARLY DEBT RETIREMENTS

Company	Increase in Earnings Attributed to Early Debt Retirement (in millions)	2nd Quarter	
		Reported Earnings (in millions)	Retirement Earnings as a Percent of Reported Earnings
Pfizer, Inc.	$ 5.0	$ 80.6	6.2%
Ohio Edison Co.	20.0	54.0	37.0
Armstrong World Industries	2.1	9.6	21.8
U.S. Home Corp.	2.0	4.1	48.7
California First Bank	6.8	4.3	158.1
Florida Coast Banks	1.3	2.4	54.1
Textron	6.0	24.7	24.2
City Investing	9.9	35.0	28.2
Kroger Co.	1.1	35.8	3.0
Phillips Petroleum Co.	15.0	140.0	10.7
Sherwin-Williams Co.	5.1	18.0	28.2
CPC International	6.0	57.0	10.5
Revlon, Inc.	6.6	39.7	10.6
Houston Natural Gas Corp.	13.9	59.0	23.5

the debt. The recognition of these cost savings (i.e., future cash savings) as a gain, however, violates one of the basic tenets of accounting: a penny saved is not a penny earned.

Methods of Early Retirement. The early retirement of outstanding debentures can be executed in a variety of ways: a cash-for-debt repurchase, a debt-for-debt swap, an equity-for-debt swap, or via defeasance. The cash-for-debt retirement is the traditional method of retirement. Indeed, many companies regularly enter the bond market and buy back portions of their outstanding debt as mandated by the sinking fund requirements of the debt agreement. Because such transactions are mandated by a debt contract, any gain (or loss) on a sinking fund repurchase may be treated as ordinary (as opposed to extraordinary) income.

In a debt-for-debt swap, a company effectively trades, for example, $40 million of 12 percent debt for $80 million of 6 percent debt, such that the total interest payments associated with the outstanding debt often remain unchanged. But, as a consequence of the swap, the company's total level of debt is reduced, and its equity increased by the approximately $40 million in before-tax gain reported as a consequence of the transaction. Obviously, this kind of transaction can have a significant effect in terms of "dressing up" a company's income statement and balance sheet, in spite of the adverse tax consequences.

Another means of financing an early debt retirement is by an equity-for-debt swap. This type of retirement is rarely initiated by the company itself, and instead has been most often instigated by a brokerage firm. Typically, it happens as follows. A brokerage firm will enter the bond market and buy substantial quantities of a firm's deep-discounted bonds. The broker then contacts the issuer and proposes to "swap" the bonds for shares of the issuer's common stock. Assuming that the issuer obliges, the broker receives a fee for the exchange, and then earns additional commissions by selling the newly issued common stock on the open market. Like all retirements, the swap substantially enhances the retiring company's financial statements—the level of outstanding debt is reduced, a gain is recorded (and is subject to taxation), and the level of equity increased.

But are these transactions economically justified? The answer in most cases is a resounding "No!" Consider, for example, the swap negotiated by Salomon Brothers with U.S. Steel in 1982. Salomon Brothers purchased $178 million of U.S. Steel's deeply discounted debt (the coupon rates varied from 4 5/8 percent to 7 3/4 percent and the maturity dates from 1996 to 2001) for approximately $90 million. The firm then exchanged the debt for 5 million shares of U.S. Steel common stock, enabling U.S. Steel to record an $87 million gain in its second quarter results. The reaction of the financial press to this transaction, and others like it, was clearly unfavorable. One financial writer observed:[5]

> U.S. Steel's multibillion dollar debt is so huge that reducing it by a mere $178 million is all but meaningless. However, issuing 5 million shares of stock...represents a rather meaningful dilution of its equity.... Would you want to buy back a 7 percent mortgage on your home with another 15 to 20 years to run, even at a sizable discount, and pay for it with shares at prices near their lowest in a decade? I don't think I would, but scores of companies are doing it now. Why? To make a paper profit.

To conclude our discussion of early debt retirements, we consider one final approach—defeasance. In legal circles, defeasance refers to "rendering null or void of an existing condition." In the case of debt retirement, a

---

[5] H. H. Biel, "Bad News, Good Opportunity," *Forbes* (August 2, 1982).

defeasance is executed by first creating a trust fund of low-risk securities, usually U.S. government debt, having a yield sufficiently high and a sequence of maturity dates to enable the trust fund to exactly cover the interest and principal payments on a company's older, lower yielding debt. By mandating that the trust is exclusively for the future retirement of the outstanding debt, current GAAP permits the "defeased" debt to be offset by the trust assets and effectively removed from the balance sheet.

The analyst should note several important subtleties associated with a defeasance. First, even though the debt is removed from a company's balance sheet, it has not been retired. And, legally, if the trust is impaired and consequently unable to fully service or retire the debt, the issuing company retains its liability to do so. Second, the transaction violates one of the very basic tenets of accounting—never offset liabilities with assets. At the extreme, offsetting assets and liabilities would leave financial statement users with a very uninformative balance sheet composed only of net assets and owners' equity. Third, since a "retirement" has not actually occurred (i.e., the debt is still outstanding), the "gain" reported on the defeasance will produce no current cash flows, but also neither is the gain taxable (which explains its popularity with management). The interest income on the trust, however, is taxable to the company, but this income is partially offset by the interest expense on the still outstanding debt.

To illustrate, consider the defeasance executed by Exxon Corporation in 1982. Exxon defeased six long-term debt issues that had been sold between 1969 and 1972 at coupon rates of 5.8 to 6.7%, by acquiring a portfolio of U.S. treasury bills issued in 1982 that were yielding approximately 14%. Exxon invested $313 million for the low risk government securities and placed them in a trust account with Morgan Guaranty Trust Company of New York. The six debt issues had a maturity (and book value) of approximately $515 million, consequently enabling Exxon to report a gain on retirement of $132 million (after providing for income taxes of $66 million on the anticipated excess trust earnings). One obvious question is "Why didn't Exxon use the $313 million invested in U.S. treasuries to simply repurchase and retire the debt?" The answer is two-fold. First, it is often quite difficult to retire an entire bond issuance. For a variety of reasons, bondholders are often reluctant to redeem securities before their natural maturity. Under defeasance it is possible to "retire" an entire outstanding issue. Second, under defeasance, the gain is not currently taxable; the excess earnings of the trust assets over the interest charges associated with the still outstanding debt is taxable, but only as earned, whereas the gain on a cash retirement is currently taxable. Thus, there is a time value of money consideration.

In conclusion, to quote an old but appropriate cliche, "There are many ways to skin a cat." In this case, the "cat" is the financial statements, and the "skinning" is the early retirement of debt.

———————————— **Debt Restructuring** ————————————

A not uncommon problem that many companies faced in the decade of the 1980s involved excessive borrowing relative to the ability of their earnings and cash flow to support such debt levels. Indeed, the banking and thrift crisis of the 1990s appears at least partially attributable to overzealous lending decisions on the part of some financial institution managers.

When a company is unable to fully service its debt, the lender is faced with a decision: either restructuring the obligation with the hope of recovering most of the loaned funds in the future, or calling the obligation, with the hope of recovering all of the funds immediately or at least minimizing the losses currently. Unfortunately, calling an obligation often leads to a voluntary bankruptcy declaration by the borrower, which may prevent the lender from recovering its loaned funds for many months or even years. Thus, many lenders opt for the first solution—a troubled-debt restructuring.

A debt restructuring essentially involves yielding certain concessions associated with the debt agreement to the borrower. Typically, the concessions granted involve either a settlement of the obligation at an amount less than its book value, or a modification of the terms of the debt instrument. In the event of the latter, a modification may involve any of the following:

1. A reduction in the stated rate of interest.
2. An extension of the maturity date.
3. A reduction in the maturity (or loan) value.
4. A reduction in any interest accrued to date.

If the debt is settled at a discounted amount, the borrower will recognize an extraordinary gain for the amount of the discount (and the lender, an ordinary loss) for income statement purposes. If, on the other hand, only the terms of the debt agreement are modified, the method of accounting will be dictated by the borrower's total future cash outflows (as opposed to the present value of the future cash outflows). Where the total future cash outflows exceed the debt's book value, no recognition of the restructuring is required in the borrower's financial statements. The debt will simply be amortized at the new interest rate or over the new term. However, where the debt's book value exceeds the total future cash outflows associated with the debt, the value of the debt must be written down to the lower value, and a corresponding extraordinary gain recognized on the income statement.[6]

———————————

[6] The accounting entry to recognize this write-down would appear as:

Debit: Loan payable $XXX
      Credit: Extraordinary gain on
      Debt Restructuring $XXX

Perhaps one of the most famous troubled-debt restructurings involved the Chrysler Corporation. By year-end 1979, Chrysler was in default on most of its institutional borrowings. In an effort to save the company and the jobs of its employees, Congress passed the Chrysler Corporation Loan Guarantee Act, providing the company with guarantees of new borrowings of up to $1.5 billion. To qualily for the guarantees, however, Chrysler had to obtain certain waivers from its existing lenders, which it did. During 1980, Chrysler's creditors converted over $900 million of short-term debt into long-term loans and over $340 million of long-term debt into newly issued preferred stock. In total, Chrysler was relieved of over $400 million in debt. The success of the Chrysler restructuring is now well-recognized. By August of 1983, Chrysler had fully repaid the funds borrowed under the Loan Guarantee Act and reported positive profits beginning as early as 1982.

Conclusions

The valuation of long-term debt is based upon the present value (or discounted value) of the future cash flows needed to satisfy an obligation. This valuation approach is consistent with the time frame implicit in any balance sheet—it reflects the value of a company's assets, liabilities, and owners' equity as of the balance sheet date. Hence, liabilities are valued at their present value, rather than at their maturity or future value.

From an analytical perspective, financial statement users should recall that liabilities, unlike assets, are never revalued on the balance sheet to reflect underlying changes in their fair market value. Even liabilities acquired in a business combination, although revalued at that point, are never again revalued to reflect their fair market value. Thus, the current discounted value of a long-term liability may be either greater or less than its reported balance sheet value. This misvaluation should not present problems for most analysts, however, unless early debt retirement is an issue.

Perhaps the greatest concern for an analyst is not those liabilities which are reported in the balance sheet, but rather those which are not. In the following chapter, we focus on a common set of liabilities which, for a variety of reasons, are carried off-balance sheet.

CHAPTER NINE

Special Topics in Debt Valuation

When analyzing the debt position of a company, either for lending or investment purposes, the analyst should direct at least as much attention to those obligations which are not reported on the balance sheet, as to those which are. Indeed, it often comes as a shock to new analysts (and, frequently when it is too late) that many of the obligations of a company are simply not required to be presented on the face of the balance sheet under existing GAAP. Some of these off-balance sheet obligations are disclosed, however, in the footnotes, while others are simply not disclosed at all.

Thus, the principal focus of this chapter is on those off-balance sheet debt items. Most off-balance sheet obligations involve financing arrangements, typically in the form of executory contracts. These off-balance sheet agreements are usually disclosed in the footnotes as "commitments and contingencies." A second group of off-balance sheet obligations involve debts which have, in most cases, simply been ignored by accounting standard-setters, and thus no current disclosure requirements exist. Obviously, the latter group is more problematic because there exists little or no information about them.

Commitments and Contingencies

Commitments and contingencies refer to a set of pending obligations which are disclosed in the footnotes to the financial statements. In some cases, as in a lawsuit, the value of the future obligation (i.e., the lawsuit settlement) may be unknown, as well as the expected date of settlement. The disclosure of these contingent liabilities, even though they don't currently exist, reflects the well-honored accounting convention of conservatism. In other cases, as in a signed contract to buy certain quantities of inventory at specified prices in the future, both the value of the obligation and the date of settlement are known. These commitments reflect a contractual future obligation, but not an existing one as of the balance sheet preparation date.

Contingent Liabilities

Contingencies, or *contingent liabilities*, represent a category of expected liabilities. Whether a contingent liability is reported in the footnotes or not, is largely determined by management's assessment of the probability of the liability's occurrence. If the liability is "probable," it should be formally reported on the balance sheet. If, on the other hand, the liability is only "reasonably possible," or if probable the amount of the liability cannot be reasonably estimated, only footnote disclosure is required. Finally, if realization of the liability is judged only to be "remote," then no disclosure whatsoever is required.

Unfortunately, just what conditions indicate a probable liability versus a reasonably possible liability vary between managers, and often between auditors. More often than not, "probable" liabilities end up being reported only in the footnotes, or unfortunately, not at all.

Consider, for example, the case of Westinghouse Electric Corporation. During the mid-1960s, Westinghouse became a manufacturer of nuclear reactors, and in an effort to secure customers, offered as an inducement the opportunity to buy processed uranium from the company for a period of up to 20 years at a price not exceeding $10 per pound. Historically, the price of uranium had never exceeded $4.50 per pound, and thus the option to buy nuclear material from Westinghouse was essentially worthless unless the price per pound escalated above $10.

From 1966 to 1973, Westinghouse signed supply options representing approximately 80 million pounds of uranium. Unbeknownst to the company, a cartel of uranium producers had been secretly formed; and by early 1974, the cartel had driven the price of uranium to nearly $45 per pound. At that time, Westinghouse had 15 million pounds on hand, and thus was exposed to a potential liability in excess of $2 billion (i.e., 65 million pounds × $35 per pound). Unfortunately, it was not until late 1975, or nearly two years later, that Westinghouse lenders and shareholders learned of this cash outflow exposure; and, only then after multiple lawsuits had been filed against the company by its former customers seeking to enforce the supply contracts.

In essence, it was not until a legal action was taken by one of the parties involved that Westinghouse perceived the potential loss and associated liability as being "reasonably possible." Given available courtroom evidence, it might be argued that Westinghouse could have reasonably estimated the potential loss in early 1974, or even late 1973, and that the probability of at least some loss was quite likely.[1] Westinghouse's customers eventually won the litigation, forcing the company to make a settlement in cash, processed uranium, and other consideration (e.g., free reactor servicing).

In another litigation liability case, Energy Transportation Systems, Inc. (ETSI) filed anti-trust litigation in 1984 against seven railroads, following the failure of the company's coal-slurry pipeline project. ETSI charged the railroads with conspiring to defeat the project due to the potential competition that the project presented to the railroads in the Southwest U.S. utility coal market. By February, 1989, five of the defendants had settled out of court for approximately $285 million. In March, 1989, a Texas jury determined that a conspiracy had caused damages of $345 million to ETSI, and after trebling for punitive damages, the total judgment was established at $1.04 billion.

In July, 1989, the remaining defendants, the Santa Fe Railroad and its parent, the Sante Fe Pacific Corp. (SFPC), motioned for retrial but were rejected; however, the judge in the proceeding did reduce the outstanding award by the amount of the prior settlements, leaving only $750 million owing to ETSI. SFPC appealed again, but before a verdict could be reached, settled out of court with ETSI for $350 million in April of 1990. At issue is whether the potential loss by SFPC was "probable" or only "reasonably possible" at year-end 1989. Given the prior settlements by the other defendants and the adverse courtroom decisions during 1989, many analysts could quite properly argue that a loss of some amount should have been accrued in 1989, with a deduction taken against 1989 earnings and a liability created on the balance sheet—SFPC chose to disclose the lawsuit exposure only in its footnotes.

These cases illustrate the all-too-often reluctance by management to recognize a loss, and the related liability. Although the desire to avoid unpleasant news is quite natural, it suggests that the analyst should be prepared to take an aggressive stance in regard to restating published financial statements with respect to contingent liabilities. In the case of SFPC, for

---

[1] Under newly issued GAAP, when a company has outstanding contractual commitments (e.g., a supply contract) which have cash flow implications, the existence of the commitment and its cash flow effects for the following five years must be disclosed in the footnotes. Thus, analysts are now provided sufficient information to conduct sensitivity (or "What if") analysis on these contracts.

example, the footnotes to the financial statements did reveal the existence of the $750 million judgment against the company. Thus, the analyst could easily incorporate this information into the published financial statements to assess, in a worst case scenario, how adversely the company would be affected if subsequent appeals failed.[2]

A final (non-litigation) example is the frequent-flyer programs adopted by most U.S.-based airlines, as well as similar programs by hotel chains, car rental agencies, and even video rental chains.[3] In the early 1980s, most major airlines established frequent-flyer plans as a means to attract and retain customers. Under the plans, passengers earned points for each air-mile flown (or for each dollar spent in affiliate programs such as the Citibank AAdvantage program for American Airlines frequent-flyers). The points could subsequently be converted into free airline tickets. According to a study by Salomon Brothers, by year-end 1988, the number of points earned was equivalent to $940 million in revenues for the eight leading airlines, with American Airlines facing the largest potential liability of $190 million.

Clearly, for these obligations, not only was the amount estimable but their occurrence reasonably possible, or even probable. But, no-where in American's financial statements was the liability revealed, not even in the footnotes. The reason—beginning in 1989, the airlines placed increasing restrictions on the utilization of frequent-flyer awards (e.g., restricting the number of available seats per flight), such that the probability of displacing a revenue-paying customer was statistically insignificant. Thus, the value of the potential liability could justifiably be argued to be only the incremental cost of an additional passenger (e.g., the cost of a meal or snack), rather than the revenue lost due to passenger displacement. And hence, when viewed from the perspective of the potential incremental cost versus that of potential revenue lost, the discounted value of the future liabilities for a frequent-flyer program was immaterial, and thus did not require disclosure.

Commitments

A commitment is a contractual obligation to provide goods or services at some future date. These contracts generally fall under the rubric *executory contract* because they are dependent upon the occurrence of some future event. And, since a dependency exists, the obligation to perform is disclosed

---

[2] The accounting entry to incorporate a potential legal liability would appear as follows:

Debit: Loss on litigation	$750 million
Credit: Liability under litigation	$750 million

When restating the income statement for such losses, the tax effects (if any) should be considered.

[3] The sale of accounts or notes receivable with recourse also represents a contingent liability. Even though this practice is widespread, it is rarely reported in the footnotes due to materiality questions.

via the footnotes, rather than on the face of the balance sheet. Examples of commitments include operating leases, purchase or supply agreements (as in the case of Westinghouse), loan guarantees on the borrowings of related companies, take-or-pay contracts, and working capital maintenance agreements, to name only a few.

To illustrate the accounting conundrum created by these contracts, consider the following two contractual relationships:

1. A company borrows $1 million from a bank, agreeing to repay the borrowed amount, plus interest of $150,000 over a 12-month period.

2. A company signs a noncancellable, nontransferable lease on retail space, agreeing to pay $1.15 million in rent payments over the next 12 months.

In both cases, the company has incurred an economic liability of approximately equivalent amounts (i.e., $1.15 million over the one year period, ignoring the small differential associated with the time value of money); however, only in the first relationship is the company obligated to record an accounting liability for the future payments.

The second relationship depicts a typical operating lease, which requires no balance sheet disclosure of the future lease payments. Instead, the lease payments are recognized only on the income statement as a lease expense, when paid. Current GAAP does require, however, that the minimum future lease payments be disclosed in the company's footnotes.

It is often difficult for cash flow-minded analysts to understand why the accounting profession differentiates operating leases (and similar executory contracts) from other accounting liabilities. Perhaps the best explanation of this can be seen by examining the similarities and differences in the above two relationships. While both contracts involve approximately equivalent cash outflows, they differ as to the amount of consideration received at contract signing. With the bank loan, consideration of $1 million was immediately received, and thus a liability for the repayment of that amount must be recorded. With the operating lease, however, only a promise of future consideration (i.e., the opportunity to utilize the retail space) was received.

For many analysts, this subtle distinction is irrelevant, and what matters is that the company has a noncancellable obligation to make future cash payments. Similarly, in the eyes of many statement users, this condition alone is sufficient justification to merit inclusion of the economic liability in the accounting statements. Given this particular viewpoint, and current GAAP footnote disclosures, it is a simple matter to restate a company's financial statements for these unreported obligations.

Operating Leases. To illustrate how this restatement can be undertaken, consider the financial data of Jack Eckerd Corporation (JEC) presented in Exhibits 9.1 and 9.2. These exhibits reveal that JEC leases substantial quantities of retail space, all via operating leases. Alternatively stated, JEC engages in off-balance sheet financing of its revenue-producing retail assets to an apparently substantial degree.

To assess the impact of these operating leases on the financial statements of JEC, an alternative approach is to treat the leases as a *capital lease*, which involves capitalizing the present value of the future lease payments on the balance sheet as both a liability and as an asset. Under GAAP, a lease agreement must be capitalized if any one of the following four criteria are satisfied at the time of lease inception:

1. The lease transfers ownership of the property to the lessee by the end of the lease term.
2. The lease contains an option to purchase the property at a bargain price.
3. The lease term is equal to 75 percent or more of the estimated economic life of the property.
4. The present value of the rentals and other minimum lease payments is equal to 90 percent or more of the fair value of the leased property (less any related investment tax credit retained by the lessor).

Given the specificity of the above criteria, however, it is a relatively easy matter to construct a long-term, noncancellable lease which does not violate any of the above criteria, and thus is entitled to off-balance sheet treatment.

Assuming that JEC's incremental cost of borrowing at July 30, 1983, is 10 percent (other footnotes reveal that JEC's short-term weighted average cost of capital was 9.3 percent and its long-term notes carried interest rates of 9.75 percent), an estimate of the present value of the minimum future lease payments (see Exhibit 9.2) after 1983 would total approximately $350.8 million. Using this estimated figure, the analyst would then increase the long-term assets (i.e., leased property) by $350.8 million and the liabilities by an equivalent amount.[4] The analyst should note that this restatement process is an accceptable, but not exacting process. Moreover, it should be

---

[4] More specifically, the accounting entry would appear as:

Debit: Leased assets	$350.8 million
Credit: Short-term lease obligation	$ 50.8 million
Credit: Long-term lease obligation	300.0 million

The analyst should note that restating the balance sheet with the above entry also requires a consideration of the effect of the restatement on the income statement. Thus, with capitalization, the lease expense will need to be replaced by depreciation expense (on the newly capitalized asset) and interest expense. Hence, capitalization will require that the analyst make certain assumptions regarding depreciation on the asset (i.e., method, salvage value, expected life).

Exhibit 9.1 _____

JACK ECKERD CORPORATION AND SUBSIDIARIES
CONSOLIDATED BALANCE SHEETS
JULY 30, 1983
(in thousands, except per share amounts)

	1983
Assets	
Current assets:	
Cash and short-term investments, at cost plus accrued interest, which approximates market . . . . $	2,194
Receivables, less allowance for doubtful receivables of $1,465 in 1983	76,024
Merchandise inventories	442,878
Prepaid expenses and other current assets	8,448
Total current assets	529,544
Property, plant and equipment, at cost:	
Land	22,206
Buildings	74,056
Furniture and equipment	182,976
Transportation equipment	17,368
Leasehold improvements	49,256
Construction in progress	12,349
	358,211
Less accumulated depreciation	94,093
Net property, plant and equipment	264,118
Excess of cost over net assets of subsidiaries acquired, less applicable amortization	60,597
Other assets and deferred charges, at cost less applicable amortization	10,626
Total assets . . . . $	864,885
Liabilities and Stockholders' Equity	
Current liabilities:	
Short-term debt	71,199
Current installments of long-term debt	1,678
Accounts payable	131,449
Accrued payroll	15,095
Other accrued expenses	34,751
Federal and state income taxes-current	9,162
Federal and state income taxes-deferred	7,959
Total current liabilities	271,293
Deferred Federal and state income taxes	14,167
Long-term debt, excluding current installments	11,133
Stockholders' equity:	
Common stock of $.10 par value. Authorized 100 million shares; issued 37,461,475 in 1983	3,746
Capital in excess of par value	108,971
Retained earnings	455,575
Total stockholders' equity	568,292
Total liabilities and stockholders' equity . . . . $	864,885

Exhibit 9.2 ————————————————————————

JACK ECKERD CORPORATION AND SUBSIDIARIES
FACILITY LEASE DISCLOSURES

The company conducts the major portion of its retail operations from leased store premises under leases that will expire within the next 25 years. Such leases generally contain renewal options exercisable at the option of the company. In addition to minimum rental payments, certain leases provide for payment of taxes, maintenance, and percentage rentals based upon sales in excess of stipulated amounts.

Total rental expense was as follows:

	1983
Minimum rentals	$ 55,980
Percentage rentals	10,735
	$ 66,715

At July 30, 1983, minimum rental commitments under non-cancellable leases were as follows:

Year	
1984	$ 55,892
1985	54,884
1986	53,434
1987	52,107
1988	50,606
1989-1993	210,166
1994-1998	129,807
1999-2003	54,572
After 2003	4,918
	$ 666,386

——

noted that the restatement assumes that the leases were contracted for as of the balance sheet date.

Not surprisingly, the capitalization of the lease payments substantially increases JEC's debt ratios:

	As reported	Adjusted
Total debt/total equity	0.52	1.12
Total debt/total capitalization	0.34	0.53

An important question at this point is "Why wouldn't JEC want to capitalize its leases?" After all, lease capitalization will add significant new asset values to the balance sheet.

Exhibit 9.3 ───────────────────────────────────

THE USE OF OPERATING LEASES IN THE
RETAIL INDUSTRY: 1981

	Unadjusted Debt-to-Capitalization Ratio	Debt-to-Capitalization Ratio Adjusted for Operating Leases
Allied Stores	52.1%	58.4%
Edison Brothers	16.4	56.7
Federated Department Stores	33.1	35.7
K Mart	49.4	59.8
Melville	19.1	51.7
J.C. Penney	32.4	44.5
Revco	19.5	51.7
Wal-Mart Stores	50.0	62.3

Implicit in the issue of off-balance sheet financing is the belief that if substantial quantities of debt can be kept off-balance sheet, a company can be leveraged to a greater extent than would otherwise be possible. Whether this belief is valid or not is an empirical question; however, many investment analysts would argue that since the stock market is informationally efficient, it cannot be fooled by the use of operating leases or other forms of off-balance sheet debt. A similar argument might be made by lenders because operating lease payments are reflected in the income statement as a lease expense and thus on any cash flow analysis prepared therefrom. While both of these points are meritorious, the fact remains that if the analyst is making an investment or lending decision solely, or even principally, on the basis of unadjusted debt ratios, then that decision is being made without an explicit consideration of the off-balance sheet debt.

As a concluding point in our discussion of leases, whether or not an analyst should undertake a restatement of the balance sheet is largely a function of the extent to which a company relies on the use of operating leases as a means to access revenue-producing assets. As the data in Exhibit 9.3 reveals, not all companies rely heavily on operating leases, and for those companies, restatement is unnecessary.

Other Executory Contracts. Before departing the topic of commitments, an explanation of some of the more prevalent forms of these contracts is instructive; these include loan guarantees, take-or-pay contracts, and working capital maintenance agreements.

Frequently, when a subsidiary or affiliate company undertakes a bank lending arrangement, additional guarantees for the loan may be sought from a parent company or a majority shareholder. Like a co-signer on a note, the parent company effectively assures the lender that if the subsidiary is unable to fulfill the debt contract, it will assume responsibility for the debt servicing and repayment. From the perspective of a parent company, this type of guarantee is an executory contract—no obligation arises until some future event (i.e., default by the subsidiary) occurs—and thus must be disclosed in the parent company's footnotes if the commitments are material in amount.

As noted in Chapter 6, a new GAAP consolidation rule (SFAS 94) became effective year-end 1989, which requires a parent company to consolidate the financial results of all majority-owned subsidiaries (including foreign subsidiaries) unless the subsidiary is only a temporary holding (e.g., a sale is pending) or unless the subsidiary is not under the control of the parent (e.g., the subsidiary has declared bankruptcy and is effectively under the control of a court-appointed trustee). Thus, beginning in 1989, much of the guaranteed debt that was previously reported only via a parent company's footnotes will now appear directly on the parent's balance sheet.

Nonetheless, significant quantities of guaranteed debt may still remain off a parent's balance sheet. For example, SFAS 94 does not cover joint ventures. Thus, if a parent company is involved in a number of joint ventures which have significant outstanding lines of credit guaranteed by the parent, the debt will only appear on the financial statements of the joint venture (which will be equity-method accounted by the parent). In the view of many seasoned analysts, it is imperative to consider a worst-case scenario in which the joint venture fails and the parent is legally obligated to assume the guaranteed debt.[5] Obviously, the worst-case scenario may never arise; however, if the investment or lending opportunity appears viable even under worst-case conditions, the analyst can gain a certain degree of confidence through such information.

Another important source of off-balance sheet (but guaranteed) debt involves the increasingly popular leveraged ESOP (or employee stock ownership plan). While this topic is addressed in Chapter 10, it is sufficient to point out at this time that should an ESOP engage in any banking relationship, that relationship would almost certainly be guaranteed by the company sponsoring the ESOP.

---

[5] Given the workings of the equity method, to restate a parent's balance sheet to reflect the level of guaranteed debt, the following accounting entry is necessary:

Debit: Investment in Joint Venture	$XXX	
Credit: Guaranteed Subsidiary Borrowings		$XXX

In the event that a joint venture fails, the value of the asset account "Investment in Joint Venture," must be seriously questioned; and alternatively, a debit to a loss account on the income statement may be appropriate.

The leveraged ESOP creates a particularly incestuous set of relations if the ESOP's only source of cash is the company-sponsor. Note that if the sponsor experiences financial difficulties, not only is the sponsor's own debt placed in jeopardy, but so too will be the debt of the ESOP if the dividend payments on the sponsor's stock (and thus the ESOP's assets) are impaired. If the ESOP holds investments (and hence cash flow sources) other than the sponsor's stock, there is clearly a greater margin for error; but, if the ESOP's only asset is the sponsor's stock, the analyst would be wise to treat the debt of the ESOP as that of the company-sponsor.

Another executory contract deriving its existence from banking relations is the *working capital maintenance agreement*. Instead of guaranteeing the full performance of a debt contract, a parent company may only guarantee certain aspects of a contract. For example, since most debt contracts specify that the existing financial condition of a borrower be maintained, a working capital maintenance agreement (WCMA) may be negotiated wherein a parent or affiliate company commits to maintaining the level of working capital of the borrower. Note the executory aspect of this agreement—in the event that a borrower's working capital falls below the level specified by the debt covenant, the guarantor is obligated to provide the necessary cash infusion to maintain the working capital level for the remaining life of the agreement.

Most managers view a WCMA as a bottomless "black hole" in that there are seldom any limits (other than the life of the debt contract) on the required cash infusions. On more than one occasion, a guarantor has found it less costly to merely pay off the debt contract as a means to escape the perpetual cash flow drain created by a WCMA. Thus, analysts would be wise to note this view, and given that current GAAP disclosures require the presentation of the basic elements of an existing WCMA in the guarantor's footnotes, to be certain to consider the impact of such commitments on the future cash flows of a company.

A final example is the *take-or-pay contract*, which is also sometimes called a thru-put contract. Under a take-or-pay contract, one company agrees to make specific future cash payments to another for a predetermined minimum quantity of products or services. Payment for the minimum quantity is required regardless of whether a buyer desires, or is even able to accept, the product. Hence, if a buyer ceases operations, either temporarily or permanently, the cash outflow required by the take-or-pay contract must be maintained. Existing GAAP requires that a company disclose the existence of, and the minimum cash flows required under such contracts thereby enabling the financial statement user to more accurately project the future cash flows of a company under various operating scenarios.

Financial Instruments with Off-Balance Sheet Risk. A recently adopted disclosure standard (SFAS 105) now requires that companies (principally financial institutions) issuing financial instruments whose characteristics expose the issuing company to potential future losses, must disclose the nature and terms of the instruments in their financial statements. The types of financial instruments covered by this new ruling include letters of credit, loan commitments, futures contracts, interest rate and foreign currency swaps, and "repo" agreements (i.e., an obligation to repurchase securities sold). For these instruments, the issuing company is required to disclose the contract amount, the nature and terms of the cash requirements, and the credit and/or market risk of the instrument. In essence, SFAS 105 expands the list of commitment and contingent liabilities that a company must disclose to its financial statement users. In so doing, the user can obtain a fuller and fairer assessment of the future cash flows associated with the operations of a given entity.

Off-Balance Sheet Debt

In the first part of this chapter, we focused on those liabilities which are effectively carried off-balance sheet as provided under existing GAAP. Many of these obligations represented various forms of off-balance sheet financing. We now turn to a set of obligations which are carried off-balance sheet as a consequence of an absence of GAAP. Until recently, this category of off-balance sheet debt was comprised of unfunded pension obligations and unfunded postretirement benefits. Effective year-end 1989, the problem of unreported pension obligations was largely rectified by the imposition of SFAS 87. The problem of unreported postretirement benefit obligations, however, remains, at least until 1994.

As a means of explaining the current status of these reporting problems, let us begin with a brief history of employee benefits in the U.S. The union movement in the United States produced a number of notable outcomes, one of which was the adoption of private pension and postretirement benefit plans by many large domestic companies. In effect, the longer an employee worked for a given employer, the greater the retirement benefits that he/she could earn. Unlike wages, however, which required current payment (and thus were immediately expensed on the income statement), retirement benefits were viewed as an obligation of the future when an employee actually retired. And, in the absence of any legislation requiring the current funding of those "future commitments," many, if not most, companies adopted a funding scheme known as "pay as you go." In effect, a company only placed funds in the pension or retirement plan sufficient to cover the expected cash outflows to retired employees for that period.[6]

This strategy suffered from a number of flaws. First, from an accounting perspective, the pay-as-you-go concept failed to recognize that retirement benefits, like wages, were really an expense of the period in which they were earned, even though they remained unpaid. Thus, in spite of the fact that funding of the earned benefits may have been delayed for many years, the benefits themselves should have been recorded as an expense and as a liability in the period earned. Second, from a funding perspective, the pay-as-you-go scheme was premised in the unjustified philosophy that currently funding such benefits was economically irrational. Once funds are placed in a pension trustee account, they are no longer available for use by the company. Thus, companies argued that fully funding a pension plan was irrational; employees would (in theory) be better off if the funds were invested in the operations of the company, in expectation of producing greater future returns and enabling even higher retirement benefits.

In the absence of an insurance plan to back up the pay-as-you-go approach, financial difficulty for a company could spell financial disaster for both retired and current employees. After a number of corporate failures in the early 1970s, which were accompanied by private pension plan failure attributable to the pay-as-you-go scheme, the U.S. government enacted the Employee Retirement Income Security Act (or ERISA). This 1974 act achieved several important goals. First, it disallowed the use of any pay-as-you-go schemes for employee pension benefits, and instead mandated that beginning in 1975, all pension benefits earned by employees in a given year were to be currently funded. Further, any unfunded pension benefits earned prior to 1975 were to be amortized and funded over a period not to exceed 40 years. Second, it created the Pension Benefit Guarantee Corporation (PBGC) to act as an insurer of employee benefits in the event of corporate failure. Funding for any underfunded plan would come from insurance premiums collected by the PBGC from companies sponsoring qualified retirement plans. The PBGC was also empowered to act as an advocate of the employees and to file suit against any corporation in the event of a failure of an underfunded plan. Through various legislation passed since 1975, the PBGC has become empowered to sue for up to 100 percent of any unfunded pension benefits. Moreover, various court rulings have placed the status of any PBGC claims above that of secured lenders (but below that of the IRS) in the event of a corporate liquidation.

While ERISA made significant headway toward improved funding of employee retirement plans, it failed to cover the issue of information disclosure to various interested parties. In 1979, however, the FASB issued

---

[6] A company may establish either a *defined benefit* or a *defined contribution* pension plan. Defined contribution plans specify the dollar amount that is to be contributed to a plan by a company, and it is the least risky of the two types of plans in that the value of a company's obligation is certain. A defined benefit plan, on the other hand, specifies the amount of future benefits that an employee will receive during retirement. This latter type of plan is far riskier in that assessing a company's future obligation requires many assumptions that frequently prove to be incorrect. Thus, the future obligation under a defined benefit plan can only be estimated, and cannot be known with certainty.

SFAS 36, which required companies to disclose via the footnotes the present value of the accumulated (vested and nonvested) pension benefits and the value of the net assets available in the pension plan to cover those obligations. Thus, users were given information to determine whether a plan was fully funded (or not). Note that if a plan was underfunded, SFAS 36 did not require that a liability for the underfunding be placed on the financial statement. It was not until 1989, with the adoption of SFAS 87, that a liability for underfunding became a required balance sheet disclosure, and thus, that the liability for any underfunded pension obligations formally became part of a company's listed liabilities.

To illustrate the current disclosures for pension plans, consider Exhibit 9.4, which presents Valhi, Inc.'s footnote disclosure relating to employee benefit plans at year-end 1989. The analyst should observe that Valhi maintains a number of pension plans, some of which are overfunded (i.e., assets exceed projected benefits) and some which are underfunded. There are several key comparisons that analysts should consider when analyzing a company's pension situation:

		1989	
		Overfunded Plans	Underfunded Plans
1.	Accumulated benefit obligation (ABO)	$ 75,457	$ 139,901
	Less: Plan assets at fair value	(117,221)	(82,102)
	Net ABO position	(41,764)	57,799

The accumulated benefit obligation, or ABO reflects a company's discounted pension obligation (vested and nonvested benefits) based upon current employee salary levels.[7] Thus, assuming no salary increases, Valhi's pension plans were underfunded by approximately $16 million net (i.e., $57.8 – $41.8 million), or $57.8 million gross, at year-end 1989.

2.	Projected benefit obligation (PBO)	$ 86,879	$ 153,696
	Less: Plan assets at fair value	(117,221)	(82,102)
	Net PBO position	$ (30,342)	$ 71,594

The projected benefit obligation, or PBO, on the other hand, reflects a company's future discounted pension obligation incorporating expected

---

[7] Pension accounting involves the use of several interest rates. Pension obligations, for example, are discounted using an interest rate—usually the settlement rate offered by insurance companies when selling retirement annuities—and pension assets are valued using future expected rates of return. Both the selection of a discount rate and the selection of the expected rate of return on pension assets are effectively a management decision, subject to review by the independent auditor. Obviously, the prudent analyst will check to ensure that these rates are not out of line with industry norms.

Exhibit 9.4 _____

VALHI, INC.
1989 PENSION DISCLOSURES

The funded status of the Company's defined benefit pension plans is set forth below. The rates used in determining the actuarial present value of benefit obligations were (i) discount rate—7% to 12%, and (ii) rate of increase in future compensation levels—nil to 10%. The expected long-term rates of return on assets used ranged from 7% to 12%. Plan assets at December 31, 1989 are primarily investments in U.S. and non-U.S. corporate equity and debt securities, short-term cash investments, mutual funds and goup annuity contracts.

	Assets exceed projected benefits December 31,		Projected benefits exceed assets December 31,	
	1989	1988	1989	1988
		(In thousands)		
Actuarial present value of benefit obligations:				
Vested benefits . . . . $	69,933	$ 23,718	$ 136,427	$ 31,713
Nonvested benefits	5,524	2,392	3,474	662
Accumulated benefit obligations	75,457	26,110	139,901	32,375
Effect of projected salary increases . .	11,422	5,403	13,795	3,408
Projected benefit obligations	86,879	31,513	153,696	35,783
Plan assets at fair value	117,221	40,961	82,102	18,277
Plan assets over (under) projected benefit obligations	30,342	9,448	(71,594)	(17,506)
Unrecognized net loss (gain) from experience different from actuarial assumptions	(2,669)	(2,061)	(12,573)	129
Unrecognized prior service cost (credit)	6,542	(514)	(4,845)	(5,854)
Unrecognized net obligations (assets) being amortized over 9 to 18 years . . .	(17,279)	(5,964)	7,950	1,898
Prepaid (accrued) pension cost—SFAS No. 87 plans	16,936	909	(81,062)	(21,333)
Non-SFAS No. 87 plans	—	12,489	—	(59,496)
Total prepaid (accrued) pension cost	16,936	13,398	(81,062)	(80,829)
Current portion and reclassification	1,174	—	2,792	1,431
Noncurrent prepaid (accrued) pension cost . . . . $	18,110	$ 13,398	$ (78,270)	$ (79,398)

salary increases (of from 0 to 10 percent for Valhi). Thus, including projected salary increases, Valhi's pension plans were underfunded by approximately $41.2 million net, or $71.5 million gross, at year-end 1989.

Under GAAP, the calculation of a company's pension liability is subject to a number of pension adjustments (see Exhibit 9.4) designed to help smooth out various shocks (e.g., changes in actuarial assumptions, unusual investment gains or losses experienced from year-to-year, etc.) that may affect such plans, before arriving at the required balance sheet disclosure. As Exhibit 9.4 reveals, in 1989, Valhi's overfunded plans had a net overfunded position of $18.1 million, and its underfunded plans a net underfunded position of $78.2 million. If a company has a net underfunded position in any of its plans, even though in aggregate the net position of all plans taken as a whole is overfunded, it must present this liability in its balance sheet. Thus, in Valhi's balance sheet for 1989, a pension liability of $78.2 million reflecting the underfunded plans is reported, along with a pension asset of $18.1 million reflecting the overfunded plans.

There are differences of opinion among financial statement users as to whether analysts should focus on the magnitude of the gross (i.e., $78.2 million) or the net underfunding (i.e., $78.2 – 18.1). Assuming that a company is a going concern, we believe that the level of net underfunding (i.e., $60.1 million) is the appropriate focal point. Legally, management may terminate a pension plan and remove any overfunding; however, legislation is pending in the U.S. Congress which would restrict the use of any reverted excess pension assets to satisfying any existing underfunding amongst a company's existing pension plans. Thus, focusing on the gross underfunding fails to recognize a company's access to excess pension assets that might be available to help reduce a pension obligation.[8]

As a concluding point, the analyst would be wise to recall that prior court rulings have placed the status of any unfunded pension obligations above that of secured debt in the event of corporate liquidation. And, a good way to gauge the pension exposure of a particular company is by calculating the unfunded pension debt-to-equity ratio. This ratio reveals the proportion of shareholder equity which would be consumed if current funding of all unfunded committed benefits was required.

Other Postretirement Benefits

While the disclosure problem relating to pension obligations was resolved with the implementation of SFAS 87, a similar unresolved problem contin-

---

[8] In the event that a company terminates a pension plan, and it may do so only with the approval of the PBGC, a gain due to previous overfunding, or a loss due to underfunding, may be recognized. Under current GAAP, the termination gain or loss is recognized in the period of termination as "other income."

Exhibit 9.5 _____

VALHI, INC.
POSTRETIREMENT BENEFITS DISCLOSURES

In addition to providing pension benefits, certain subsidiaries currently provide certain health care and life insurance benefits for eligible retired employees...The cost of postemployment benefits is expensed as health care claims and life insurance premiums are paid. The aggregate net cost to the company of these benefits approximated $8 million in each of 1989, 1988, and 1987...

---

ues to exist with regard to other postretirement benefits, such as dental care, health care, and life insurance. According to a report by the General Accounting Office released in 1989, the total future liability for health benefits exceeds $400 billion. Thus, U.S. corporations face future payments in excess of $400 billion for health care benefits, plus the cost of any other committed benefits.

As an interim solution, the FASB issued SFAS 81 in 1984, requiring only minimal disclosures relating to these costs. For example, Exhibit 9.5 presents the 1989 footnote disclosure for Valhi, Inc. relating to that company's other postretirement benefits. It is easy to compare and contrast the degree of information contained in Exhibit 9.5 versus that contained in Exhibit 9.4. Clearly, at the moment, analysts have insufficient information to assess the severity of a company's postretirement benefit problem (if any). To deal with this issue, the FASB has proposed that beginning with financial statements issued after December 15, 1993, a company would disclose sufficient information in its financial statements to permit a user to discern the existence of any unfunded ABO for other postretirement benefits. Accumulated benefits that are unfunded as of year-end 1993 can be accounted for either by a one-time charge to income (and the creation of a liability) or by amortizing the benefits against income over a 20-year period. Obviously, for companies concerned about the adverse effect on earnings, the latter approach will be preferred.

While there exists little data with regard to the severity of this problem at the individual firm level, some companies have provided preliminary information regarding the magnitude of their other postretirement benefits. DuPont, for example, estimates that its annual cost for medical and other postretirement benefits exceeds $160 million; and, in 1987, Ford Motor Company reportedly paid over $340 million for such expenses. To our knowledge, one of the few companies that has anticipated the FASB ruling on postretirement benefits and recognized an actual balance sheet liability for future costs is LTV Corporation. In 1988, LTV took a $2.6 billion charge against earnings, and created a corresponding liability, for these committed expenditures.

──────────────────── **Conclusions** ────────────────────

When investigating the financial condition of a company, a credit or investment analyst will spend considerable time understanding the nature of the company's existing debt. An equivalent effort, however, should also be spent investigating a company's unreported obligations. In most cases, the off-balance sheet debt is reported in the commitments and contingent liabilities footnote. In the case of postretirement benefit obligations, however, there may be no debt disclosure whatsoever until 1994.

Given the required cash flow disclosures associated with operating leases, take-or-pay contracts, leveraged ESOPs, etc., it is a simple matter to restate a company's balance sheet to fully reflect these obligations. In some cases, the restated results will only marginally differ from the unadjusted results, whereas in other cases, significantly different results may be obtained. Naturally, the purpose of such restatement is to ensure that any calculated debt ratios fully reflect a company's current and future obligations.

In the following chapter, we consider the basics of owners' equity, and its relationship to reported assets and obligations of a company.

CHAPTER TEN

Owners' Equity

This chapter focuses on the owners' or shareholders' equity. In the view of many credit and investment analysts, there is relatively little new or important information contained in the owners' equity section of the balance sheet, and thus it can be readily ignored. For many companies, this is indeed the case, but for others, it is possible to obtain important data about the owners' financing of a company only in this section. Moreover, a number of important accounting adjustments (i.e., foreign currency translation adjustments and long-term investment valuation adjustments) are reported in the owners' equity section, and thus without an examination of these accounts, the analyst will have only a partial picture of a company's financial condition.

By definition, *owners' equity* represents the residual interest in the assets of a company after deducting its liabilities and any minority interest. As a consequence, there are few new valuation concepts associated with the equity accounts. In effect, the valuation of the equity accounts is driven by the valuation methods adopted for the assets and liabilities. Thus, our focus in this chapter will be upon identifying and explaining the various elements that comprise owners' equity. A secondary objective is to briefly overview the determination of primary and fully diluted earnings-per-share.

The Components of Owners' Equity

Owners' equity, or net worth, may be conveniently thought of as the sum of the contributed and earned capital of a company. Some financial institutions constrain the definition of owners' equity to only tangible net worth, or alternatively owners' equity less the value of any intangible assets (and occasionally, prepaid expenses). Owners' equity is also sometimes thought of as the net book value of a company, particularly when the focus is one of investment or acquisition. The principal components of owners' equity include the capital stock accounts, retained earnings, and various adjustments that bypass the income statement and consequently are reported as elements of owners' equity.

Capital Stock Accounts

The contributed capital of a company is largely composed of the common and/or preferred stock sold by a company to the investing public. In the U.S., a corporation may be formed only after receipt of an approved (by a state incorporating commission or agency) charter of incorporation. Among other things, the charter specifies the type, number, and par or stated value of any capital stock to be issued by the incorporated entity.

Most states in the U.S. require that corporations maintain some minimum legal capital which cannot be distributed to shareholders. The original purpose of the concept of legal capital was to specifically set aside a buffer which would exist for creditors in the event that a company failed and was liquidated. In the 1930s, when those security laws were created, they were undoubtedly well justified; however, in today's sophisticated financial environment, the legal capital of a company has little or no meaning.

Nonetheless, those laws are still in effect, and the primary means of establishing legal capital is through the issuance of par value or stated value stock. The value of a company's legal capital is thus determined by multiplying the number of shares issued by the par or stated value-per-share. The par or stated value (hereafter, par value) is simply the value which is printed on the share certificate itself. The analyst should note, however, that there is absolutely no relation between the par value of a stock and its fair market value, except perhaps in the rare event of liquidation due to bankruptcy.[1]

Since most companies tend to set the par value of their capital stock at some nominal level (e.g., $.01 in Exhibit 10.2), most stock will sell at a price far in excess of this value. To account for this excess capital contribution,

---

[1] A company may issue no-par or no-stated value stock; however, if such stock is issued in a state whose securities laws require the issuance of par or stated value stock, then the stock cannot be initially sold there. Legally, the stock may be sold in such a state only after a secondary market develops.

an additional paid-in capital account is created.[2] Together, the par value account and the additional paid-in capital account represent the contributed capital of a company.

The two most common types of capital stock are *common stock* and *preferred stock*. In most corporations, common stock is distinguished from preferred stock in that common shareholders have the right to elect members to the board of directors. In some cases, preferred shareholders may also be granted voting rights, although this tends to be the exception rather than the norm. Preferred stock, on the other hand, is distinguished from common stock in that preferred shareholders, whose stock usually carries a specific dividend, must receive their regular full dividend before common shareholders receive any. Thus, in the event that the earnings available for dividends are limited, the preferred shareholders may receive all or part of their regular dividend while common shareholders receive none. Preferred shareholders also have preferential access to corporate assets upon liquidation of the corporation; however, if the liquidation is associated with a bankruptcy declaration, it is unlikely that this preferential access will yield much in the way of cash return.

Some preferred stocks also carry features which are of particular value to investors, and some features which are not. For example a preferred stock may be convertible into common stock at some pre-specified conversion ratio. Or, the preferred stock may be participating, in which case if a significant amount of earnings is made available for dividend payments, preferred shareholders may be entitled to receive dividend payments above and beyond their regular dividend. Finally, a preferred stock may be cumulative. Before any dividend is paid to either common or preferred shareholders, it must first be declared as payable by the board of directors; thus, dividend payments are never guaranteed, even to the preferred shareholders. Nonetheless, in the event that a regular dividend is missed, the cumulative preferred stockholder carries the right to receive all prior unpaid dividends before any current dividends can be paid to the common or preferred shareholders. Prior unpaid dividends on cumulative preferred stock are not a liability of a company until a dividend is declared by the board of directors; however, any unpaid prior dividends must be disclosed in the footnotes and are called dividends in arrears. From a future investor's perspective, dividends in arrears should be thought of as a contingent liability, and a constraint on the receipt of any future dividends.

---

[2] To illustrate the accounting for a stock issuance, assume that $100,000 of $.01 par value stock, representing 5,000 shares is sold:

Debit: Cash	$100,000	
Credit: Capital stock, $.01 par value		$ 50
Credit: Additional paid-in capital		99,950

Note how the value of a company's legal capital can quite effectively be minimized by setting the par value per share at an extremely low value.

Clearly, the convertible, participating, and cumulative features are valuable characteristics for a preferred stock, and indeed, investors will find that they typically will be required to pay a premium for stock carrying any of these features. A less desirable feature, however, is the call feature, which enables a company to retire any outstanding preferred stock at management's discretion (subject to constraints documented in the stock indenture agreement). While such retirements or redemptions are usually done at a premium above the original issuance price of the preferred, if the company has been successful, the call price is rarely equivalent to the current market value of the stock.

Options, Subscriptions, and Warrants. While most capital stock is obtained by purchasing shares from other investors with the assistance of a broker, some shares may be purchased directly from a company.

Many corporations, for example, grant *stock options* to selected employees as part of a compensation package or to encourage loyalty by making the employees co-owners of the firm. A stock option permits the holder to buy a specified number of common shares at a specified price (called the exercise price) during a specified period of time. Stock options are usually granted at the existing market price of the stock, and thus, since no immediate value can be realized by the employee, no expense is recorded and the existence of the option is recognized only in the footnotes to the balance sheet. If, on the other hand, the options are granted at a price below the existing market value, and the options are currently exercisable, value has been distributed to the employee and a new equity account (common stock options) is created. When either type of option is exercised, the par value and the additional paid-in capital accounts will be increased.

Somewhat similar to a stock option plan is an employee stock ownership plan, or *ESOP*. If an ESOP exists, the board of directors will meet annually to determine how many shares (if any) will be contributed to the ESOP. Obviously, the distribution of these shares is another form of compensation for the employees, and the capital accounts must be increased by the value of the newly issued shares. Frequently a special class of common stock is created for ESOP purposes, often called Class B common stock. Class B stock is usually inferior to regular common stock (or class A stock) with respect to the dividend paid and with respect to its voting power (i.e., ten shares of Class B may be needed, for example, to equal one share of Class A).

If an ESOP exists, analysts should investigate to determine if the plan is a leveraged ESOP. Consider, for example, the case of Texas, Inc., a disguised Dallas-based company. Texas, Inc. created an ESOP for its employees and placed its CEO in a capacity to direct the activities of the ESOP (a not uncommon event). The ESOP then borrowed significant sums from one of Dallas' regional banks. The loans were guaranteed by Texas, Inc., and the borrowed funds were used by the ESOP to buy additional shares of capital stock from Texas, Inc. Not surprisingly, the dividend rate on the purchased shares was set annually to exactly cover the principal and interest payments on the ESOP's bank debt. It should be apparent that the form and substance of this transaction are not equivalent. While it may appear that the ESOP is simply borrowing to buy stock, the reality is that Texas, Inc. has effectively created a form of off-balance sheet debt (which appears as equity on its financial statements).

Also similar to a stock option is a *stock warrant*. Stock warrants are like stock options in that they grant the warrantholder the right to purchase a stated quantity of common stock at a specified price. Warrants are often distributed to shareholders as a means to not only raise additional future capital, but also to create shareholder goodwill. Sometimes warrants are sold in conjunction with a nonconvertible preferred stock offering or a nonconvertible debt offering, principally as a so-called "sweetener" to help ensure the success of the offering. When warrants are sold for value, an owners' equity account must be created (i.e., common stock warrants), whereas if they are distributed for no consideration, they are only acknowledged via the footnotes. In any case, when warrants are exercised, the par value and additional paid-in-capital accounts are increased.

A final means of bypassing a broker and acquiring shares directly from a company is by subscription. Out of courtesy, and occasionally due to the existence of a preemptive right to purchase a pro rata number of any new shares issued, a company will offer to its existing shareholders the opportunity to buy, in total or in part, a new offering of capital stock. In effect, a company will solicit its shareholders and offer them the opportunity to "subscribe" to the offering on a first-right-of-refusal basis. Any undersubscription is then sold to various brokerage houses, which in turn place the shares with their clients. When shares are subscribed, but not yet purchased, a new equity account is created—capital stock subscribed.[3] Ultimately, the subscribed stock account will be closed when payment is received and the capital stock account increased when the new shares are actually issued.

Share Repurchases. In today's capital markets, a quite frequent transaction involves a share repurchase. If available excess cash exists, a company may choose to buy back its own common stock for a variety of reasons, including: (1) to reduce the probability of success of a hostile takeover attempt; (2) to acquire shares for issuance to an ESOP or other stock compensation plan; (3) to acquire shares for issuance in connection with a conversion of preferred stock or convertible debentures; or (4) simply because the company's stock represents (in the eyes of management) the best available investment for its idle cash.

---

[3] The issuing of shares directly to shareholders via subscription is effectively a form of private placement, although private placements may be negotiated with either existing or potential shareholders.

Other reasons also exist. For example, on November 17, 1989, General Electric Company announced the largest ever corporate buy-back in U.S. business history—a repurchase of up to $10 billion of its common stock. According to a company spokesperson, the repurchase would result in a significantly higher return on equity and significantly improved earnings-per-share value. Thus, although this represents an extreme example, some companies undertake a share repurchase to positively impact their market-based indicators of performance (e.g., ROE, EPS, P-E ratio, etc.). There are at least two reasons why this decision makes sense. First, with fewer shares outstanding and a higher per-share stock price, a company will need to distribute fewer shares to effect a merger or acquisition by stock exchange (i.e., a pooling); in effect, less dilution of the existing equity positions will occur. Second, since share repurchases and sales by the issuing entity are not subject to taxes, once the price has been driven up, the shares can be (discreetly) sold back into the market for nontaxable cash gains.

When stock is repurchased with the intent to reissue, it is called *treasury stock* and usually accounted for at the cost basis of the repurchased shares. Treasury stock is most properly reflected on a company's balance sheet as a contra-owners' equity account, since it represents stock that is no longer outstanding. (In unaudited financial statements, the debit balance in treasury stock may be erroneously carried as an asset, which is clearly in contradiction with the GAAP definition of an asset.) When shares are repurchased for retirement, the capital accounts (par and additional paid-in capital) are reduced by the value of the reacquired shares.

Stock Dividends and Splits. Two final capital stock transactions that may be reflected in owners' equity include the issuance of a stock dividend and a stock split. These transactions are similar in one important respect—while the shareholder ends up owning more shares of stock, in reality he or she has received no assets or other consideration from the company.

Consider the case of a stock dividend. In lieu of a cash dividend, a company's board of directors may declare the distribution of a stock dividend, or a distribution of new shares based on the pro rata holdings of existing shareholders.[4] For example, a company may declare a 10 percent stock dividend in which each shareholder receives an additional share of stock for each 10 shares currently held. Whereas a cash dividend is accounted for by reducing both total assets (specifically, cash) and total owners' equity (specifically, retained earnings), a stock dividend leaves both total assets and total equity unchanged. In general, a stock dividend is accounted for by shifting an amount equal to the fair market value of the newly distributed shares from retained earnings to the capital stock accounts. Thus, while

---

[4] Although it is extremely rare, a company may also issue a property dividend in which various assets (perhaps its own products) are distributed to sharcholders.

total owners' equity is unchanged, the balances of the individual equity accounts are redistributed.

Occasionally, a company may feel that its stock price is too high. The most effective way of reducing its share price is through a (forward) stock split. In a two-for-one stock split, for example, the total number of shares outstanding is doubled, and the transaction is accounted for by proportionately reducing (i.e., halving) the par or stated value of the stock. Note that in this case, none of the equity account balances are affected, but in all likelihood the market value of the stock will also halve. To illustrate an extreme case of a stock split, Schuchardt Software Systems declared a 2,000-for-one stock split in 1984. The company's common stock had been trading at a whopping $5,000 per share; the post-split per share price was expected to trade around $3 per share.

Although quite rare, a reverse stock split may be employed in an attempt to raise the market value of a stock. A one-for-five reverse split, for example, will reduce the number of shares outstanding by 80 percent, and is accounted for by proportionately increasing the par or stated value of the stock. Thus, again, none of the individual equity account totals are affected.

Retained Earnings: Earned Capital

Retained earnings refers to the amount of corporate earnings that have not been distributed to the shareholders of a company, and instead, have been retained in the company to support various corporate objectives. It is, in effect, the earned capital of a company that has been involuntarily retained (from the perspective of the shareholders) by the company.

Many investors wonder why all of the earnings of a company are not paid out in the form of dividends. In some cases, dividend payments are restricted by the borrowing agreements entered into by a company. In effect, lenders try to secure as much protection as possible for their loaned assets—collateralizing the loan with various company assets and restricting the payment of dividends are two effective means of doing this. Moreover, a widely held view in the financial community is that it is simply not very prudent to pay all of a company's earnings out in dividends. Clearly, the perceived riskiness of such a company would be higher than if some level of earnings were retained.

Generally speaking, retained earnings is affected by two types of equity transactions—income increases the retained earnings balance, and the payment of dividends decreases it.[5] If, however, a company undertakes a change

---

[5] There are two types of dividends: regular and liquidating. Regular dividends are paid out of existing balances in current earnings and retained earnings. Liquidating dividends, on the other hand, represent a distribution of contributed capital. This tax-free distribution only arises after a company has paid out all of its current and retained earnings to shareholders; and hence, such distributions are made from previous capital contributions.

in its accounting methods, the change may require a retroactive adjustment for all prior periods affected by the change. For example, if a company changes its method of accounting for inventories from LIFO to FIFO, the change requires a retroactive adjustment to the earnings of prior periods, which is reported as an adjustment to retained earnings. Thus, retained earnings may also be affected by the accounting procedures associated with a change in GAAP.

Earnings, dividends, and prior period adjustments are thus the principal determinants of retained earnings. If, however, a company is experiencing financial difficulties, as evidenced by significant losses and a negative retained earnings balance, it may undertake a quasi-reorganization in which the negative balance in retained earnings is offset against the additional paid-in capital account, and the par value account if necessary. As a consequence of a reorganization, the retained earnings balance will be returned to zero and the level of shareholders' equity substantially reduced. In effect, the creditors' increasing ownership in the assets of the company is recognized by restating (i.e., lowering) the value of the owners' equity accounts.

Consider, for example, the case of Telecom Corporation, a company involved in the wholesale distribution of air conditioning and heating components and the manufacture of bulk conveying and processing equipment. Telecom's largest subsidiary, Spector Red Ball, was a trucking company which had been adversely affected by the deregulation of the trucking industry in 1981. As a consequence, Telecom's consolidated financial statements in 1981 and 1982 revealed significant losses, accumulating to a deficit in retained earnings of over $22 million by year-end 1982. During 1985, Telecom's shareholders approved a quasi-reorganization in which over $16.9 million was transferred from the additional paid-in capital account to retained earnings to eliminate the remaining accumulated deficit (see Exhibit 10.1).

Adjustments to Owners' Equity

In addition to the contributed and earned capital accounts, owners' equity may be impacted by two special valuation accounts. Under SFAS 12 (see Chapter 5), if the market value of a company's portfolio of long-term equity investments declines relative to its aggregate cost, the balance sheet value of the portfolio is reduced (under L.C.M.) along with total shareholders' equity. This treatment reflects the notion that since the investments are long-term in nature, the current decline in value is likely to be recovered in the future; and hence, to avoid adding unnecessary volatility to reported earnings, the write-down for the current period bypasses the income statement and is carried directly to owners' equity. If the unrealized deficit in value is recovered in future periods, the contra-owners' equity account is reduced by the unrealized gain until the balance reaches zero.

Exhibit 10.1

TELECOM CORPORATION AND SUBSIDIARIES
CONSOLIDATED STATEMENTS OF SHAREHOLDERS' EQUITY
FOR THE YEARS ENDED DECEMBER 31, 1985, 1984 AND 1983
(In Thousands)

	Number of Shares	Par Value of Common Shares	Paid-in Capital	Accumulated Deficit Eliminated in Capital Restatement	Retained Earnings since January 1, 1985	Unrealized Appreciation (Depreciation) on Investments	Treasury Stock
Balances, January 1, 1983	3,707	$ 3,707	$ 24,172	$ (22,159)	$ —	$ 3,590	$ (73)
Net income				2,678			
Net change in unrealized appreciation (depreciation) on investments						(775)	
Balances, December 31, 1983	3,707	3,707	24,172	(19,481)	—	2,815	(73)
Net income				2,535			
Net change in unrealized appreciation (depreciation) on investments						(2,153)	
Balances, December 31, 1984	3,707	3,707	24,172	(16,946)	—	662	(73)
Restatement of capital accounts (Note 7)			(16,946)	16,946			
Net income					2,990		
Net change in unrealized appreciation (depreciation) on investments						(2,234)	
Utilization of net operating loss carryforwards			1,703				
Balances, December 31, 1985	3,707	$ 3,707	$ 8,929	$ —	$ 2,990	$ (1,572)	$ (73)

Another equity adjustment account may arise when the foreign assets of a company are consolidated with its U.S. assets in the preparation of U.S. dollar-denominated consolidated financial statements. Under SFAS 94, the financial results of all majority-owned subsidiaries, including foreign subsidiaries, must be consolidated with those of the parent company. This consolidation process is impeded, however, when the exchange rate between the U.S. dollar and the currency of the foreign-host country change over time. In effect, the U.S. dollar-equivalent value of a company's foreign net assets will fluctuate as the exchange rate with the U.S. dollar fluctuates.

Under SFAS 52, a change in the U.S. dollar-equivalent of a company's overseas net assets is reflected in an adjustment to the parent's total shareholders' equity (see Exhibit 10.2). The foreign currency translation adjustment account thus merely accommodates the consolidation process, and is of little informational value unless, and until, the sale or liquidation of the foreign subsidiary is expected.

An Illustration

Presented in Exhibit 10.2 is the stockholders' equity section of the consolidated balance sheet of Valhi, Inc. as of December 31, 1989. Note that while Valhi's charter of incorporation has authorized the sale of both common and preferred stock, none of the preferred stock has as yet been sold to investors. Note also that of the 150 million common shares authorized to be sold, 123.5 million have been issued, but only 113.7 million are actually outstanding. The difference between the shares issued and the shares outstanding is reflected in the 9.8 million shares held in treasury.

During 1989, Valhi's additional paid-in capital account declined by over $10 million, despite an increase in the number of shares issued and outstanding. This decline reflects the net effect of a $1.6 million increase in additional paid-in capital from new stock issuances and a $11.6 million decrease associated with the repurchase of outstanding common stock warrants.

During 1989, Valhi's retained earnings also increased by a net of $74.8 million, reflecting net income of $103.3 million and dividend payments of $28.5 million. Finally, Valhi's stockholders' equity was revalued downward in 1989 as a consequence of two factors. First, the company's long-term marketable equity security portfolio experienced an unrealized decline of over $34 million, principally due to a decline in the value of Valhi's 17.9 percent shareholding in Lockheed Corporation. Second, Valhi's foreign operations (principally in Canada and Europe) were subject to a currency exchange rate adjustment in the amount of $46.8 million. Since the value of the U.S. dollar strengthened during 1989 against the Canadian dollar and most European currencies, when Valhi's foreign subsidiaries were consolidated with the U.S. parent into U.S. dollar-equivalents, the net book value of

Exhibit 10. 2

VALHI, INC.
CONSOLIDATED STOCKHOLDERS' EQUITY
(in thousands)

	as of December 31	
	1989	1988
Shareholders' equity:		
Preferred stock, $.01 par value; 5,000 shares authorized; none issued	$ 0	$ 0
Common stock, $.01 par value; 150,000 shares authorized; 123,567 and 123,309 shares issued	1,236	1,233
Additional paid-in capital	27,763	37,811
Retained earnings	374,711	299,881
Adjustments:		
Currency translation	(15,089)	31,717
Marketable equity securities	(34,057)	—
	354,546	370,642
Less: common stock reacquired—at cost (9,838 and 9,412 shares)	67,131	60,006
Total stockholders' equity	$ 287,433	$ 310,636

the foreign assets were written down. The decline of $46.8 million offset the beginning balance of $31.7 million to produce a net negative translation adjustment of $15.1 million as of year-end 1989. The analyst should note that all of the above information was obtained from Valhi's annual 10-K filing with the SEC.

Earnings Per Share

Generally accepted accounting principles require that earnings-per-common share (EPS) be disclosed as part of the income statement. EPS can be defined as net income less preferred dividends divided by the weighted average number of common shares outstanding; however, there are actually three types of EPS numbers that may be disclosed in the financial statements, depending upon the capital structure of the corporation: basic EPS, primary EPS, and fully-diluted EPS.

Firms with a complex capital structure (i.e., those which have issued potentially dilutive securities such as convertible debentures, convertible preferred stock, stock options, or stock warrants that upon conversion or exercise could, in the aggregate, materially dilute or decrease EPS) are required to disclose both primary and fully-diluted EPS. Firms with simple capital structures (i.e., those having no such dilutive securities) are only required to disclose basic EPS.

Basic earnings per share can be expressed as:

$$\frac{\text{Net Income} - \text{Preferred Dividends}}{\text{Average Number of Outstanding Common Shares}}$$

Both primary and fully-diluted earnings per share adjust the numerator and denominator of basic EPS according to a set of somewhat arbitrary accounting rules (i.e., APB Opinion No. 15, and SFAS Nos. 55 and 85). Primary EPS, for example, attempts to capture the dilutive effects of common stock equivalents. *Common stock equivalents* are defined to be stock options, stock warrants, and convertible securities (debentures and preferred stock) whose effective yield is less than two-thirds of the corporate Aa rating when the convertibles were originally issued. These potentially convertible securities are treated as common stock when calculating EPS even if at year-end they have not been converted. Fully-diluted EPS, on the other hand, attempts to capture the dilutive effects of all potentially dilutive securities in the capital structure of a corporation (common stock equivalents and non-common stock equivalents). In effect, fully-diluted EPS attempts to capture the maximum potential dilution of earnings, and hence is always the lowest earnings-per-share number. It is important for the analyst to note that neither primary nor fully-diluted EPS are actual EPS numbers; they are merely hypothetical calculations of possible EPS that could have been reported if various conversions had actually taken place during the accounting period.

To illustrate, consider again Valhi, Inc. According to Exhibit 10.2, Valhi had over 113 million shares of common stock outstanding at year-end 1989. According to the company's financial statements, however, the weighted average number of shares was 113,996,000, reflecting that many of the over 400,000 common shares repurchased in 1989 were outstanding most of the year. Valhi's income statement reveals the following data:

	(in millions)
Income before extraordinary items	$ 102.3
Extraordinary items	1.1
Net income	$ 103.4
Per share data:	
Income before extraordinary items	$ .90
Extraordinary items	.01
Net income	$ .91

GAAP requires that EPS for continuing operations be disclosed separately from the EPS for discontinued operations (if any) and the EPS for extraordinary items. The value of this data is obvious—it enables the analyst to project recurring EPS more readily. By virtue of Valhi's disclosure of only basic EPS, we can infer that the effect of any outstanding dilutive securities was immaterial.

Conclusions

By virtue of the definition of owners' equity—it is the residual interest in the net assets of a company—most of the information content of the equity accounts is contained in any analysis of a company's asset and liability accounts. Nonetheless, since the contributed capital accounts reflect the owners' vested interest, and since retained earnings is a summary of the effectiveness and success of a company's prior operations, it is shortsighted to ignore these accounts. Moreover, important adjustments relating to the value of any foreign-based operations and the value of any long-term investments are reported in the owner's equity section.

Most analyses of owners' equity are premised in comparisons with other measures. The value of owners' equity is often compared, for example, to the current market value of outstanding capital stock. Naive conventional wisdom suggests that if the market value of equity is less than its accounting book value, then the purchase of a company's capital stock is advisable. But, if one unquestioningly adheres to that wisdom, all that has been said about accounting values in the prior nine chapters will have been ignored, and the analyst may fall victim to the "greater fool theory."[6] Another frequently utilized analysis of equity compares the level of owners' equity to either the total assets or the level of debt. These latter comparisons attempt to assess the degree of risk assumed by the owners, versus the degree of risk assumed by creditors. Obviously, the higher the risk absorption by existing owners, the more appealing will be future credit or other owner investments.

In the following chapter, we investigate the question of risk from the perspective of the cash flows of a company.

---

[6] The "greater fool theory" conjectures that there is always a greater fool waiting to buy a given company's stock.

PART IV

The Statement of Cash Flows

A major objective of this book to this point has been to discuss the analytical and valuation issues associated with the income statement and the balance sheet, and by implication the accrual system of accounting. Few will deny that while the accrual system is largely an effective system of measuring and portraying firm performance and financial condition, it suffers from certain limitations which are of particular importance to credit and financial analysts.

In recognition of these limitations, and of the financial community's desire and need for increased information regarding a firm's cash flows, the FASB adopted SFAS 95 in 1987. Under SFAS 95, companies preparing audited financial reports must present as one of the basic financial statements, a statement of cash flows disclosing the cash flows used for (or generated from) operations, investing activities, and financing activities.

In this section, we review the content, analysis, and use of the statement of cash flows. We view the information contained in this statement as perhaps the most critical of any of the basic financial statements. After all, there is only one asset that a company cannot operate without—cash.

CHAPTER 11

Cash Flow Analysis

Over the last decade, no other model has been advocated more to assess the financial health of a company in lending and investment decisions than the concept of cash flow. The importance of cash flow stems, in part, from its invariant nature. As one scans the balance sheet, almost every account is subject to multiple valuations under GAAP—all, that is, except cash. Accounts receivable, for example, is dependent upon the revenue recognition model adopted, inventory upon the cost flow assumption, fixed assets upon the depreciation method, and liabilities upon the interest rate used. Shareholder equity, through income, is similarly affected by all of these items. Only cash is invariant with regard to the various accrual (GAAP) assumptions made.

Many surrogate measures have been used, at one time or another, to proxy a company's cash flow. And, one of the most prevalent ones used in financial analysis is net income plus depreciation and amortization, sometimes called *recurring cash earnings*. As more and more accrual adjustments were called for by the authoritative accounting literature (as witnessed by the plethora of balance sheet accounts), this surrogate, and others like it, have become less and less representative of a company's actual cash flow. It is of interest to note that the authoritative accounting literature now calls for properly prepared financial statements to also include a cash flow statement. Obviously, even in the eyes of the FASB, accrual-based financial statements do not convey all of the information considered necessary to assess the financial health of a firm, at least not also without a cash flow statement.

This chapter has two principal purposes. The first is to demonstrate that, in the absence of a computer, it is quite easy to prepare a cash flow statement, even with only a rudimentary knowledge of accounting. Second, and more importantly, it provides insights to the analysis and interpretation of a statement of cash flows. Many analysts lack the knowledge to prepare even a simple cash flow statement, much less the more important skill of interpretation. This chapter is devoted to building those skills.

Definitions of Cash Flow

To begin, it is important to recognize that there are a variety of definitions of cash flow that are used in practice today. At the broadest definitional level, there are the total cash inflows and total cash outflows, which net to the cash flow of a company for any given period. One of the principal components of a company's net cash flow is its *cash flow from operations*, or CFFO. As we shall see, the CFFO is a highly significant indicator of the overall financial health of a company. Ideally, a company should maintain a positive CFFO. Where the CFFO is negative, a company will eventually be forced to borrow, to generate new equity, or to sell assets just to remain in operations. Obviously, a prolonged period of negative CFFO is a pre-cursor to bankruptcy.[1]

A final measure of cash flow is called the *free cash flow*, or alternatively, the *discretionary cash flow*. Free cash flow is a derivative of the CFFO; that is, it is the CFFO less any required cash disbursements in the subsequent periods, for example, for dividends, currently maturing debt payments, or the like (e.g., a sinking fund payment). The free cash flow thus represents the portion of a company's CFFO that is available to fund discretionary corporate actions, such as a merger or takeover, some form of capital asset expansion, or perhaps a stock buyback or early debt retirement. This residual measure is important to investors because it represents the source of new dividend payments and internal growth investment, and to lenders because it is the source of principal repayment for any new debt agreements. Clearly,

---

[1] As noted in Chapter 2, a company undertaking a significant growth effort is very likely to experience a negative CFFO, largely because of the cash investment in receivables and inventory necessary to sustain and support such growth. Unless the growth period is indefinite (an unlikely event), the CFFO must eventually turn positive. Thus, our principal concern is with those companies experiencing a negative CFFO for prolonged periods, or ones experiencing a negative CFFO in a nongrowth period.

the larger the free cash flow, the more a company will be able to undertake new opportunities when they arise.

─────────── Cash Flow Preparation ───────────

A Four-Step Procedure

The current financial media are wrought with stories concerning the complexity of today's business environment. On the surface, many businesses may indeed seem quite complex, but internally they are in fact relatively simplistic. Most businesses, for example, perform only seven basic activities; they are:

Activity	Effect on Cash	Transaction Type
(1) Operate (produce/sell a product or service)	–/+	Operations
(2) Acquire resources (invest in assets)	–	Investment
(3) Sell resources (disinvest in assets)	+	Investment
(4) Obtain equity proceeds (sell stock)	+	Financing
(5) Return equity (pay dividends, purchase treasury stock)	–	Financing
(6) Obtain debt proceeds (issue debt)	+	Financing
(7) Return debt proceeds (retire debt)	–	Financing

These activities form the fundamental structure of the cash flow statement required under SFAS 95; namely, the cash flow of an entity is trichotomized into its principal sources and uses of operations, investment, and financing transactions (see, for example, Exhibit 11.4).

The preparation of a cash flow statement would be easy if one had access to the general ledger of a company. It would simply be a matter of going down the list of cash transactions reported in the ledger and identifying the amount and type of transaction involved. Using a general ledger T-account, a cash flow statement might look as follows:

Type		Cash				Type
	Beginning balance	$30,000				
Operations	Cash sale	10,000	15,000	Purchase product	Operations
			6,000	Purchase computer	Investment
Financing	Issue debt	5,000	1,000	Pay rent	Operations
Investment	Sell old computer	1,000	5,000	Pay dividends	Financing
	Ending balance	$19,000				

The problem is that a corporation of even small size would have a general ledger which could go on for hundreds of pages, and in any case, would not be made available to an outside analyst. An alternate methodology, which would effectively allow the analyst to see into a company's cash T-account, is thus needed.

In the above example, the change in the company's total cash balance was a negative $11,000. The sources of cash totaled $16,000 and uses $27,000, again revealing a decrease of $11,000. Thus, if an analyst can determine the beginning and ending balances of cash, as would be the case with comparative balance sheets, there is sufficient information to determine the total sources and uses of cash from the three types of activities: operations, investment, and financing. With just a little simple algebra, the change in the cash balance between two periods can be seen to equal the change in all other balance sheet accounts:

$$\begin{aligned}
& \text{Cash}_1 + \text{Other Assets}_1 = \text{Liabilities}_1 + \text{Owners' Equity}_1 \\
& \underline{-(\text{Cash}_0 + \text{Other Assets}_0 = \text{Liabilities}_0 + \text{Owners' Equity}_0)} \\[4pt]
& (\text{Cash}_1 - \text{Cash}_0) = -(\text{Other Assets}_1 - \text{Other Assets}_0) \\
& \qquad + (\text{Liabilities}_1 - \text{Liabilities}_0) \\
& \qquad + (\text{Owners' Equity}_1 - \text{Owners' Equity}_0)
\end{aligned}$$

Thus, the cash flow statement is simply a listing of the changes in all the balance sheet accounts, except cash.

A four-step method can be used to assist the analyst in quickly creating a useful but very basic cash flow statement. These steps are:

1. Calculate the changes in all balance sheet accounts. This, of course, is done by subtracting the beginning balance from the closing balance for each balance sheet account.

2. Identify the total change in cash. This number represents a "check figure" to be used to test the accuracy of the results of the cash flow statement created.

3. Take each of the balance sheet accounts and associate it with one of the activity types—operations, investment, and financing—using the following guidelines: (a) Any asset or liability related to an income statement account is categorized as operations; examples of this include accounts receivable and income taxes payable. (b) Other assets besides those related to income statement accounts are classified as investments. (c) Other liabilities are classified as financing transactions. (d) Equity accounts fall either into financing (i.e., capital stock, additional paid in capital, preferred stock, dividends, etc.) or operations (the net income portion of retained earnings).

4. Place each of the individual balance sheet accounts (except cash) under one of the three categories reflecting whether the transaction was a source or use of cash. Remember, the net of the total sources and uses must aggregate to the check figure identified in step 2.

An Illustration: Centex Corporation

To illustrate this four-step process, let us return to the financial statements of Centex Corporation. Centex is a Texas-based company which, as its principal business activity, engages in residential, commercial, and general construction and the sale of construction products. Exhibits 11.1 and 11.2 contain the comparative balance sheets and income statements for Centex Corporation, respectively, for the years ended March 31, 1987 and 1988. These statements will be used to illustrate how a cash flow statement can be developed, and then how to interpret the available information.

Following the four-step method, the following is done:

Step 1: Calculate the change in all the balance sheet accounts, as shown in Exhibit 11.1. The change in each account reflects the subtraction of the 1987 balance from the 1988 balance.

Step 2: The "check figure" for the cash flow statement for 1988 is a decrease of $6,887. Thus, uses of cash must have exceeded sources of cash by $6,887. Any cash flow statement created must have a total change equal to a negative $6,887.

Step 3: The last column of Exhibit 11.1 identifies the activity associated with the individual accounts. Judgment calls must be made at this step. For example, under the general classification "accounts and notes receivable," three specific categories exist: Trade, Construction contracts, and Notes. Clearly, the Trade and Construction contracts are accounts associated with the operations of Centex; but, what of the Notes? Without specific knowledge of the transactions which gave rise to these receivables, it is difficult to be certain as to their classification into operations or investment activities. A misclassification will not lead to an unbalanced cash flow statement, but simply a misspecification of the relative amounts of operations, financing, and investment cash flow. Since Notes could arise from the types of products Centex sells, the Notes will be assumed to be related to operations. Similarly, the retained earnings account has two activity types associated with it: 0 for the operations component (income) and F for the financing (dividends) component.

Step 4: Exhibit 11.3 contains the changes in the balance sheet accounts placed under the three activity headings.[2] Note that the total of the three activity categories equals the total change in cash (i.e. a negative $6,887). This total provides assurance that the cash flow statement is in balance.

Any difference between Exhibit 11.3 and Centex's published cash flow statement (Exhibit 11.4) is simply a matter of refinement and presentation preferences. Looking at Exhibit 11.3, certain accounts actually reflect more than one change in cash. For example, the change in the net Property and Equipment account reflects both purchases of property and equipment and also the sale of, or retirement of, property and equipment no longer in service. Thus, a more useful cash flow statement would disaggregate this information and contain both the cash spent on purchases and the cash received from sales of property and equipment. The net property and equipment account also reflects the current period's depreciation charges. In the current form of Exhibit 11.3, this item has been netted-out, and using the disaggregated gross amounts is likely to be more useful for projecting future cash flows. Similarly, the change in the retained earnings account reflects the net of at least two potential transactions—dividends and net income.

For the cash flow of Exhibit 11.3 to be more useful to the user, these net changes should be disaggregated and considered separately. Remember, these refinements will not change the overall statement, but simply lead to a reclassification, or disaggregation, of certain components of the cash flow. Exhibit 11.3 is a perfectly valid, useful form of cash flow statement and one that may be the best that can be constructed when limited data is available.

Published Cash Flow Statements

SFAS 95 requires that issuers of publicly disseminated financial statements present a cash flow statement prepared under either the direct or indirect method. The *indirect method* is merely a refinement of Exhibit 11.3, reflecting a disaggregation of some of the accounts. The *direct method*, on the other hand, is a simple refinement of the indirect method, providing yet further disaggregated information.

---

[2] In Exhibit 11.3, the sequence of the presentation of individual accounts merely follows that of the balance sheet. To help decide whether a given account balance change represents a source or use of cash, it is often helpful to try to relate the change to the economic events that are likely to have caused the change. For example, if trade receivables increased by $705, Centex has effectively extended loans to its customers in the additional amount of $705, therefore using cash.

Exhibit 11.1

CENTEX CORPORATION AND SUBSIDIARIES
CONSOLIDATED BALANCE SHEET
(000'S)

	March 31			Activity * Type
	1988	1987	Change	
ASSETS				
Cash	$ 9,443	$ 16,330	$ (6,887)	—
Accounts and notes				
Receivable				
Trade	23,765	23,060	705	O
Construction contracts	154,791	144,372	10,419	O
Notes	17,853	20,093	(2,240)	O
Inventories				
Housing Projects	457,127	322,498	134,629	O
Land held for development & sale	76,458	71,400	5,058	O
Construction products	16,408	12,950	3,458	O
Investments				
Joint ventures and unconsolidated				
subsidiaries	45,758	170,815	(125,057)	I
Centex Development				
Company, L.P.	76,573	75,951	622	I
Property and equipment, net	133,736	115,441	18,295	I
Other assets and deferred charges	26,640	20,812	5,828	I
Total Assets	$ 1,038,552	$ 993,722	$ 44,830	
LIABILITIES AND STOCKHOLDERS EQUITY				
Accounts payable and				
accrued liabilities	$ 310,977	$ 268,037	$ 42,940	O
Notes payable	44,100	1,263	42,837	F
Long-term debt				
Subordinated debentures	119,144	99,126	20,018	F
Other	59,718	34,335	25,383	F
Deferred income taxes	139,767	227,947	(88,180)	O
Stockholders' equity				
Common stock $.25 par value;				
authorized 50,000,000 shares;				
issued 15,048,264 and				
17,747,113 shares, respectively	3,762	4,437	(675)	F
Capital in excess of par value	—	19,326	(19,326)	F
Retained earnings	361,084	339,251	21,833	O,F
Total stockholders' equity	364,846	363,014	1,832	
Total Liabilities and				
Stockholders Equity	$ 1,038,552	$ 993,722	$ 44,830	

* O - operations, I - investing, and F - financing

Exhibit 11.2 ————————————————————————————————

CENTEX CORPORATION AND SUBSIDIARIES
STATEMENT OF CONSOLIDATED EARNINGS
(dollars in thousands except per share data)

| | For the years ending March 31 | | |
	1988	**1987**	**1986**
REVENUES			
Home building and real estate	$ 552,501	$ 591,593	$ 593,887
Construction products	128,820	152,706	160,969
General construction	778,740	559,598	672,345
	$ 1,460,061	$ 1,303,897	$ 1,427,201
COST AND EXPENSES			
Home building & real estate incl. interest of			
$8,955, $71,550 & $26,006, respectively	527,964	535,764	534,911
Construction products	116,167	126,628	132,451
General Construction	770,360	555,154	665,434
Corporate General & Admin.	8,913	8,252	6,817
Minority stockholders' interest	486	847	739
Interest incurred, net	4,366	7,816	13,169
Interest capitalized	(4,366)	(7,816)	(13,169)
	1,423,890	1,226,645	1,340,352
EARNINGS BEFORE INCOME TAXES &			
1988 ACCOUNTING CHANGE	36,171	77,252	86,849
PROVISIONS FOR INCOME TAXES	12,108	33,048	39,280
EARNINGS BEFORE 1988 ACCOUNTING			
CHANGE	24,063	44,204	47,569
CUMULATIVE EFFECT OF CHANGE IN			
ACCOUNTING FOR INCOME TAXES	50,100	—	—
NET EARNINGS	$ 74,163	$ 44,204	$ 47,569
EARNINGS PER SHARE			
Before 1988 accounting change	$ 1.50	$ 2.47	$ 2.62
Cumulative effect of accounting change	3.13	—	—
	$ 4.63	$ 2.47	$ 2.62

Exhibit 11.3 _____

CENTEX CORPORATION AND SUBSIDIARIES
SIMPLIFIED CASH FLOW STATEMENT
(000'S)

	Sources (Uses)
Operations:	
Change in Trade Receivables	$ (705)
Change in Construction contracts	(10,419)
Change in Notes Receivable	2,240
Change in Housing Projects	(134,629)
Change in Land held for development & sale	(5,058)
Change in Construction products	(3,458)
Change in Accounts payables & accrued liabilities	42,940
Change in Deferred Income tax	(88,180)
Change in Retained earnings	21,833
Total Operations	$ (175,436)
Investments:	
Change in joint ventures & unconsolidated subsidiaries	$ 125,057
Change in Centex Development Company, L.P.	(622)
Change in Property and Equipment, net	(18,295)
Change in Other Assets & deferred charges	(5,828)
Total Investment	$ 100,312
Financing:	
Change in Notes Payable	$ 42,837
Change in Subordinated debentures	20,018
Change in Other (Long-term debt)	25,383
Change in Common stock	(675)
Change in Capital in excess of par value	(19,326)
Total Financing	$ 68,237
Total Changes in Cash	$ (6,887)

The Indirect Method

Exhibit 11.4 presents the published cash flow statements of Centex Corporation for the years ended March 31, 1988, 1987, and 1986, using the indirect method of presentation. It contains the gross changes for most of the net account changes identified in Exhibit 11.3. The totals are the same, so it is a simple manner to reconcile the aggregated data in Exhibit 11.3 with the disaggregated data in Exhibit 11.4. Exhibit 11.5 presents a partial reconciliation of Exhibits 11.3 and 11.4.

Exhibit 11.4 ──────────────────────────────────────

CENTEX CORPORATION AND SUBSIDIARIES
STATEMENT OF CONSOLIDATED CASH FLOWS
(dollars in thousands)

	For the years ending March 31		
	1988	**1987**	**1986**
CASH FLOWS-OPERATING ACTIVITIES			
Net earnings	$ 74,163	$ 44,204	$ 47,569
Adjustments			
Cumulative effect of change in accounting for income taxes	(50,100)	—	—
Depreciation, depletion & amortization	11,765	12,484	15,322
Deferred income taxes	(34,543)	19,658	38,130
Equity in earnings of joint ventures and unconsolidated subsidiaries, net	7,075	2,572	(4,055)
Minority stockholders' interest	486	847	739
Increase in payables & accruals	42,952	9,008	24,235
Increase in receivables	(8,884)	(12,173)	(31,772)
(Increase) decrease in inventories	(74,399)	(6,835)	13,620
Other, net	(10,947)	(2,253)	(2,461)
	$ (42,432)	$ 67,512	$ 101,327
CASH FLOWS-INVESTING ACTIVITIES			
Contribution of plant and equipment to Texas-Lehigh joint venture	$ —	$ 78,009	$ —
Acquisitions of John Crossland	(69,506)	—	—
Property & equipment additions, net	(28,838)	(31,563)	(32,396)
Decrease (increase) to joint ventures & unconsolidated subsidiaries	117,982	(127,623)	(24,950)
	$ 19,638	$ (81,177)	$ (57,346)
CASH FLOWS-FINANCING ACTIVITIES			
Increase (decrease) in notes payable & long-term debt, other	$ 68,220	$ (84,796)	$ (17,280)
Increase in subordinated debentures	20,018	99,126	—
Cash dividends	(3,962)	(4,464)	(4,533)
Dividend of securities related to Centex Development Company, L.P.	(1,272)	—	—
Common stock issued	377	1,254	1,145
Retirement of stock	(67,474)	(5,772)	(18,343)
	$ 15,907	$ 5,348	$ (39,011)
Net (decrease) increase in cash	(6,887)	(8,317)	4,970
Cash at beginning of year	16,330	24,647	19,677
Cash at end of year	$ 9,443	$ 16,330	$ 24,647

Exhibit 11.5

CENTEX CORPORATION AND SUBSIDIARIES
MAJOR ITEM RECONCILIATION OF EXHIBIT 11.3 AND EXHIBIT 11.4
(000'S)

Exhibit 11.3

Operations:

Change in Trade Receivables	(705)
Change in Construction contracts	(10,419)
Change in Notes Receivable	2,240
Change in Housing projects	(134,629)
Change in Land held for development/sales	(5,058)
Change in Construction products	3,458
Change in Accounts payables & accrued liabilities	42,940
Change in Deferred Income tax	(88,180)
Change in Retained earnings	21,833

Investments:

Change in joint ventures & unconsolidated subsidiaries	125,057
Change in Centex Development Company, L.P.	(622)
Change in Property and Equipment, net	(18,295)
Change in Other Assets & deferred charges	(5,828)

Financing:

Change in Notes Payable	42,837
Change in Subordinated debentures	20,018
Change in Other (Long-term debt)	25,383
Change in Common stock	(675)
Change in Capital in excess of par value	(19,326)

Total	(6,887)

Exhibit 11.4

Operations:

Net earnings	74,163
Cumulative change	(50,100)
Depreciation, depletion, amortization	11,765
Deferred income taxes	(34,543)
Equity in earnings of joint ventures & unconsolidated subsidiaries	7,075
Minority stockholders' interest	486
Increase in payables & accruals	42,952
Increase in receivables	(8,884)
Increase in inventories	(74,399)
Other, net	(10,947)

Investments:

Acquisitions of John Crossland Company	(69,506)
Property & equipment additions, net	(28,838)
Decrease in advances to joint ventures & unconsolidated subsidiaries	117,982

Financing:

Increase in notes payable & long-term debt, other	68,220
Increase in subordinated debentures	20,018
Cash dividends	(3,962)
Dividend of securities related to Centex Development Company L.P.	(1,272)
Common stock issued	377
Retirement of stock	(67,474)

Total	(6,887)

When possible the analyst should attempt to use the most disaggregated information available, in that the greatest insights can be obtained from disaggregated data. Published cash flow statements are usually quite aggregated, given management's preference for the indirect method. And thus, a conversion of an indirect method cash statement to the direct method (i.e., a less aggregated statement) can be quite beneficial.

The Direct Method

As can be seen in Exhibit 11.5, the indirect method involves replacing many of the net changes from the balance sheet with gross changes. The cash flow statement created under the direct method is yet a further disaggregation of the indirect statement method, principally by replacing the net earnings number with the individual income statement accounts which compose it.

Exhibit 11.6 presents a direct method cash flow statement for Centex Corporation. The insertion of the individual income statement accounts will sometimes lead to such accounts as depreciation, depletion, and amortization appearing twice—once as a source of cash and once as a use. In some direct method statements, the depreciation, depletion, and amortization accounts do not appear at all, since these items are neither sources nor uses of cash. In Exhibit 11.6, they are added back to net income to correct the situation wherein they are subtracted in arriving at (accrual) net income but do not really involve a cash outflow. Adding them back, in effect, corrects the subtraction. If a direct method statement begins with sales revenue and only includes those accounts which really affect cash, no adjustment for depreciation (or other non-cash items) is necessary.

Analyzing Cash Flow Statements: Centex Corporation Revisited

To effectively interpret a direct method cash flow statement, certain accounts which are related should be jointly analyzed. For example, in Exhibit 11.6, the Provision for Income Taxes, the Cumulative Effect of Accounting Change, and the Deferred Income Tax accounts are all related. Placing them together within the cash flow statement gives more insight into the cash sources and uses involving taxes for Centex. Exhibit 11.7 represents a direct method cash flow statement where admittedly judgmental associations have been made. This exhibit will be used to develop a methodology for interpreting a cash flow statement.

The analysis and interpretation of a cash flow statement centers on the basic question of what sources and uses of cash are likely to recur in the future. The cash flow statement, like the balance sheet and the income statement, is historical in focus, but the analyst must attempt to use this data to

Exhibit 11.6

CENTEX CORPORATION AND SUBSIDIARIES
DIRECT METHOD CASH FLOW STATEMENTS
(000'S)

Cash Flows – Operating Activities

Home building & real estate revenues	$	552,501
Construction products revenues		128,820
General construction		778,740
Home building and real estate expenses	(	527,964)
Construction products expenses	(	116,167)
General construction expenses	(	770,360)
Corporate general & administrative expenses	(	8,913)
Minority stockholders' interest expenses	(	486)
Interest expense incurred, net	(	4,366)
Interest capitalized		4,366
Provision for Income Taxes	(	12,108)
Cumulative Effect of Accounting Change		50,100

Adjustments

Cumulative Effect of Change in Income Tax	(	50,100)
Depreciation		11,765
Deferred Income Taxes	(	34,543)
Equity in earnings of joint ventures & unconsolidated subsidiaries, net		7,075
Minority stockholders' interest		486
Increase in payables and accruals		42,952
Increase in receivables	(	8,884)
(Increase) decrease in inventories	(	74,390)
Other, net	(	10,947)
	$ (	42,432)

Cash Flows – Investing Activities

Acquisition of John Crossland Companies	(	69,506)
Property & equipment additions	(	28,838)
Decrease in advances to joint ventures & unconsolidated subsidiaries		117,982
	$	19,638

Cash Flows – Financing Activities

Increase (decrease) in notes payable & long term debt, other		68,220
Increase in subordinated debentures		20,018
Cash Dividends	(	3,962)
Dividend of securities related to Centex Development Company, L.P.	(	1,272)
Common stock issued		377
Retirement of stock	(	67,474)
	$	15,907

Net (decrease) increase in cash	(	6,887)
Cash at beginning of year		16,330
Cash at end of year	$	9,443

Exhibit 11.7 ─────────────────────────────────────

CENTEX CORPORATION AND SUBSIDIARIES
INTERPRETED DIRECT METHOD CASH FLOW STATEMENT
YEAR ENDED MARCH 31, 1988
(000'S)

	Source (Use)	Classification
Cash Flows – Operating Activities		
Revenues	$ 1,460,061	R,LT
Increase in Receivables	(8,884)	NR,ST
Cash from sales	$ 1,451,177	
Cost of Sales	(1,414,491)	R,LT
Increase in payables and accruals	42,952	NR,ST
Increase in inventories	(74,399)	NR,ST
Depreciation, depreciation & amortization	11,765	R,LT
Cash product expenses	(1,434,173)	
Corporate general and administrative expense	(8,913)	R,LT
Other, net	(10,947)	NR,ST
Cash general and administrative expense	(19,860)	
Equity in earnings of joint ventures & unconsolidated subsidiaries, net	7,075	NR,LT
Cash from investments	7,075	
Provision for Income Tax	(12,108)	
Cumulative Effect of Accounting Change	50,100	
Cumulative Effect of Accounting Change	(50,100)	
Deferred Income Taxes	(34,543)	
Cash for taxes	(46,651)	R,LT
Cash flow from Operations	$ (42,432)	
Cash Flows – Investing Activities		
Acquisition of John Crossland Companies	(69,506)	NR,LT
Property & equipment additions, net	(28,838)	R,LT
Decrease in advances to joint ventures & unconsolidated subsidiaries	117,982	NR,LT
Cash Flows from Investing Activities	$ 19,638	

Exhibit 11.7 (continued)

	Source (Use)	Classification
Cash Flows – Financing Activities		
Increase in notes payable & long-term debt, other	$ 68,220	NR,LT
Increase in subordinated debentures	20,018	NR,LT
Cash Dividends	(3,962)	R,LT
Dividend of securities related to		
Centex Development Company, L.P.	(1,272)	R,LT
Common stock issued	377	NR,LT
Retirement of stock	(67,474)	NR,LT
Cash Flow from Financing Activities	$ 15,907	
Net (decrease) increase in cash	$ (6,887)	
Cash at beginning of year	16,330	
Cash at end of year	$ 9,443	

predict the future cash flows of the company. A major objective of the analysis of any cash flow statement should focus on the (current and projected) adequacy of the CFFO, as this is the one cash source that the firm must ultimately use to repay the principal and interest of a loan or dividends on an equity investment. A second objective should be the identification of the actual free cash flow for the current period, and a projection of the expected future recurring free cash flows.

The first step in any cash flow analysis should involve a comparison of the CFFO with the net income for the same period. The CFFO is effectively a measure of the accrual net income of a company on a cash basis. This measure is of significance not only because of its relationship to dividend and debt payments, but also because, as noted at the beginning of this chapter, it is a relatively invariant measure, far less easily "managed" by a company's executives.[3] Centex Corporation, for example, had net income of $74.1 million (Exhibit 11.4), but a negative CFFO of $42.4 million for the same period. The historical surrogate for CFFO, namely net income plus depreciation, is $85.9 million ($74.1 + $11.8). Note that this surrogate measure is more highly correlated with net income than with the CFFO—a good reason to avoid it.

---

[3] While it is possible to manage the CFFO, the effect is very short-term. A company, for example, might delay payment on its accounts payable. Similarly, a company may extend longer payment terms to its own customers—a fact which will be obvious from the average day's receivable collection period. Note that if these practices are followed over a number of periods, their effect is negated after a period or two when the payables are ultimately paid and the receivables collected. A more common approach to the management of CFFO involves the selective inclusion (or exclusion) of adjustments to net income.

The CFFO is a complex number and deserves detailed analysis because it can substantially differ from accrual net income. From Exhibit 11.7, the major differences between the CFFO and net income can be easily identified, which is one of the principal reasons for using the direct method. The two major differences between Centex's income and its CFFO centered on an inventory realignment which required a cash investment of $74.4 million, and a cash payment of $46.6 million for income taxes; while the income component for taxes was only $12.1 million. (For further information on Centex's tax situation, see Chapter 4.)

What the analyst must now do is relate the past, as reflected in the historical cash flow statement, with expectations regarding the future. In order to do this, the line items of Exhibit 11.7 have been classified along two dimensions. The first dimension is the frequency of *occurrence*. If a cash flow item occurs regularly, it is classified with an R, meaning recurring, whereas if its occurrence is sporadic, then it is labeled NR, or nonrecurring. The other dimension is *longevity*, as revealed by the nature of the account with which an item is associated. Revenues, for example, are part of income which go into retained earnings, a long-term account, and are therefore classified as LT. An increase in receivables, on the other hand, is associated with accounts receivable, a short-term account, and classified as ST.

Some very simple rules, coupled with these classifications, can make cash flow analysis relatively straightforward:

1. Long-term cash sources should be used to fund long-term cash uses. In general, the term of cash sources should always exceed the term for the cash uses.
2. Long-term cash sources may be used to fund short-term cash uses; however, short-term cash sources should never be used to fund long-term cash uses.
3. Recurring cash sources should be used to fund recurring uses.
4. Recurring cash sources may be used to fund nonrecurring uses; but nonrecurring sources should never be used to fund recurring uses.

The logic of these rules is, hopefully, transparent. If, for instance, operations is truly the only source of cash flow to draw upon for loan or investment repayment, then operations must occur before payback can take place. If a company fails to follow the above rules, it may lead to a situation in which operations will be inadequate to generate needed cash flows on a timely basis, thus necessitating the acquisition of cash from other sources (e.g., investors, creditors, or via asset sale).

Let us now investigate whether Centex, for example, follows these rules. If not, are there likely to be cash flow problems in Centex's future?

Summing up the recurring items (marked R) from Exhibit 11.7, it would appear that a good estimate of Centex's 1988 free cash flows would be:

FREE CASH FLOWS
(000'S)

Revenues	$ 1,460,061
Product expense	(1,414,491)
General and administrative	(8,913)
Taxes	(46,651)
Depreciation, depletion, amortization	11,765
Recurring CFFO	$ 1,771
Property and equipment additions	(28,838)
Cash Dividends	(3,962)
Free Cash Flow	$ (31,029)

Note that the property and equipment additions were considered to be re-curring in this case because this type of investment is considered necessary for the entity's continued survival. Dividends, though discretionary, are in most firms held to be sacrosanct, and thus are best treated as a recurring cash outflow. Note also that the recurring CFFO calculated above does not equate to the CFFO in Exhibits 11.3 through 11.7, which include both recur-ring and nonrecurring elements of the CFFO.

Centex appears to be facing a relatively rocky path in the coming pe-riod. Given the need to cover recurring cash uses, if Centex follows our guideline as to where these funds should be obtained, the only recurring source is operations. Thus, Centex must find some way to improve its opera-tions (for example, through cost savings or greater revenue) to adequately cover its recurring cash outflows.

But what of Centex's balance of short-term and long-term nonrecur-ring items? The following table shows this split:

CLASSIFICATION OF
NONRECURRING CASH SOURCES AND USES BY EXPECTED LONGEVITY
(000'S)

Short-term Sources:		Short-term Uses:	
Increase in Payables	$ 42,952	Increase In Inventory	$ 74,399
Long-term Sources:		Long-term Uses:	
Decrease in advances		Acquisition of	
to joint ventures	$ 117,982	Crossland Companies	$ 69,506
Increase in notes pay-			
able and long-term debt	68,220	Retirement of Stock	64,474
Increase in subordinated			
debentures	$ 20,018		

In general, it appears as if Centex has followed our basic guidelines. The short-term uses are greater than the short-term sources, but long-term sources should be, and were used, by Centex to cover the excess short-term uses. This will give Centex's inventory time to work through its operating cycle before payback is expected. One other issue of importance is noteworthy—Centex is retiring its common stock. Long-term funds (i.e., cash flow from joint ventures) were used to retire the stock and this is in line with our rules. And, in the absence of a better investment opportunity for Centex, this seems appropriate.

In general, Centex has balanced its nonrecurring sources and uses of funds, but is still in a critical situation due to its lack of cash generated from operations. Operations must turn around if repayment of short to intermediate term debt is to be made by Centex. Alternatively, the company will need to downsize by the liquidation of existing assets, which is not a highly desirable alternative. Hence, any further investment or credit analysis of Centex should center on the company's ability to improve its operations

——————— Phoenix Technologies: An Illustration ———————

To help reinforce these concepts, let us consider another example involving Phoenix Technologies, Ltd., a high-tech firm offering BIOS (Binary Input-Output System) chips and other hardware and software components to the personal computer (PC) industry. The year 1989 was a difficult one for firms in the PC industry. Although Phoenix Technologies witnessed an almost 18 percent growth in revenues ($52.6 million in 1989; $44.7 million in 1988), income fell by over $15 million, from $8.057 million in 1988 to a negative $7.684 million in 1989. How did this happen and what was the effect on Phoenix's cash flow for the year?

Exhibits 11.8 and 11.9 present Phoenix Technologies' 1988 and 1989 balance sheets and income statements, respectively. Exhibit 11.11 presents a direct method cash flow statement derived by substituting the underlying revenue and expense accounts for net income and rearranging accounts in the published cash flow statement for 1989, which is presented in Exhibit 11.10. Also, Exhibit 11.11 presents the associated classifications of NR/R and ST/LT as discussed earlier.

Exhibit 11.8 _____

PHOENIX TECHNOLOGIES, LTD.
CONSOLIDATED BALANCE SHEETS
SEPTEMBER 30, 1989 AND 1988

	1989	1988
Assets		
Current Assets:		
Cash and Cash Equivalents (Note 2)	$ 15,929,000	$ 32,026,000
Accounts Receivable, Net of Allowance for Doubtful Accounts of $1,763,000 in 1989 and $375,000 in 1988	27,523,000	18,892,000
Income Taxes Receivable (Note 7)	2,028,000	2,165,000
Other Current Assets	4,441,000	1,418,000
Total Current Assets	49,921,000	54,501,000
Property and Equipment, Net (Notes 2 and 3)	8,924,000	3,699,000
Computer Software Costs, Net (Note 2)	4,991,000	3,071,000
Computer Software License (Note 6)	4,000,000	2,800,000
Accounts Receivable, Net of Allowance For Doubtful Accounts of $729,000 at September 30, 1989	4,206,000	1,861,000
Other Assets	220,000	156,000
Total Assets	$ 72,262,000	$ 66,088,000
Liabilities		
Current Liabilities:		
Notes Payable (Notes 5 and 8)	$ 6,603,000	$ 261,000
Current Portion of Computer Software License Payable (Note 6)	3,000,000	2,100,000
Accounts Payable	5,373,000	1,811,000
Accrued Liabilities	1,706,000	3,513,000
Salaries, Commission, and Related Items	2,853,000	3,409,000
Accrued Restructuring Costs (Note 13)	4,439,000	—
Deferred Income Taxes (Note 7)	—	652,000
Total Current Liabilities	23,974,000	11,746,000
Notes Payable (Notes 5 and 8)	419,000	169,000
Computer Software License Payable (Note 6)	1,000,000	700,000
Deferred Income On Sale/Leaseback (Note 4)	1,182,000	—
Total Liabilities	26,575,000	12,615,000

Exhibit 11.8 (continued) ────────────────────────────────

	1989	1988
Commitments (Note 8)		
Stockholders' Equity		
Preferred Stock, $.10 Par Value, 500,000 Shares		
Authorized, Issued and Outstanding 9,979,653		
at September 30, 1989, and 9,381,015 at		
September 30, 1988 (Notes 10 and 11)	10,000	9,000
Additional Paid-In Capital	44,369,000	43,909,000
Retained Earnings	1,871,000	9,555,000
Less: Treasury Stock at Cost, 30,013 Shares	(563,000)	—
Total Stockholders' Equity	45,687,000	53,473,000
Total Liabilities and Stockholders' Equity	$ 72,262,000	$ 66,088,000

The following table summarizes the recurring free cash flows for Phoenix Technologies in 1989:

RECURRING FREE CASH FLOWS

Revenue	$ 52,639,000
Royalties and other costs	(10,990,000)
Research and Development	(14,858,000)
Depreciation and Amortization	3,183,000 *
General and Administrative	(16,923,000)
Selling and Marketing	(14,115,000)
Interest Income	1,815,000
Interest Expense	(594,000)
Taxes	277,000
Deferred Gain and Sales Leaseback	1,182,000 *
Purchase of Property and Equipment	(7,169,000)
Additions to Computer Software Costs	(3,159,000)
Total Recurring Free Cash Flow	$ (8,712,000)

* Adjustments for these accounts were necessary since they were aggregated within other line items.

On the basis of our determination of free cash flows, it appears that Phoenix Technologies has not, nor will it, have operating cash flow in the near-term. Obviously, this condition must be remedied if the company is to remain a viable entity. Undoubtedly, the management of Phoenix Technologies is attempting to correct this problem through restructuring; whether this will help remains to be seen.

Exhibit 11.9

PHOENIX TECHNOLOGIES, LTD.
CONSOLIDATED STATEMENTS OF OPERATIONS
YEARS ENDED SEPTEMBER 30, 1989 AND 1988

	1989	1988
Revenue (Notes 2 and 12)	$ 52,639,000	$ 44,756,000
Costs and Expenses:		
Royalties and Other Costs (Notes 2 and 6)	10,990,000	9,261,000
Selling, Marketing and Support	14,115,000	7,238,000
General and Administrative (Note 13)	16,923,000	5,804,000
Research and Development (Note 2)	14,858,000	10,179,000
Restructuring Costs (Note 13)	5,450,000	—
Total Costs and Expenses	$ 62,336,000	$ 32,482,000
Operating (Loss) Income	(9,697,000)	12,274,000
Interest Income	1,815,000	813,000
Interest Expense	(594,000)	(351,000)
(Loss) Income Before Income Taxes and Extraordinary Credit	(8,476,000)	12,736,000
(Credit) Provision For Income Taxes (Note 7)	(792,000)	4,883,000
(Loss) Income Before Extraordinary Credit	(7,684,000)	7,853,000
Extraordinary Credit, Tax Benefit of Net Operating Loss Carryforwards (Note 7)	—	204,000
Net (Loss) Income	$ (7,684,000)	$ 8,057,000
(Loss) Income Per Common Share (Note 2):		
(Loss) Income Before Extraordinary Credit	$ (.79)	$ .86
Extraordinary Credit	—	.02
Net (Loss) Income	$ (.79)	$ .88
Weighted Average Number of Common and Common Equivalent Shares Outstanding (Note 2)	$ 9,712,000	$ 9,198,000

Exhibit 11.10 _____

PHOENIX TECHNOLOGIES, LTD.
CONSOLIDATED STATEMENTS OF CASH FLOWS
YEAR ENDED SEPTEMBER 30, 1989

	1989
Operating Activities:	
Net (Loss) Income	$ (7,684,000)
Adjustments to Reconcile Net Income to Net Cash	
Provided by Operating Activities:	
Depreciation and Amortization	3,183,000
Change in Assets and Liabilities Net of Effects	
From Purchases of Subsidiaries:	
(Increase) in Accounts Receivable	(10,976,000)
Decrease (Increase) in Income Taxes Receivable	137,000
(Increase) in Other Current Assets and Other Assets	(3,087,000)
Increase in Accounts Payable and Accrued Liabilities	1,755,000
Increase in Accrued Restructuring	4,439,000
(Decrease) Increase in Salaries, Commissions and	
Related Items	(556,000)
(Decrease) Increase in Income Taxes Currently Payable	—
(Decrease) Increase in Deferred Income Taxes	(652,000)
Total Adjustments	(5,757,000)
Net Cash (Used) Provided By Operating Activities	(13,441,000)
Investing Activities:	
Deferred Gain on Sale/Leaseback	1,182,000
Purchase of Property and Equipment	(7,169,000)
Net Cash Received From Acquisition of Subsidiaries (Note 11)	—
Additions to Computer Software Costs	(3,159,000)
Net Cash Used by Investing Activities	(9,146,000)
Financing Activities:	
Proceeds From Initial Public Offering, Net of Issuance Costs	—
Proceeds From Sale of Preferred and Common Stock	—
Proceeds From Sale of Warrants	—
Proceeds From Exercise of Common Stock	
Options and Warrants	461,000
Tax Benefit Related to Option Shares	—
Proceeds From Notes Payable	27,905,000
Repayment of Notes Payable	(21,313,000)
Purchase of Treasury Stock	(563,000)
Net Cash Provided by Financing Activities	6,490,000
Net (Decrease) Increase in Cash	(16,097,000)
Cash and Cash Equivalents at Beginning of Year	32,026,000
Cash and Cash Equivalents at End of Year	$ 15,929,000

Exhibit 11.11

PHOENIX TECHNOLOGIES, LTD.
DIRECT METHOD CASH FLOW STATEMENT FOR 1989

		Classification
Cash Flow From Operations:		
Revenue	$ 52,639,000	R, LT
Change in Accounts Receivable, Net	(10,976,000)	NR, ST
Cash From Sales	41,663,000	
Royalties and Other Costs	(10,990,000)	R, LT
Research and Development	(14,858,000)	R, LT
Depreciation and Amortization	3,183,000	R, LT
Cash Production Costs	(22,665,000)	
General and Administrative	(16,923,000)	R, LT
Increase in Other Current Assets	(3,087,000)	NR, LT
Increase in Accounts Payable and		
Accrued Liabilities	1,755,000	NR, ST
Cash General and Administrative Costs	(18,255,000)	
Selling, Marketing and Support	(14,115,000)	R, LT
Decrease in Salaries, Commissions and		
Related Items	(556,000)	R, LT
Cash Selling, Marketing and Support	(14,671,000)	
Restructuring Costs	(5,450,000)	
Increase in Accrued Restructuring	4,439,000	
Cash Restructuring Costs	(1,011,000)	NR, LT
Interest Income	1,815,000	R, LT
Interest Expense	(594,000)	R, LT
Cash Interest Costs	1,221,000	
Provision For Income Taxes	792,000	
Decrease in Deferred Income Taxes	(652,000)	
Decrease in Income Tax Receivable	137,000	
Cash Flow From Taxes	277,000	R, LT
Total Cash Flow From Operations	(13,441,000)	
Investing Activities:		
Deferred Gain on Sale/Leaseback	1,182,000	R, LT
Purchase of Property and Equipment	(7,169,000)	R, LT
Additions to Computer Software Costs	(3,159,000)	R, LT
Cash Flow Used By Investing Activities	(9,146,000)	

Exhibit 11.11 (continued) —————————————————————————————

		Classification
Financing Activities:		
Proceeds From Exercise of Common Stock Options and Warrants	461,000	NR, LT
Proceeds From Notes Payable	27,905,000	NR, ST
Repayment of Notes Payable	(21,313,000)	NR, ST
Purchase of Treasury Stock	(563,000)	NR, ST
Cash Flow Provided By Financing Activities	6,490,000	
Net Decrease in Cash	(16,097,000)	
Cash and Cash Equivalents at Beginning of Year	32,026,000	
Cash and cash Equivalents at End of Year	$ 15,929,000	

One important issue is whether Phoenix Technologies has structured its nonrecurring cash flows in such a way as to help ensure its continued existence. The following analysis presents a breakdown of the nonrecurring cash sources and uses by their associated longevity:

CLASSIFICATION OF NONRECURRING CASH SOURCES AND USES BY EXPECTED LONGEVITY

Short-term Sources:		Short-term Uses:	
Change in Accounts Payable	$ 1,755,000	Change in Accounts Receivable	$ 10,976,000
Proceeds from Notes Payable	27,905,000	Repayment of Notes Payable	21,313,000
Long-term Sources:		Long-term Uses:	
Proceeds from Exercise of Stock Options and Warrants	461,000	Change in Other Assets	3,087,000
		Decrease in Salaries, Commissions and Related Items	556,000
		Restructuring Costs, Net	1,011,000
		Purchase of Treasury Stock	563,000

Although this type of analysis involves considerable judgment on the part of the analyst, our figures above suggest that a definite imbalance exists for the company. Phoenix Technologies has many long-term uses which should have been funded by long-term sources, but instead were funded by short-term sources and beginning cash balances (see the change in the cash account). The consistency of this funding scheme with the long-term survival of Phoenix must be questioned. If the CFFO is impaired in 1990, as it was in 1989, the remaining cash balance will be depleted and serious consequences inevitable. Thus, it appears that Phoenix Technologies must improve its CFFO and its mix of sources and uses to give its investments in R&D and software a chance to generate new cash flows from operations.

An analysis of Phoenix Technologies is not complete at this stage (although many analysts stop here) because the particular needs of the company must be evaluated in light of the economic events causing the cash flow problems. Knowing that a company has cash flow problems is not the same as knowing why a company has such problems. In the next section, we attempt to provide some understanding of the relationship between a company's products, its life cycles, and the resulting cash flows.

Product Life Cycles and Cash Flows

Ultimately, the only recurring long-term source of cash which can be used in all aspects of a business is operations. Companies which borrow cash and make investments simply are expecting these investments to be used in operations to generate a return which will compensate the lender/investor with a return of principal and interest or dividends. Since the CFFO is intimately tied to the products or services which a company offers, understanding a company's product life cycle will be invaluable in helping the analyst understand the cash sources and uses of a company.

The traditional graph of a product's life cycle appears as follows:[4]

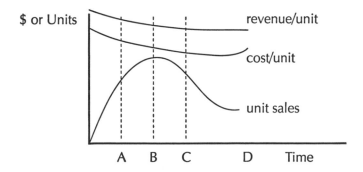

---

[4] The product life cycle concept is described in detail in many textbooks on marketing, economics, and business policy. The form of the model may vary in these presentations, not in terms of the stages, but in their labeling. The particular model used herein is found in R. Kerin and R. Peterson, *Strategic Marketing Problems* (Allyn and Bacon, 1990), pp. 183-193.

The life of a product, after design and development, can be segmented into four stages: A—Adoption, B—Growth, C—Maturity Saturation, D—Decline. During the adoption stage, revenue and costs per unit are (not surprisingly) very high. Even though revenues run higher than costs, the company will still have a high need for cash as the volume of sales are typically insufficient to recover the cash previously invested in design and developmental costs, as well as in receivables and inventory. As unit sales increase and costs per unit fall due to the learning curve effect and economies of scale, the company will eventually become cash rich, returning all that it had previously borrowed and becoming a net cash source (stages B and C). As the product reaches the decline stage, D, the production facilities usually become less efficient, with costs increasing and revenues decreasing concurrently with a decline in unit sales. Although a company should be able to sustain itself on the cash generated in the decline stage, frequently the owners will seek "permanent" debt financing, which effectively allows them to take some value out of the business. Lenders and investors must be watchful that such cash withdrawals do not put these "permanent" loans in jeopardy (as in some unsuccessful leveraged buyouts).

Companies frequently experience critical cash needs when the life cycles of their individual products do not overlap. Phoenix Technologies, for example, would appear to be in this situation. The diagram below shows a situation of overlapping product life cycles. As long as there is sufficient overlap, a decline in a company's CFFO should not occur. If, however, the distance between product cycles grows, a need for cash and a negative CFFO are likely to arise.

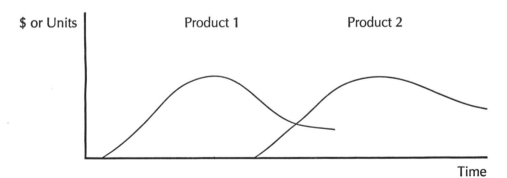

The Special Case of the Single Product Firm

The relationship of the product life cycle to income measurement and cash flow becomes particularly acute when a firm has only a single product (or type of product). This is true of many small to medium-sized businesses.

Many times, the owners/managers of these single-product firms do not understand that an updated product, for example, does not constitute a new product. An updated version of a product may simply enter the product life cycle at the same stage as the product it replaces or may move through the various life stages in an abbreviated manner. As a consequence, the CFFO of the firm may not be noticeably improved, in spite of the product updating and the associated cash investment. Consequently, payback of the product costs of a replacement product requires as detailed an assessment of the life cycle as for a new product.

Likewise, many small to medium-sized businesses aware of the tie between their cash flow and their single product will attempt to diversify their cash flow by increasing their product lines. Diversification of cash flows will only occur, however, if the new products' sales patterns differ from those of the older products. Usually, the new products are in the same genre of products as the old and do not really lead to any real cash flow diversification.

In either of the cases described above, more frequent monitoring of cash flows (preferably monthly, at maximum quarterly) will be necessary to follow the greater inherent riskiness of the single product firm. More frequent monitoring is also appropriate for any firm which has seasonal sales or sales cycles.

Conclusion

That cash flows are important can be no better illustrated than by the following full-page advertisement that appeared in *The Wall Street Journal* during July, 1990:

NEVER UNDERESTIMATE THE POWER OF CASH

It's no secret that when we bought Great Northern Nebraska, we took on some debt. Wall Street noticed. But, it's also no secret that we acquired a world-class paper company with a very large cash flow. Wall Street noticed.

Add to that our own substantial cash flow, and the picture gets clearer. Because the simple fact is, the new Georgia-Pacific will be capable of generating $1.5 billion in annual cash flow from operations. And when combined with the possible sale of non-strategic assets, we should retire our debt far quicker than many expected.

And that's the sort of news all kinds of people notice. Especially our shareholders.

GEORGIA-PACIFIC

The statement of cash flows can be used to gain valuable insights into the activities of a business. A good analysis will start with a direct method statement and a categorization of the individual line items into recurring/

nonrecurring and short-term/long-term classifications. These classifications can then be used to help predict the strengths and weaknesses of an entity's cash flows using a set of simple rules and guidelines.

The cash flow statement itself must be linked to the economic events which it portrays, and this is best accomplished by integrating the product life cycle model with it. The cash flow statement, if properly interpreted, can help the analyst identify critical problem areas. It should not be used in isolation, but must be integrated with other analytical tools. The one fact that the past decade has revealed is that the cash flow statement is not the panacea that it was once believed to be. In the next chapter, other useful models will be discussed which, when combined with the cash flow statement, can effectively highlight a company's problem areas.

PART V

The Quality of Reported Earnings and Assets

Throughout this book we have followed what may be considered a traditional approach to the analysis and interpretation of financial statements. We have considered the various financial statement accounts, how they are measured, and how the alternative measurement and valuation approaches may interact with the interpretation of financial ratios. We have tried to highlight where aberrations are likely to occur, and how to identify them.

In the following and final section of this book, we move from the traditional to the nontraditional. Our focus in this section is on the subtleties of financial analysis, many of which have been introduced in prior chapters, and the organization of these information cues to arrive at an assessment of the quality of reported earnings and assets of a company.

In Chapter 12, some alternative ways to approach financial statement analysis are introduced. In addition, the chapter describes the computer software accompanying this book, which we feel will not only enable the user to process large quantities of financial data faster, but can also be entertaining when doing so. Finally, in Chapter 13, we attempt to summarize the keys and "red flags" to financial analysis, and offer some parting advice.

CHAPTER TWELVE

Alternative Models of Financial Analysis

Although the concept of cash flow is typically stressed in credit and investment decision analysis, other analytical models can and also should be used as part of the credit/investment review process. The use of such models, however, must be predicated on a realization that any model is merely an abstraction of reality, and not reality itself. Thus, the use of any analytical model usually leads a user to identify important questions, but seldom direct answers.

In this chapter, two groups of analytical models are considered. The first group belongs to those models traditionally used in financial statement analysis, namely models focusing on the use of ratio analysis, common-sized statements, and trend analysis. As an illustration of this group, we present a graphical user interface model, or GUI, which uses financial ratio analysis and comparative direct method cash flow statements to present various relationships of interest to an analyst. A second group of non-traditional models, developed from the so-called DuPont model, is also presented.

———————————— **Traditional Analytical Models** ————————————

Introduction to Ratio Analysis

A curious characteristic of human beings is their attempt to find and use patterns of information. The brain, in learning to speak, read, and write, basically acts as a pattern recognition processor. The analyst likewise demonstrates the search for patterns when he or she uses financial ratio analysis.

A ratio, of course, is simply two numbers placed in relationship to each other by using the division operation. For the analyst, this means taking a set of financial statement numbers (e.g., total assets or sales) and dividing it by another financial statement number. Over the closed set of numbers representing the basic financial statements, the division operation is non-linear. This non-linearity, and the resulting non-normality of the distributions of the ratios formed from financial statement data, is important. As mentioned previously, human beings search for patterns in much of what they do, and most recognized patterns are assumed to be linear in form. Since financial ratio analysis deals with ratios which are neither linear nor normal, it becomes problematic for the analyst to rely on financial ratio analysis, either principally or exclusively. Thus, the remainder of this first section is devoted to exploring the proper use of traditional ratio analysis with a digression upon the use of a special graphics model for displaying multiple period ratios.

Finding Patterns in Ratios: Some Concerns

Traditional ratio analysis involves the investigation of three perspectives: (1) direction of change; (2) magnitude of change; and, (3) interpretation of change.

Direction of Change. The easiest perspective to measure with financial statement ratios is direction of change. One needs only to compare a ratio from one period to the next in order to capture a directional change. The value of the current period ratio is either greater than, equal to, or less than the previous period's ratio. An analysis which explores the directional change perspective is usually called a *time-series analysis*.

In time-series analysis, the analyst is usually attempting to establish a trend of a particular ratio. If, for example, the asset turnover ratio has been 2, 3.3, 4.2, and 5.5 over the last four periods, respectively, the analyst might conclude that a company has established a trend in utilizing its assets more effectively. Basically, this trend is the correlation of the change in the ratio with time; however, a correlation does not communicate a magnitude perspective. And, consequently, if an analyst uses a correlation to predict that a company will again have a higher asset turnover ratio in a subsequent

Exhibit 12.1 ————————————————————————————————

**TREND STATEMENTS OF SELECTED FINANCIAL ITEMS FOR GENERAL MOTORS:
1984-1988 (1984 BASE YEAR)***

	1984	1985	1986	1987	1988
Net Sales and revenues	100	114.5	124.1	123.3	132.7
Cash and Marketable securities	100	74.1	68.8	73.2	95.3
Total assets	100	132.1	152.6	165.0	166.7
Long-term debt	100	103.4	156.0	155.5	163.6
Expenditure for special tools	100	125.4	147.8	95.7	89.5
Earnings attributable to common stock	100	86.3	58.0	70.7	98.1

* Source: 1988 General Motors Annual Report

period, the analyst will be unable to predict the magnitude of the expected change or the importance of that change.

Another way to use time series analysis in conjunction with financial statements is to create *trend statements*. These statements are constructed by choosing a base year and setting the financial statement numbers equal to a baseline of 100. For each year prior to or after the baseline year, the individual financial statement number is presented in percentage terms relative to the base-year number. Exhibit 12.1 contains a trend statement for selected items from General Motors' financial data for the period 1984 to 1988.

As noted above, a trend statement provides directional changes but not magnitude changes. While both total assets and long-term debt, for example, appear to be approximately 60 (or more) percent greater for G.M. in 1988 than in 1984, it is important to note that total assets started at $98,414.9 million and long-term debt at $2,772.9 million in the base year. Thus, cross comparisons of numbers in trend statements must be undertaken with some caution.

Another consideration is that any time-series analysis presupposes stationarity of the underlying relationships of the financial statement numbers. Consequently, any event which disturbs an underlying relationship will also affect the results of the analysis. Although not an exhaustive listing, examples of events that will disturb underlying relationships include:

(1) a structural change in the accounting entity (e.g., a merger or acquisition);

(2) a change in accounting method or principle (e.g., the adoption of SFAS No. 96);

(3) a change in accounting estimate or classification (e.g., an extension of the estimated life of any depreciable asset; the segregation of income or loss from a plant closing from the ordinary income from operations);

(4) an extreme observation used as the base period or found within the trend statement (e.g., data on a quarterly basis may be influenced by the seasonality of a company's product line).

Any use of time-series data for ratios or trend statements is subject to constraint by any of the above mentioned events. Thus, the analyst must be careful to ensure that any changes in the time-series properties of a ratio or trend statements are caused by true economic events, and not merely cosmetic changes in the relationship of the data items. A thorough reading of the footnotes to the financial statements is probably the best way to investigate for this.

Magnitude of Change. In order to measure the magnitude of change, a standard must be developed. For ratio analysis, the standard is often an industry average for a given period. Unfortunately, the use of any standard is subject to many of the same constraints that characterize time-series analyses. Moreover, the use of a standard involves many limiting assumptions, which include:

(1) The individual company is assumed to be structurally similar to the average of the industry. Unfortunately, given the degree of corporate diversification of many firms today, this is rarely the case.

(2) The industry and the company are assumed to use a common set of accounting principles. If, for example, the industry uses FIFO inventory costing, whereas a company under review uses LIFO, large differences could occur with any ratio involving inventory, cost of goods sold, current assets, or net earnings.

(3) The industry and the company are assumed to use a similar set of accounting estimates. In 1988, for example, Blockbuster's change to a three-year estimated life for its "hit" movies may have created a policy that dramatically differed from the industry as a whole. Consequently, income-based ratios would therefore be predictably higher for Blockbuster than for the industry in general.

(4) The industry and the company are assumed to experience a common set of external influences. A given company, however, may have undergone an unusual economic event (e.g., a labor strike) having multiple period implications which are not reflected in the industry standard.

When an industry average or other companies' data is used as a standard, the analysis is often called *cross-sectional analysis*. Cross-sectional analysis, however, is wrought with more problems than time-series analysis because the stationarity assumptions are more easily broken when more than one company is involved.

Interpretation of a Ratio Change. The most difficult task in traditional ratio analysis involves the interpretation of a change in a ratio either on a time-series basis or a cross-sectional basis. The interpretation problem results because a ratio change has the potential of being caused by either the numerator, the denominator, or both. Moreover, the change may be either cosmetic or based on a real change in economic events.

The analyst must always look beyond the ratio itself to the underlying economic events causing a change. Ratios and their change are merely signals that the analyst may use to identify the underlying cause of those changes. Not withstanding the many problems inherent in the use of ratios in recognizing patterns for an entity, the analyst has little choice but to rely on them for insights. In the following section, we identify some ratios of particular interest and discuss their use in financial statement analysis. At the conclusion of this section, a graphical presentation of ratios is explored.

Ratio Analysis

Ratio analysis is undoubtedly the most widely used analytical technique employed by investment and credit analysts. Ratio analysis involves computing the relationship between various elements of the financial statements and the comparison of this relationship with a standard from another time period of either the same entity or other entities in the same or similar industry.

Numerous ratios have been developed to assist in the analysis of financial statements. Research on the plethora of available ratios has led to the identification of nineteen ratios that have been found to be particularly useful in investment and credit decisions. Unfortunately, even for this set of nineteen, research has found them to be distributed in a non-normal, non-linear manner. Nonetheless, prior experience suggests that the calculation of these ratios can be beneficial to financial statement users.

These ratios fall loosely into seven categories:

1. Cash position
2. Liquidity
3. Working capital/cash flow
4. Capital structure
5. Debt service coverage
6. Profitability
7. Turnover

The significance of each of these categories and the respective ratios to be calculated are discussed below. The ratios are illustrated using the financial statements of Chili's Incorporated, a chain of theme restaurants, as presented in Exhibits 12.2 and 12.3.

Cash Position. Cash and marketable securities form an important reservoir that an entity may use to meet current and future operating obligations as they fall due. Three ratios that can be used to measure the cash position of an entity include:

1. $$\frac{\text{Cash and marketable securities}}{\text{Current liabilities}}$$

2. $$\frac{\text{Cash and marketable securities}}{\text{Sales}}$$

3. $$\frac{\text{Cash and marketable securities}}{\text{Total assets}}$$

For Chili's in 1989 and 1990, respectively, the three ratios were:

	1989	1990
1.	$\frac{6,506}{26,028} = .250$	$\frac{7,067}{41,569} = .170$
2.	$\frac{6,506}{285,943} = .023$	$\frac{7,067}{347,127} = .020$
3.	$\frac{6,506}{154,024} = .042$	$\frac{7,067}{197,718} = .036$

These results indicate that Chili's cash position ratios have decreased. Whether this is a concern requires an interpretation of both the numerator and denominator of each ratio. In this instance, the amount of cash and marketable securities has increased, but not in proportion to the change in the denominator. Consequently, the result is positive in ratios (2) and (3) because one would hope that an increase in sales and assets would not require a proportionally equivalent increase in cash. On the other hand, ratio (1) shows more cash, but less coverage of current liabilities. Thus, in terms of cash, Chili's can be seen to be experiencing certain economies of scale but also less coverage of current liabilities.

Liquidity. Liquidity refers to the ability of an entity to meet its short-term financial obligations as they fall due. While the cash position ratios highlight one dimension of liquidity, they fail to capture the relative coverage of current debt from all current asset sources. Two liquidity ratios that are frequently examined include:

4. $$\frac{\text{Cash, Marketable Securities, and Accounts Receivable}}{\text{Current Liabilities}}$$

5. $$\frac{\text{Current Assets}}{\text{Current Liabilities}}$$

Ratio (4) is commonly known as the *quick ratio* or *acid test*, and ratio (5) as the *current ratio*. Historically, some rules of thumb have been used to judge the adequacy of these measures—.5:1 for the quick ratio and 2:1 for the current ratio. These rules of thumb have no foundation in reality, however, and are industry-dependent. Thus, they should be used cautiously by the analyst.

For Chili's in 1989 and 1990, respectively, these ratios were:

	1989		1990	
4.	$\frac{11,360}{26,028}$	$= .436$	$\frac{11,314}{41,569}$	$= .272$
5.	$\frac{23,020}{26,028}$	$= .884$	$\frac{23,180}{41,569}$	$= .558$

Although Chili's ratios have again decreased from 1989, the decrease may not necessarily be a concern for the analyst. The food service business is generally quite liquid, and consequently, the need to hold cash is significantly less than in other industries. Thus, these ratios are probably indicative of improved cash management, and whether they represent good cash management can only be discerned by comparing these ratios to other food service companies noted for the quality of their cash management.

Working Capital/Cash Flow. Increasing attention to cash flow in recent years has caused the importance of these ratios to increase. Inferences about an entity's cash-generating ability may be gained through the calculation of these ratios:

6. $$\frac{\text{Cash flow from operations}}{\text{Net sales}}$$

7. $$\frac{\text{Cash flow from operations}}{\text{Total assets}}$$

8. $$\frac{\text{Working capital from operations}}{\text{Net sales}}$$

9. $$\frac{\text{Working capital from operations}}{\text{Total assets}}$$

The numbers used in the numerator of these ratios for Chili's were derived from the company's financial statements as presented in Exhibits 12.3 and 12.4. The Chili's ratios for 1989 and 1990 were:

	1989		1990	
6.	$\frac{31,257}{285,943}$	= .109	$\frac{39,733}{347,127}$	= .114
7.	$\frac{31,257}{154,024}$	= .203	$\frac{39,733}{197,718}$	= .201
8.	$\frac{29,086}{285,943}$	= .102	$\frac{35,474}{347,127}$	= .102
9.	$\frac{29,086}{154,024}$	= .189	$\frac{35,474}{197,718}$	= .179

Chili's cash flow from operations appears to be strong—obviously, a very positive sign for any company. Even with a large increase in sales and assets, cash flows (and working capital) from operations were also up significantly. For most inventory-intensive industries, a significant growth in sales and assets is usually accompanied by at least one period of declining (and sometimes negative) cash flows from operations due to the heavy investment of cash in inventory and receivables normally necessary to achieve the sales growth. This was apparently not true for Chili's, largely because of the rapid inventory turnover and the relatively low level of receivables characteristic of the food service industry.

Capital Structure. Capital structure ratios are calculated to provide insight as to the extent to which non-equity capital is being used to finance the resources of a company. Two widely accepted capital structure ratios involve the relationship of debt-to-equity capital, with the latter commonly known as the debt-to-equity ratio:

10. $$\frac{\text{Long-term debt}}{\text{Stockholders' Equity}}$$

11. $$\frac{\text{Total debt}}{\text{Stockholders' Equity}}$$

For Chili's, these ratios for 1989 and 1990 were:

1989	1990

10. $$\frac{49,682}{78,314} = .634 \qquad \frac{23,755}{132,394} = .179$$

11. $$\frac{75,710}{78,314} = .967 \qquad \frac{65,324}{132,394} = .493$$

On the basis of these results, it appears that the largest change in Chili's financial structure occurred in the area of its capital base. Chili's apparently made a conscious decision to reduce debt and replace it with equity, both earned and contributed. A comparison of these ratios with other restaurant companies would be beneficial to see if Chili's has merely come into line with other companies or is strategically placing itself in a position to expand its use of alternative forms of debt financing.

Debt-Service Coverage. Debt-service coverage refers to the ability of an entity to service from operations its interest payments due on non-equity sources of capital. Two common ratios in this area include:

12. $$\frac{\text{Operating income + Annual interest payments}}{\text{Annual interest payments}}$$

13. $$\frac{\text{Cash flow from operations}}{\text{Annual interest payments}}$$

For Chili's, these ratios for 1989 and 1990 were:

1989	1990

12. $$\frac{13,938 + 2,920}{2,920} = 5.77 \qquad \frac{18,090 + 2,132}{2,132} = 9.48$$

13. $$\frac{31,257}{2,920} = 10.70 \qquad \frac{39,733}{2,132} = 18.64$$

Due to Chili's reduction of its long-term debt in 1990, and the increase in cash flows from operations and operating income, the interest coverage ratios appear to be quite good. Consequently, the company would appear to be well positioned to undertake additional debt financing should it choose to do so.

Profitability. Profitability refers to the ability of an entity to generate revenues in excess of expenses. These ratios use net income as the principal measure of profitability, which is then related to the various resources used to generate profit. The general label for any of these ratios is a "return" ratio. For example, if total assets is the activity base, then the ratio is known as the return on assets. The return ratios include:

14. $\dfrac{\text{Net income}}{\text{Net sales}}$

15. $\dfrac{\text{Net income}}{\text{Stockholders' equity}}$

16. $\dfrac{\text{Net income}}{\text{Total assets}}$

For 1989 and 1990, Chili's return ratios were:

	1989	1990
14.	$\dfrac{13,938}{285,943} = .049$	$\dfrac{18,090}{347,127} = .052$
15.	$\dfrac{13,938}{78,314} = .178$	$\dfrac{18,090}{132,394} = .137$
16.	$\dfrac{13,938}{154,024} = .090$	$\dfrac{18,090}{197,718} = .091$

The growth in Chili's return ratios reflect the company's increase in net income from operations from 1989 to 1990. Whether these return ratios are poor, adequate, or excellent, requires a comparison against either an industry average or perhaps the top quartile of the industry. The decline in the return on equity would be of concern if the return on sales and the return on assets had not increased over the same period.

Turnover. Various aspects of the efficiency of asset utilization by an entity are measured by turnover ratios. A turnover ratio is characterized by an income statement number divided by a balance sheet number related to it. For example, accounts receivable turnover is measured by dividing net sales by accounts receivable, with the ratio usually named for its balance sheet account component. The three major turnover ratios are assets, accounts receivable, and inventory:

17. $\dfrac{\text{Net sales}}{\text{Total assets}}$

18. $\dfrac{\text{Net sales}}{\text{Accounts receivable}}$

19. $\dfrac{\text{Cost of goods sold}}{\text{Inventories}}$

The turnover ratios for Chili's were:

	1989		1990
17.	$\dfrac{285{,}943}{154{,}024} = 1.86$		$\dfrac{347{,}127}{197{,}718} = 1.76$
18.	$\dfrac{285{,}943}{4{,}854} = 58.91$		$\dfrac{347{,}127}{4{,}247} = 81.73$
19.	$\dfrac{83{,}472}{4{,}388} = 19.02$		$\dfrac{101{,}712}{3{,}512} = 28.96$

Chili's turnover ratios reflect improved receivable and inventory control. For example, Chili's lowered its receivable collection period from 6.2 days to only 4.47 days. With the sales and asset growth experienced in 1989-1990, the company's ability to maintain these turnover levels will be critical to its continued success.

Overall, Chili's appears to be in a stable but slightly improving financial position, even after sustaining substantial growth in 1990. In general, the calculated ratios appear to be consistent with economic events that are favorable for a restaurant chain.

Other Considerations. When undertaking ratio analysis, it is often useful to consider certain rules of thumb. First, when performing ratio analysis using balance sheet accounts, the average value (of receivables or inventory, for example) sometimes makes a ratio more meaningful, especially if a known anomaly exists in the ending balance. Using an average of the beginning and ending account balance allows the analyst to smooth out any seasonal aberrations. Second, the number of ratios investigated is often less important than the interpretation of the ratios. Remember that most of the ratios are related, and an increase in one ratio is likely to mean an increase in another. Thus, numerous ratios will often point out the same change in an entity's economic situation. Third, ratios should not be used in isolation. A current ratio of .8 to 1 means little unless it is anchored in a context. The context can be provided by the entity itself, another company, or the industry. And finally, because of seasonality factors, it is usually best to compare ratios over time using comparable time periods (e.g., first quarter 1990 versus first quarter 1991, etc.)

Other Traditional Analyses

In addition to trend analysis, two other types of financial statement analyses are frequently performed—horizontal analysis (percentage of change analysis) and vertical analysis (common-size statement analysis). Like trend analysis, both horizontal and vertical analysis are tied to an internal base (or standard), although the individual components may be compared to industry or other company measures.

Horizontal Analysis: Percentage of Change. When comparative balance sheets are presented side-by-side, these statements can be made more meaningful if the dollar amount of increase or decrease and the percentage change is shown. This percentage analysis is called horizontal analysis because the comparisons are made on a horizontal plane from left to right. In a two-year comparison, for example, the earlier year is the base year and the percentage change is usually rounded to the nearest tenth of a percent.

Exhibits 12.2 and 12.3 illustrate a horizontal analysis for Chili's Inc., using a comparative balance sheet and income statement. Although only two years of data are presented, for most analyses three or more years is desirable. An interpretation of the horizontal analysis statements for Chili's would center on the company's growth in property and equipment and the funding of this growth. While Chili's was growing in both sales and assets, the source of growth, namely its capital structure, was also undergoing large changes both in quantity and mix. The horizontal analysis reveals, for example, that long-term debt dropped by over $28 million, or 69.7%, relative to its balance in 1989. Hence, given the growth in sales and assets, and the drop in debt, how did Chili's finance its growth?

The large change in equity accounts—both contributed and earned—represents the major sources of funds used to support the company's growth and the reduction in long-term debt. As mentioned in Chapter 11, the use of permanent long-term sources of funds, such as issuing common stock and retention of earnings, represents a proper balance in the source of funds versus the obvious uses of funds by Chili's.

Exhibit 12.2 _____

CHILI'S INCORPORATED*
COMPARATIVE BALANCE SHEETS WITH HORIZONTAL ANALYSIS
JUNE 30, 1990 AND 1989
(in 000's)

	1990	1989	Amount of Increase \<Decrease\> During 1990	Percentage Increase \<Decrease\> During 1990
Assets				
Current Assets:				
Cash and Cash Equivalents	$ 7,067	$ 4,052	$ 3,015	$ 74.4%
Short term Investments	—	2,454	< 2,454>	<100.0>
Accounts Receivable	4,247	4,854	< 607>	< 12.6>
Federal Income Taxes Receivable	—	316	< 316>	<100.0>
Assets Held for Sale and Leaseback	1,417	1,003	414	41.3
Inventories	3,512	4,388	< 876>	< 20.0>
Prepaid Expenses	6,937	5,953	984	16.5
Total Current Assets	23,180	23,020	160	.7
Property & Equipment at Cost				
Land	28,986	16,498	12,488	75.7
Building & Leasehold Improvements	97,362	69,044	28,318	41.0
Furniture and Equipment	66,203	51,342	14,861	28.9
Construction-in-Progress	6,210	5,830	380	6.5
	198,761	142,714	56,047	39.3
Less Accumulated Depreciation and Amortization	52,327	39,476	12,851	32.6
Net Property and Equipment	146,434	103,238	43,196	41.8
Other Assets				
Deferred Costs	6,946	6,741	205	3.0
Investment in Joint Ventures at Equity	5,660	4,428	1,232	27.8
Long-term Marketable Securities	8,610	10,043	< 1,433>	<14.3>
Long-term Notes Receivable	4,007	3,995	12	.3
Other	2,881	2,559	322	12.6
Total Other Assets	28,104	27,766	338	1.2
Total Assets	$ 197,718	$ 154,024	43,694	28.4

Exhibit 12.2 (Continued) _____

	1990	1989	Amount of Increase <Decrease> During 1990	Percentage Increase <Decrease> During 1990
Liabilities and Stockholders' Equity				
Current Liabilities:				
Short-term Debt	$ 8,900	$ —	8,900	—
Current Installments of				
Long-term Debt	93	662	< 569>	< 86.0>
Accounts Payable	14,291	10,343	3,948	38.2
Accrued Liabilities	15,621	12,843	2,778	21.6
Deferred Income Income Taxes	2,664	2,180	484	22.2
Total Current Liabilities	41,569	26,028	15,541	59.7
Long-term Debt, Less Current				
Installments	12,185	40,279	<28,094>	< 69.7>
Deferred Income Taxes	7,778	5,858	1,920	32.8
Deferred Gain on Sale and Leaseback	102	155	< 53>	< 34.2>
Other Liabilities	3,690	3,390	300	8.8
Stockholders' Equity				
Preferred Stock	—	—	—	—
Common Stock	1,138	1,002	136	13.6
Additional Paid in Capital	73,220	37,213	36,007	96.8
Unrealized Loss on Marketable				
Securities	(1,685)	(1,501)	184	12.3
Retained Earnings	59,721	41,600	18,121	43.6
Total Stockholders' Equity	132,394	78,314	54,080	69.1
Total Liabilities and				
Stockholders' Equity	$ 197,718	$ 154,024	$ 43,694	28.4%

The horizontal analysis of the income statement reveals a consistency in the change in costs in approximately the same percentage change as in sales. The percentage change of cost of sales and restaurant expenses in approximately the same percentage as sales implies that these costs are variable, while general and administrative costs must contain a fixed component. A more explicit analysis of the cost structure of an entity follows in a later section of this chapter. Suffice it to say at this juncture that a horizontal analysis of an income statement may give the analyst some insight into the cost structure of an entity; however, given the growth in property and equipment as well as sales for Chili's, the consistency of the change in costs is unexpected. Typically, as entities grow, their costs would not be expected to grow at a rate consistent with the growth in sales, but rather would be

Exhibit 12.3

CHILI'S INCORPORATED
COMPARATIVE INCOME STATEMENTS WITH HORIZONTAL ANALYSIS
FOR YEARS ENDED JUNE 30, 1990 AND 1989

	1990	1989	Amount of \<Decrease\> During 1990	Percentage \<Decrease\> During 1990
Revenues	$ 347,127	$ 285,943	$ 61,184	21.4
Operating Expenses:				
Cost of Sales	101,712	83,472	18,240	21.9
Restaurant Expenses	180,168	148,326	31,842	21.5
Depreciation and Amortization	17,406	15,161	2,245	14.8
Total Operating Expenses	299,286	246,959	52,327	21.2
General and Administrative	19,684	16,835	2,849	16.9
Interest Expense	2,132	2,920	< 788>	< 27.0>
Other, Net	(1,387)	(1,509)	122	< 8.1>
Total Cost and Expenses	319,715	265,205	54,510	20.6
Income Before Promise for Income Taxes and Cumulative Change	27,412	20,738	6,674	32.2
Provision for Income Taxes	9,322	6,800	2,522	37.1
Income Before Cumulative Effect on Accounting Change	18,090	13,938	4,152	29.8
Cumulative Change	—	—	—	—
Net Income	$ 18,090	$ 13,938	$ 4,152	29.8%

expected to grow at a higher or lower rate of change. Thus, a concern regarding the possible manipulation of expenses and costs must be raised—a point to which we will return shortly.

Vertical Analysis: Common Size Statements. Another traditional method of analyzing financial statements calls for a vertical analysis of the accounts which make up the financial statements. In vertical analysis, three financial statement numbers are converted to a base of 100 percent; these are: (1) Total Assets; (2) Total Equities; and (3) Net Sales. Each item within the various sections of the financial statements associated with these three accounts is then expressed as a percentage of these bases. Since for any given set of financial statements the bases represent 100 percent, the restated financial statements are called common-size statements.

Comparisons can be made within an entity, with other entities in the same industry, or with the entire industry with this method. The financial statements for Chili's are again used to illustrate this technique in Exhibits

Exhibit 12.4 ────────────────────────────────────

CHILI'S INCORPORATED
COMPARATIVE BALANCE SHEETS WITH VERTICAL ANALYSIS
JUNE 30, 1990 AND 1989
(in 000's)

	1990	1989	Common Size Percentages 1990	Common Size Percentages 1989
Assets				
Current Assets:				
Cash and Cash Equivalents	$ 7,067	$ 4,052	3.6	2.6
Short-term Investments	—	2,454	0.0	1.6
Accounts Receivable	4,247	4,854	2.1	3.1
Federal Income Tax Receivable	—	316	0.0	.2
Assets Held for Sale and Leaseback	1,417	1,003	.7	.7
Inventory	3,512	4,388	1.8	2.8
Prepaid Expenses	6,937	5,953	3.5	3.9
	23,180	23,020	11.7	14.9
Property and Equipment, at Cost				
Land	28,986	16,498	14.7	10.7
Building and Leasehold Improvements	97,362	69,044	49.2	44.8
Furniture and Equipment	66,203	51,342	33.5	33.3
Construction-in-Progress	6,210	5,830	3.1	3.8
	198,761	142,714	100.5	92.6
Less Accumulated Depreciation and Amortization	52,327	39,476	26.5	25.6
	146,434	103,238	74.0	67.0
Other Assets				
Deferred Costs	6,946	6,741	3.5	4.4
Investment in Joint Ventures at Equity	5,660	4,428	2.9	2.9
Long-term Marketable Securities	8,610	10,043	4.4	6.5
Long-term Notes Receivable	4,007	3,995	2.0	2.6
Other	2,881	2,559	1.5	1.7
	28,104	27,766	14.3	18.1
Total Assets	$ 197,718	$ 154,024	100.0%	100.0%

Exhibit 12.4 (Continued)————————————————————————

	1990	1989	Common Size Percentages 1990	Common Size Percentages 1989
Liabilities and Stockholders' Equity				
Current Liabilities:				
Short-term Debt	$ 8,900	$ —	4.5	—
Current Installment				
of Long-term Debt	93	662	.1	.4
Accounts Payable	14,291	10,343	7.2	6.7
Accrued Liabilities	15,621	12,843	7.9	8.3
Deferred Income Taxes	2,664	2,180	1.3	1.4
Total Current Liabilities	41,569	26,028	21.0	16.8
Long-term Debt, Less Current				
Installments	12,185	40,279	6.2	26.2
Deferred Income Taxes	7,778	5,858	3.9	3.8
Deferred Gain on Sale				
and Leaseback	102	155	.1	.1
Other Liabilities	3,690	3,390	1.9	2.2
Stockholders' Equity				
Preferred Stock	—	—	—	—
Common Stock	1,138	1,002	.6	.7
Additional Paid in Capital	73,220	37,213	37.0	24.2
Unrealized Loss on				
Marketable Securities	(1,685)	(1,501)	< .9>	< 1.0>
Retained Earnings	59,721	41,600	30.2	27.0
Total Stockholders' Equity	132,394	78,314	67.9	50.9
Total Liabilities and				
Stockholders' Equity	$ 197,718	$ 154,024	100.0	100.0

12.4 and 12.5. While only two years of data is presented for Chili's, additional years of data would be desirable.

An interpretation of vertical statements often parallels the interpretation of horizontal statements. Between 1989 and 1990, the largest percentage changes in any account occurred in property and equipment (67 to 74 percent), long-term debt (26.2 to 6.2 percent), and total shareholder equity (50.9 to 67.0 percent). As noted earlier, the shift in these percentages represents a proper balancing of sources and uses of cash flows.

In the income statement, Chili's maintained consistent ratios in the various operating expenses over the two-year period. This phenomena is

Exhibit 12.5 —————————————————————————————

CHILI'S INCORPORATED
COMPARATIVE INCOME STATEMENTS WITH VERTICAL ANALYSIS
FOR YEARS ENDED JUNE 30, 1990 AND 1989
(in 000's)

	1990	1989	Common Size Percentages 1990	Common Size Percentages 1989
Revenues	$ 347,127	$ 285,943	100.0%	100.0%
Operating Expenses:				
Cost of Sales	101,712	83,472	29.3	29.1
Restaurant Expenses	180,168	148,326	51.9	51.9
Depreciation & Amortization	17,406	15,161	5.0	5.3
	299,286	246,959	86.2	86.3
General and Administrative	19,684	16,835	5.7	5.9
Interest Expense	2,132	2,920	.6	1.0
Other, Net	(1,387)	(1,509)	< .4>	< .5>
Total Cost and Expenses	$ 319,715	$ 265,205	92.1	92.7
Income Before Provision for Income Taxes and Cumulative Change	27,412	20,738	7.9	7.3
Provision for Income Taxes	9,322	6,800	2.7	2.4
Income Before Cumulative Effect of an Accounting Change	18,090	13,938	5.2	4.9
Cumulative Change	—	—	—	—
Net Income	$18,090	$13,938	5.2%	4.9%

unexpected in a growth cycle where costs usually increase until the growth slows. Either the company's cost structure is relatively inelastic to growth or Chili's is manipulating its costs. Some indication of manipulation may be found in the increase in prepaid expenses and deferred costs. The change in these accounts represents $3 million, which could have alternatively impacted the income statement (i.e., leading to a reduction in net income as a percentage of sales). Only continued monitoring of the percentage of costs over the next few years will allow the analyst to discern which conclusion is appropriate. To this end, the monitoring of financial ratios is discussed in the next section.

Exhibit 12.6 _____

CHILI'S INCORPORATED
CONSOLIDATED STATEMENTS OF CASH FLOWS
(thousands of dollars)

	Year Ended June 30,	
	1990	1989
Cash Flows from Operating Activities:		
Net Income	$ 18,090	$ 13,938
Adjustments to Reconcile Net Income to		
Net Cash Provided by Operating Activities:		
Depreciation and Amortization	12,851	9,639
Amortization of Deferred Costs	4,555	5,522
Gain on Sale and Leaseback	(53)	(27)
Pro Forma Provision for Income Taxes	31	14
Cumulative Effect of an Accounting Change	—	—
Changes in Assets and Liabilities:		
Decrease (Increase) in Accounts Receivable	607	159
Decrease (Increase) in Federal Income		
Taxes Receivable	316	1,049
Decrease (Increase) in Inventories	876	(1,183)
(Increase) in Prepaid Expenses	(984)	(1,015)
(Increase) in Other Assets	(5,986)	(6,391)
Increase (Decrease) in Accounts Payable	3,948	3,651
Increase in Accrued Liabilities	2,778	3,376
Increase in Deferred Income Taxes	2,404	1,498
Increase in Other Liabilities	300	1,027
Net Cash Provided by Operating Activities	39,733	31,255
Cash Flows From Investing Activities:		
Payments for Property and Equipment	(56,059)	(34,872)
(Increase) Decrease in Assets Held for		
Sale and Leaseback	(414)	584
(Increase) in Investment in Joint Ventures	(1,232)	(117)
Proceeds from Sale of Investments	3,703	1,712
Net Cash Used in Investing Activities	(54,002)	(32,693)

Exhibit 12.6 (Continued) _____

	Year Ended June 30,	
	1990	1989
Cash Flows from Financing Activities:		
Short-term Debt, Net	8,900	—
Principal Borrowings on Long-term Debt	6,337	(3,766)
Stock Options Exercised	2,047	3,535
Cash Distribution to Satisfy Subchapter		
S Tax Liability	—	(78)
Net Cash Provided by (Used in)		
Financing Activities	17,284	(309)
Net Increase (Decrease) in Cash and Equivalents	3,015	(1,745)
Cash and Cash Equivalents at Beginning of Year	4,052	5,797
Cash and Cash Equivalents at End of Year	$ 7,067	$ 4,052
Cash Paid During the 12 Month Periods:		
Interest, Net of Amounts Capitalized	$ 2,443	$ 2,936
Income Taxes	$ 7,906	$ 3,300
Non-cash Items During the 12 Month Periods:		
Long-term Notes Receivable from Sale of		
Property and Equipment	$ —	$ 3,995
Conversion of 6¼% Convertible		
Subordinated Debentures	$ 35,000	$ —

——— Monitoring Financial Ratios: Graphical User Interface ———

Ratio analysis and the presentation of ratios in columnar form has frequently been found to be an inefficient form of financial evaluation. The actual relationship of the various ratios is often hidden in such presentation formats. Moreover, research in human information processing has consistently revealed that data users are able to more quickly and correctly process data presented in a graphical format, as opposed to a numeric/columnar format. Thus, to assist in the quick review of changes in various ratios of interest, a computer program displaying nineteen ratios for up to twenty-four periods has been developed and accompanies this book.

Exhibit 12.7 ————————————————————————————

CHILI'S FACES NORMALIZED AGAINST INDUSTRY

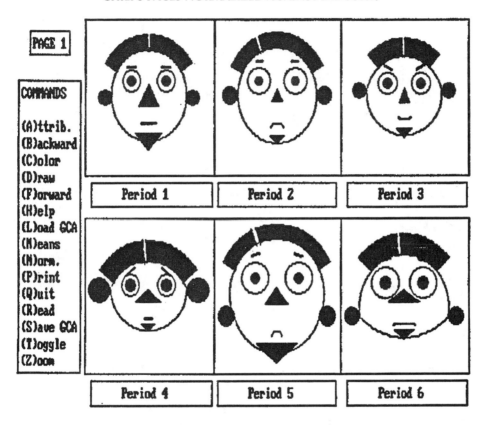

The software program is called FACES (Financial Analysts Caricature Evaluation System) and allows the analyst to compare ratios over time, against an industry or another company, and to present the images on the computer (or via hard copy). The use of the program is detailed in Appendix 3.

To illustrate the program, we again use data from Chili's Inc. The faces presented in Exhibit 12.7 relate 19 ratios for a period of six years (1985-1990) normalized against an industry norm (SIC #5812 Restaurants). As can be seen, some structural differences exist between the industry and Chili's. Industry ratios were derived from the RMA Annual Report Studies, 1985-1990.

Exhibit 12.8

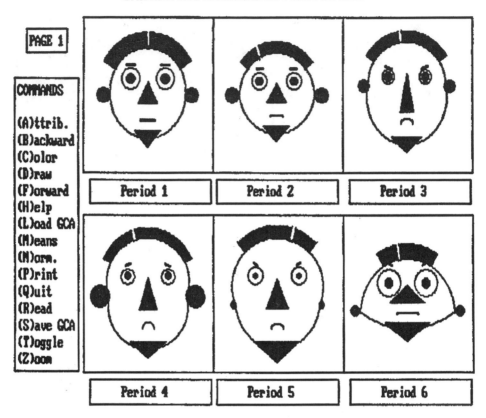

CHILI'S FACES NORMALIZED AGAINST SELF

Exhibit 12.8 displays the six faces for the Chili's data for 1985 through 1990 normalized against company data from 1985. At least five features changed sufficiently to warrant closer investigation. These include:

	Feature	Ratio
1.	Hair Coverage	Net Income Before Tax/Working Capital
2.	Hair Part	Net Income Before Tax/Net Worth
3.	Angle of Eye Brows	Long-term Debt/Working Capital
4.	Eye Pupils	Current Assets/Total Assets
5.	Face Height	Net Fixed Assets/Net Worth

Three of the five features deal with working capital and related concepts; consequently, it would appear that working capital is a potential problem area for Chili's. This is borne out in the tabular data that reveals that Chili's developed a negative working capital position as recently as 1989 (although in the food service industry, this need not indicate a financial concern). The last two features are related to net worth. The hair part moved from the right side in period 5 to the left side in period 6, revealing an increase in net worth. A comparable change occurred in the length of the face between period 5 and period 6. The associated economic event was Chili's conversion of subordinated debentures, which dramatically increased net worth and led to the large change in the features associated with these ratios.

Exhibit 12.7 displays the faces of Chili's when the company data is normalized against industry averages for the same period. Many of the salient features discussed above for the self-normalized data again appear in the industry-normalized faces. The face height in period 5 is longer than in period 1, showing that Chili's net worth is low as compared to the industry average. But by period 6, after the conversion of its subordinated debt, the ratio of fixed assets to net worth is higher than the industry average. Thus, Chili's seems to be positioned to now increase fixed assets and yet maintain this ratio at or below the industry average.

While the working capital ratios were featured when the data was self-normalized, such features as the hair part in the industry-normalized faces remained on the left side. This indicates that while Chili's current assets to total assets fluctuated over the six periods, the same phenomena occurred in the industry and Chili's generally had as good a ratio of current assets to total assets as did the industry as a whole.

Analysts are frequently faced with the responsibility of processing large amounts of data, and a graphical presentation may be critical to enable the individual to efficiently and correctly process such large data banks. It is important to note, however, that the use of graphical models does not eliminate the need for analysis. The use of graphics to highlight potentially critical changes in the underlying structure of a firm must be confirmed by further inquiry and investigation.

The DuPont Model

In the early 1950s, economists at the DuPont Corporation outlined a relationship among four financial ratios that became the foundation of a new approach to analyzing firm performance. That relationship, later named the DuPont model, was given by:

$$\frac{\text{Sales}}{\text{Average Assets}} \times \frac{\text{Average Assets}}{\text{Average Equity}} \times \frac{\text{Net Income}}{\text{Sales}} = \frac{\text{Net Income}}{\text{Average Equity}}$$

If the assumption could be made that a company's stock price was directly related to its return on equity (i.e., net income/average equity, or ROE), then the company's stock price could be increased by an overall increase in any of these individual ratios. Whether a firm's stock price is or is not directly related to its ROE is an empirical question beyond the scope of this book. Nonetheless, what can be inferred from this model is the importance of the three ratios as they relate to the overall management of a company's resources.

Decomposing the model into its individual components, the following three areas of management are highlighted: asset turnover, as measured by sales/average assets; financial leverage, as measured by average assets/average equity; and operating leverage, as measured by net income/sales. For the analyst, when the three ratios are viewed in a time series for an individual firm and in comparison with industry averages, considerable insights regarding management and its effectiveness on these three dimensions are highlighted. DuPont Corporation, as a company, did not use the model (it had no debt in its capital structure at that time), but other companies have elected to adopt the model as an operating philosophy directed at maximizing shareholders' wealth.[1]

The model is highly versatile, and applicable in a variety of industry-settings. Consider, for example, Chili's, whose ratios for the period 1985-1990 are as follows:

Year Ended June 30	(1) Sales / Avg. Assets		(2) Net Income / Sales		(3) Avg. Assets / Avg. Equity		(4) Net Income / Avg. Equity
1985	1.684	×	.086	×	1.770	=	.256
1986	1.695	×	.062	×	1.640	=	.172
1987	1.592	×	.064	×	2.270	=	.231
1988	1.715	×	.057	×	2.111	=	.206
1989	1.852	×	.073	×	1.960	=	.265
1990	1.756	×	.079	×	1.490	=	.207

Ratio (1) indicates management's utilization of assets in the generation of sales, and for Chili's, the pattern is relatively stable, but slightly upward trending. When compared to an industry standard (SIC No. 5812)—1.99, 1.34, 1.79, 1.41, 1.67, and 1.55, respectively, for 1985 through 1990—Chili's

---

[1] The interested reader is encouraged to examine, for example, the annual report of Tandy Corporation, particularly for the period 1977-1979.

asset turnover ratio is less variable, and in general indicates a higher level of asset utilization than the average for the industry.

Ratio (2), the return on sales, ranges between .057 and .086, or a variability of 50% (.029/.057). This large variability is probably a function of Chili's operating leverage in that, in general, the higher the operating leverage the greater the variability that can be expected in the return on sales. A comparison of Chili's return on sales with the industry average (i.e., .073, .013, .046, .072, .038, and .062, respectively) reveals that Chili's exceeded the industry average in all but one year (1989). Moreover, the variability of the industry average, 462% (.06/.013), again raises the spectre of potential asset/expense manipulation by Chili's. Given the operating leverage of restaurants, the return on sales pattern for Chili's is remarkably stable.

And finally, ratio (3), a measure of financial leverage, reveals considerable change over the period 1985-1990. As both asset utilization and the return on sales generally trended upward over this period, Chili's was able to maintain its return on equity (ratio 4) while increasing the relative amount of equity as compared to assets (i.e., the asset growth came from equity, not debt growth, and at a faster rate). As noted earlier, Chili's long-term debt was reduced when a convertible debt issuance was called and converted to equity. As compared to the industry average (i.e., 2.87, 2.69, 2.24, 2.05, 3.25, and 2.23, respectively), Chili's financial leverage exceeded the industry average in only two years (1987 and 1988).

Combining these three perspectives, we find that Chili's generally manages its assets well, maintains relatively stable operations, and is currently well poised to issue new debt. Chili's return on equity equalled or exceeded the industry average in all but one year (1988).

As can be seen in the Chili's data, manipulation of the ratios is, at best, difficult. Positive gains in one ratio lead to a negative effect in another. Increases in the ratios can only come about by real gains in the operations of a company. Since all components are integrated twice in the model, as both a numerator and a denominator (except average equity and net income), the model provides a built-in safety feature. For example, if an increase in sales is made at the expense of real economic gains (e.g., by liberalizing a company's credit-granting policy), the effect of the change in sales in the denominator of ratio (2) more than offsets the benefit in the numerator of ratio (1). Only a simultaneous increase in net income attributable to an increase in sales will lead to a higher return on equity, and this can only occur with a parallel management of costs.

The DuPont model contains one ratio, Net Income/Sales, which is interpreted as a surrogate measure for the operating cost structure of a firm. In the following section, another model is discussed which attempts to delineate the cost structure of a firm to the extent that the resulting numbers may be used in investment or lending decisions.

——————————— **The Cost-Volume-Profit Model** ———————————

Published financial statements have never intentionally conveyed information on a company's operating cost structure; however, the procedures described below illustrate how comparative cash flow statements can be used to derive this information, which can then be used in lending/investment decisions. An example, using information from an actual (but adapted) loan decision, illustrates how knowledge of a company's operating cost structure can be used to test the riskiness of an intermediate working capital loan. Sensitivity analysis can then be used to offer the borrower (or investor) additional insights into the risk a loan (or investment) presents to both the borrowing and lending institutions.

Operating versus Financial Leverage. *Leverage* involves the substitution of a fixed operating cost for a variable operating cost, and has historically been defined as the use of debt as a source of funds with a fixed cost component (i.e., interest). The problem with this concept of leverage is that it only partially captures management's choice in the substitution of fixed costs for variable costs. Although interest is an important cost, in most instances interest represents less than 20 percent of the total costs of most major manufacturing businesses. In short, most firms have many more costs which management may elect to convert to fixed costs. For example, the use of robots on the assembly line and the use of ATM's in banking have ramifications for labor costs, benefit costs, and maintenance costs, among others. In contrast, the use of debt impacts only the cost of interest. While financial leverage is important, it is just a member of a larger and more important set of operating leverages. For this reason, it is important to focus not only on financial leverage, but also to consider operating leverage.

Understanding Operating Leverage. The importance of operating leverage can be seen by reviewing two graphs, representing firms with contrasting operating cost structures. Assume, for example, that Company A (Exhibit 12.9) is a firm with high variable costs relative to the amount of fixed costs in its operating cost structure, while Company B is the opposite, with high fixed costs and low variable costs.

The amount of profit and loss, and therefore cash flow, can be shown to be a function of four components: 1) the selling price per unit, as revealed by the slope of the Total Revenue (TR) line; 2) the variable cost per unit, as revealed by the slope of the Variable Cost (VC) line; 3) total fixed costs (FC); and 4) the level of activity, as revealed along the horizontal axis (Q). Total costs (TC) can be seen to be the sum of VC and FC, a horizontal summation along the $ axis.

As revealed in the exhibit, Company A with a low contribution margin (i.e., selling price less unit variable cost) will make less profit as volume increases above its break-even point (Q^{BE}), but will also lose less as volume

Exhibit 12.9 ─────────────────────────────────────

A COMPANY WITH HIGH VARIABLE COSTS AND LOW FIXED COSTS

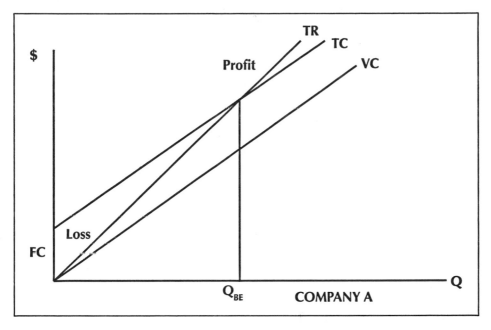

COMPANY A

A COMPANY WITH LOW VARIABLE COSTS AND HIGH FIXED COSTS

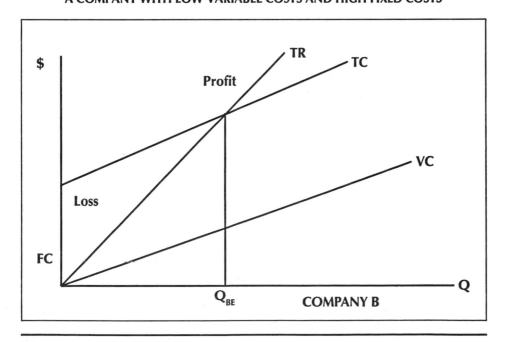

COMPANY B

Exhibit 12.10 ——————————————————————————————

PARTIAL LOAN APPLICATION

Borrower:	Boilermaker Dairy, Inc.
Address:	Anywhere, USA
Business:	Dairy Products (Production and Sale)
Amount Requested:	$3,500,000
Current Direct Debt:	$4,113,744
Rate:	Indiana State Bank Prime +1%
Compensating Balance:	5% of usage Available
Date Last Annual Statement	12/31/88 N.W. $6,153,000
Date Last Annual Statement	12/31/89 N.W. $6,666,000
Purpose:	To provide funds for working capital.
Liquidation Agreement:	

One year commitment to be structured on a promissory note with interest payable monthly and principal due at maturity. *Repayment to come from cash flow from operations.*

---

falls below the break-even point in relationship to Company B. On the other hand, Company B will make more profit than Company A for a given change in volume above the breakeven, but will lose any profit very rapidly as compared to Company A below breakeven. In addition, if Company A were to increase its fixed costs, it would need a proportionally higher level of sales to contribute toward those fixed costs than would Company B (as would be the case in a new loan).

A knowledge of the operating structure of a firm is very important in understanding the risks of making loans to and providing funds in general to any firm. Since GAAP-prepared financial statements provide few insights into the operating cost structure of a firm, the next section shows how comparative cash flow statements can be used to gain that insight.

An Illustration. Assume that the Indiana State Bank received a loan application (Exhibit 12.10) from Boilermaker Dairy, Inc., which is in the business of producing and distributing dairy products through grocery and company-owned convenience stores. The current request is for a $3.5 million working capital loan with interest set at the prime rate plus one percent. The current bank prime is 12%.

The loan decision clearly depends upon many factors; but the basic question to be asked is: Is the return offered by the Boilermaker loan commensurate with the risk associated with the loan? This question can best be addressed by breaking it down into the following three subquestions:

1. Will Boilermaker Dairy generate sufficient resources by the use of this loan to provide for the return of principal and interest to the bank?
2. Are the Dairy's projections of increased sales and growth reasonable given the cost structure of the firm?
3. At what rate of interest and principal amortization will the loan provide a threat to the liquidity and solvency of Boilermaker?

The balance sheets, income statements, and cash flow statements for Boilermaker Dairy, Inc. for the years 1987, 1988, and 1989 have been provided in Exhibits 12.11, 12.12, and 12.13, respectively. This financial data usually represents the financial information that would be available to the loan officer or the credit analyst. Although this information does give some insight into the answers to the questions above, other information will also need to be developed concerning the potential borrower.

Variable and Fixed Cost Components. In order to perform a cost-volume-profit analysis, costs and revenues must be dichotomized into their fixed and variable components. A simple method to attain this dichotomization is the high-low method. Basically this method uses two observation points to interpolate a straight-line. The slope of that straight-line is then interpreted as the variable component while the remainder (the observation less the variable cost component) is interpreted as the fixed component.

Exhibit 12.14 displays the statement of cash flows for 1988 and 1989 dichotomized into fixed and variable components. Sales revenue is set to unity and is classified as strictly variable. An adjustment to sales, the change (increase) in accounts receivable, is made (subtracted) to arrive at cash provided by sales. This adjustment amounts to $-.05873$, or $(-555 \div (87,877-78,428))$, and is classified as variable since it is an adjustment to a strictly variable component.

Cash production costs, on the other hand, contain both variable and fixed components since they are comprised of cost of goods sold as well as changes in inventory and accounts payable. The high-low method can be used to break these items into variable and fixed components. For cost of goods sold, the variable component is computed by its change from 1988 to 1989 in relation to the change in sales from 1988 to 1989: $-.79712$, or $(-(66,212-58,680) \div (87,877-78,428))$. Since the changes in inventory and accounts payable are just that, changes, their variable components are computed to be .01682, or $(-159 \div (87,877-78,428))$, and .08763, or $(828 \div (87,877-78,428))$, respectively. The total variable component is the sum of these three, $-.72631$. This implies that the fixed component of these cash production costs is the remainder, $-1,717.06$, or $(-65,543 - (-.72631 \times 87,877))$.

Exhibit 12.11

BOILERMAKER DAIRY, INC.
COMPARATIVE BALANCE SHEETS
(in 000's)

	1989	1988	1987
Assets			
Cash	$ 644	$ 36	$ 180
Net Receivables	6,254	5,699	5,665
Inventories	1,894	1,735	1,444
Other Current Assets	32	25	0
Total Current Assets	8,824	7,495	7,289
Gross Fixed Assets	22,006	20,429	18,547
Accumulated Depreciation	13,164	11,501	10,088
Net Fixed Assets	8,842	8,928	8,459
Prepaid Expenses	0	0	17
Other Noncurrent Assets	1,641	1,646	1,010
Total Assets	$19,307	$18,069	$16,775
Liabilities			
Current Portion of LT Debt	$ 1,976	$ 1,688	$ 1,451
Notes Payable	1,830	3,145	2,761
Accounts Payable	3,791	2,963	2,575
Income Tax Liability	158	45	82
Accruals	1,079	481	460
Other Current Liabilities	218	181	236
Total Current Liabilities	9,052	8,503	7,565
Deferred Income Taxes	57	6	57
Long-Term Debt	3,532	3,407	3,732
Total Liabilities	12,641	11,916	11,354
Equity			
Preferred Stock	116	29	28
Common Stock	329	82	83
Capital Surplus	510	510	510
Treasury Stock	(479)	(327)	(553)
Retained Earnings	6,190	5,859	5,353
Total Equity	6,666	6,153	5,421
Total Liabilities & Equity	$ 19,307	$ 18,069	$ 16,775

Exhibit 12.12 _____

BOILERMAKER DAIRY, INC.
COMPARATIVE INCOME AND RETAINED EARNINGS STATEMENTS
(in 000's)

	1989	1988	1987
Sales, net	$ 87,877	$ 78,428	$ 74,546
Cost of Goods Sold	(66,212)	(58,680)	(55,538)
Gross Profit	21,665	19,748	19,008
Selling and General Expenses	(17,418)	(15,945)	(14,543)
Depreciation Expense	(2,363)	(2,109)	(1,733)
Operating Profit	1,884	1,694	2,732
Interest Expense	(1,030)	(1,241)	(1,315)
Income Tax Expense	(328)	(181)	(210)
Other Revenues & Expenses	77	506	264
Net Income	$ 603	$ 778	$ 1,471
Beginning Retained Earnings	$ 5,859	$ 5,353	
Plus: Net Income	603	778	
Minus: Preferred Dividends	(272)	(272)	
Ending Retained Earnings	$ 6,190	$ 5,859	

Cash operating expenses are computed in the same manner as cash production costs. Income tax expense, cash interest costs, and dividends are assumed in this method to be strictly fixed, due to the short-run nature of the lending decision at hand. Hence, net cash income is composed of the variable component, .12236. For every incremental dollar of sales revenue, approximately twelve cents contributes to free cash flow. The fixed cost component of net free cash flow is −11,865.65. Since amortization and depreciation are included in this amount and are not cash outflows, an adjustment is made to exclude these non-cash components leading to an adjusted cash fixed cost in the amount of −9,502.65 (the negative sign represents the outflow nature of this cost).

Cost-Volume-Profit Analysis

Cost-volume-profit analysis is a technique used to examine the relationship among sales volume (expressed in cash sales dollars in this example), total costs (expressed as cash outflows), and profit (excess operating cash flow). A subset of cost-volume-profit analysis is called break-even analysis where the

Exhibit 12.13

BOILERMAKER DAIRY, INC.
COMPARATIVE CASH FLOW STATEMENTS
(in 000's)

	1989	1988
Operating Activities:		
Sales, net	$ 87,877	$ 78,428
Change in Receivables	(555)	(34)
Cash from Sales	87,322	78,394
Cost of Goods Sold	(66,212)	(58,680)
Change in Inventories	(159)	(291)
Change in Payables	828	388
Cash Production Costs	(65,543)	(58,583)
Selling and General Expenses	(17,418)	(15,945)
Change in Prepaids	0	17
Change in Accruals	598	21
Cash Operating Expenses	(16,820)	(15,907)
Cash from Operations	4,959	3,904
Other Revenues and Expenses	77	506
Income Taxes Paid	(164)	(269)
Interest Expense	(1,030)	(1,241)
Dividends (Preferred)	(272)	(272)
Net Cash Operating Income	$ 3,570	$ 2,628
Investment Activities:		
Capital Expenditures	(2,277)	(2,578)
Other Investments (current and		
non-current)	(2)	(661)
Total	(2,279)	(3,239)
Financing Activities:		
Change in Short-Term Debt	(990)	566
Change in Long-Term Debt	125	(325)
Change in Equity	182	226
Total	(683)	467
Change in Cash	$ 608	$ (144)

Exhibit 12.14

BOILERMAKER DAIRY, INC.
COST COMPONENTS
(in 000's)

Year	1989	1988	Variable Component	Fixed Component
Sales	$ 87,877	$ 78,428	$ 1	
Change in A/R	−555	−34	−0.05873	
Cash-Sales	87,322	78,394	0.94127	
Cost of Goods Sold	−66,212	−58,680	−0.79712	
Change in Inventories	−159	−291	−0.01682	
Change in A/P	828	388	0.08763	
Cash-Production	−65,543	−58,583	−0.72631	$ −1,717.06
Selling, Admin. Expense	−17,418	−15,945	−0.15589	
Change in Prepaids	0	17	0	
Change in Accruals	598	21	0.06329	
Cash-Oper. Exp.	−16,820	−15,907	−0.09260	−8,682.59
Other Revenues and Expenses	77	506	0	0.00
Income Taxes	−164	−269	0	−164.00
Interest	−1,030	−1,241	0	−1,030.00
Dividends (Pref.)	−272	−272	0	−272.00
Net Cash Inc.	$ 3,570	$ 2,628	$ 0.12236	$ −11,865.65
Amort. & Depr.	$ 2,363	$ 2,109		+ 2,363.00
Adj. Cash FC	$			−9,502.65

question of interest is usually phrased as, "How many sales dollars are necessary to earn zero profit or loss?" In our context, the question becomes, "What are the necessary increases in sales to cover the principal and interest associated with this loan?"

Cost-volume-profit analysis can easily be used to show that Boilermaker Dairy is above the "break-even" point (i.e., is making a cash profit). Dividing the adjusted cash fixed cost component (ignoring the negative sign) of 9,502.65 by the contribution-margin ratio of 0.12236 yields 77,661.41, which is less than the sales volume (measured in dollars) of 87,877 in the current year. In other words, Boilermaker Dairy has a "margin of safety" of 10,215.59 sales dollars (i.e., 10,215.59 sales dollars above the break-even point).

Boilermaker Dairy's loan application is for a working capital loan of $3.5 million at 13 percent (prime rate of 12 percent plus one point). In the first year, incremental cash interest would be $455,000. Can the firm handle this payment? A review of the Dairy's income statement shows a growing level of sales revenue each succeeding year. Even at the current level of sales, the firm should be able to handle this extra cash expense since it would still be above the break-even point ((9,502.65 + 455)÷.12236 = 81,380 < 87,877, the current level of sales). Interest coverage appears to be adequate, but what of the amortization of the loan principal?

If the bank expects to receive the total principal by year-end, an additional $3.5 million would be needed from operations. To achieve this cash throw-off, sales would need to be an additional $23,333,000 (3,500,000 ÷ .12236). At the growth rate previously experienced, this does not appear reasonable. If the loan is fully drawn, it does not appear likely that Boilermaker Dairy will be able to repay both the principal and interest.

What would be a more reasonable expectation for repayment of the principal of the loan? If sales increase another 12 percent next year as they did this last year ($10,545,000), then an additional $1,290,286 ($10,545,000 × .12236) would be available for principal repayment. At that rate, approximately 2.7 years would be required for principal repayment if no additional growth was experienced in year 2.

Using this type of analysis, the loan officer is in a better position to communicate when a loan would not be beneficial to a borrower. In the example at hand, the cash return per dollar of sales of $.12 is close to the marginal cost of borrowing of $.13. If this relationship was different, for example, with marginal cost much greater than the cash return, in the short-term it would have been too costly for Boilermaker to grow. This kind of growth information is important to the borrower, as well as to the loan officer.

By coupling the cash flow concepts of Chapter 11 with the cost structure of a firm, the analyst/investor may better understand the availability of future cash flows, and thus result in superior lending/investment decisions.

Conclusion

The models presented in this chapter should not to be used in isolation. Each model can contribute to the analyst's understanding of a given loan/investment. The DuPont model addresses three basic questions—asset management, financial leverage, and operating leverage. Moreover, comparative cash flow statements can be used to identify a company's operating cost structure (i.e., operating leverage) and how its management has elected to utilize fixed costs. Finally, the analyst must be prepared to explore alternative presentations of financial data. Specifically, a graphical interface (GUI) may be beneficial if the analyst is to review quickly and accurately the large amounts of information that must be processed in a lending/investment decision. The FACES program is an attempt to provide that interface.

CHAPTER THIRTEEN

Assessing the Quality of Earnings and Assets: Some Final Thoughts

In the prior twelve chapters we have tried to present a reasonably complete, but nontechnical description of financial statements and the environment in which they are prepared. To many individuals, financial statements will remain a confusing source of accounting data. To the analyst, however, these statements should become the most instructive and valued data resource available.

Even for the experienced analyst, financial statements and their accompanying footnotes are rarely fully understood. In part this is due to the enormous data reduction process that is involved in the preparation of these statements. Unfortunately, it is also due in part to the creative construction of such reports, which satisfy the minimal GAAP disclosure standards but are not sufficiently documented or articulated to permit even an informed user to fully understand what has transpired.

It is our belief, however, that compliance with even minimum disclosure standards is sufficient to enable the analyst to form a reasonably cogent assessment of a company's prior performance, and thereby enable a reasonably well-founded pro forma assessment of future performance to be developed. To accomplish this, we believe that an analyst must possess only a few basic skills and predispositions: (1) a willingness to carefully read the entire financial report, especially the accompanying footnotes, and a willingness to track the flow of information from statement to statement and footnote to footnote; (2) an understanding of basic GAAP rules and conventions, especially industry norms and practices; (3) an understanding of the differences between accrual and cash flows, and of the interdependencies between the balance sheet, the income statement, and the statement of cash flows; and (4) an understanding of, and an ability to calculate (or a computer software package which will do so), a set of fairly standard financial ratios. This book has focused on the latter three; needless to say, however, these skills are of limited value without the first.

As a way to bring closure to our examination of financial statements, we have prepared a list of investigative maxims. The items that comprise this list are often quite critical in assessing the quality of earnings, assets, and cash flows. A failure to identify them can, in some cases, be quite costly. Before considering these maxims, however, we define the concept of quality.

Assessing Quality

A major theme throughout this book has been that the reported accounting numbers are a direct consequence of the deliberate GAAP choices that corporate executives must make in anticipation of the preparation of a company's published financial statements. And thus, in order to assess the true earnings-generating ability of a company, the analyst must make some determination as to the quality of a company's reported earnings and assets.

Quality, however, is a very loosely, if not ill-defined concept. We prefer to think of quality, in the context of financial statements, as referring to accounting data that is substantially free of deficiencies. Moreover, we find it convenient to view this concept along a continuum from low to high.

Most professional analysts and accountants tend to equate higher quality earnings with "conservative" accounting methods (i.e., those methods that do not result in the highest level of reported profits). This view tends to be premised in the belief that a company using conservative reporting methods will be less adversely affected when faced with an industry or economy-wide downturn than a company using "liberal" reporting methods. In the words of two financial writers:[1]

> . . . the term quality of earnings is really an assessment of accounting policy. Good quality implies that current revenues are not being reported in a manner that jeopardizes future revenues, nor are costs reported so as

---

[1] M. Mendelson and S. Robbins, *Investment Analysis and Securities Markets* (Basic Books, Inc., 1976).

to benefit current profits at the expense of future profits. Poor quality implies just the opposite: accounting practices that inflate current revenues or curtail costs, postponing problems until some future day of reckoning.

Another financial writer tried to more precisely define the concept of quality by identifying those accounting methods which increased quality and those which decreased it; a partial listing is as follows:[2]

Accounting Methods Tending to Raise the Quality of Earnings	Accounting Methods Tending to Lower the Quality of Earnings
1. LIFO	1. FIFO
2. Deferral of investment tax credits	2. Flow-through reporting of investment tax credits
3. Completed contract accounting	3. Percentage-of-completion accounting
4. Pooling of interests accounting	4. Purchase accounting

While we agree with the notion that quality is really an assessment of accounting policy decisions, we disagree with the view that quality can be defined simply with respect to specific accounting methods, principally because few GAAP methods are always associated with low (or high) quality earnings. It is always necessary to evaluate the particular accounting methods in use in the context of the industry setting or market faced by a company. For example, during inflationary periods, the LIFO method does provide the highest quality of reported earnings for most companies. However, while general price levels may be rising for the economy at large, the specific price levels of a particular industry or company may be falling. Under these circumstances, LIFO would not provide a high quality of earnings, and instead FIFO would be preferred.

Thus, there is no simple solution to measuring the quality of earnings and assets of a company. Indeed, many factors—the treatment of revenues and expenses, the level of cash flows from operations, the consistent use of accounting methods and estimates, pending or contingent events and obligations, the various sources of earnings, (e.g., operating versus unusual versus extraordinary) etc., etc., etc—must all be considered. Throughout the previous 12 chapters we have tried to cover the majority of these factors. In the remaining pages we summarize some of the more important ones.[3]

---

[2] E.E. Comiskey, "Assessing Financial Quality: An Organizing Theme for Credit Analysts," *The Journal of Commercial Bank Lending* (December, 1982).

[3] Appendix 4 contains a Risk Analysis Profile checklist which allows the analyst to check off the potential risks contained in any set of financial statements.

──────────────── **Investigative Maxims** ────────────────

The Auditor's Report

It seems to us that the most natural place to begin an analysis of financial statements is with the auditor's report, assuming that the financial statements have been audited. With respect to the process of assessing quality, the independent auditor can be viewed as a first-level check on the quality of reported data. In essence, the auditor examines the financial data to ensure that it is prepared in accordance with GAAP and is free of material errors.

In Chapter 1, we reported that while the independent auditor does not review all account balances, statistical theories of sampling, testing, and inference are used to provide a reasonable degree of assurance that any unsampled and untested accounts are also accurate. In those instances where the auditor identifies the existence of significant internal control weaknesses that might permit a deception to occur, where material errors or misstatements are in fact observed, or where GAAP is not followed (or is not consistently followed), the auditor bears the professional and ethical responsibility of so notifying the reader via the audit report.

Thus, given the nature and level of effort expended by the independent auditor, we recommend that the analyst begin his or her review process with the auditor's report. The analyst should not, however, be lulled into a less rigorous analysis by the presence of a clean audit opinion. An unqualified opinion is no guarantee of a high quality of reported earnings, assets, or cash flows. Remember, *caveat emptor*.

Commitments and Contingent Liabilities

Two themes that have repeatedly surfaced throughout these pages are: (1) financial statements are essentially historical in focus, reporting what has transpired as opposed to what might transpire; and (2) credit and investment decisions should be made principally on the basis of a company's future prospects, and not its past performance. One highly important category of futuristic events is the economic obligations of a company. Economic obligations, as distinguished from accounting obligations (see Chapters 8 and 9), are not recorded in the balance sheet under GAAP. Nonetheless, because of their significance to the overall financial health of a company, these obligations are disclosed in the footnotes to the financial statements under the heading "Commitments and Contingent Liabilities."

This rubric encompasses many types of future obligations, from clearly defined, often noncancelable obligations such as operating leases payments, to highly uncertain ones such as potential damage awards under pending lawsuits. To a large measure, *commitments* constitute fairly certain future obligations, many if not most of which involve *executory contracts* (e.g., supply contracts, take-or-pay contracts, working capital maintenance agreements, etc.); whereas, *contingent liabilities* constitute obligations of fairly uncertain amounts with reasonably uncertain timing as to payment (e.g., product warranty agreements, receivables sold with recourse, guaranteed debt agreements involving a joint venture or affiliate company, etc.).

What characterizes each of these obligations, however, is that they may (or in some cases, definitely will) have a significant impact on the future earnings and cash flows of the company. Thus, since a major aspect of financial analysis is the preparation of pro forma financial statements, it is crucial for the analyst to carefully review this footnote and to be certain to include these obligations in his or her projections.

Off-Balance Sheet Debt

In addition to the problem of future obligations, the analyst must also investigate for the presence of currently legally-binding obligations that are not reported on a company's balance sheet. As noted in Chapter 9, the principal concern of this type involves post-retirement benefit obligations.

Post-retirement benefit obligations are those insurance and medical benefits committed to employees on the basis of prior service to a company. In the absence of any governmental regulations, such as ERISA, mandating the prior funding of these commitments, most companies have adopted a "pay-as-you-go" approach and consequently face substantial future cash outflows as their workforce ages and retires. Moreover, in the absence of an accounting standard requiring the recognition of such obligations, most companies have adopted the position that these obligations are future, and not current, commitments. It is now recognized that these obligations, and the associated expense, should have been recorded in the period in which the benefits were earned, and thus committed.

Analysts should be able to rectify this situation in the future by adjusting the published financial statements. Beginning in 1994, companies are expected to provide information regarding the magnitude of their unfunded postretirement benefits via the accompanying footnotes. Thus, analysts will have sufficient information to reflect a liability for any underfunding in the balance sheet if necessary.

Single-period Transactions

Another recurring theme throughout these chapters has been that while nonrecurring, single-period transactions are instructive in that they help the analyst understand how and why a company arrived at its current financial condition, they have very little future value and thus should be ignored for purposes of preparing pro forma statements. In Chapter 2, for example, we saw that the unusual and extraordinary items reported on the income statement could indeed have a material effect on the level of currently reported income, but realistically could not be expected to recur in future periods. Further, because of the flexibility in reporting various economic events permitted under GAAP, we concluded that it was incumbent upon the analyst to review all of the items disclosed on the income statement to satisfy himself or herself as to just which items could be expected to recur versus those which were unlikely to recur.

Thus, an important maxim for the analyst is to always assume an aggressive, proactive stance in the analysis and interpretation of financial statements. As noted in the Introduction, it is possible to report the financial results of a company in many different ways under GAAP. And consequently, the analyst should not passively accept the methods or format followed in the printed financial statements as the only appropriate approach to report the financial condition of a company. Indeed, a major goal of this book has been to provide the analyst with a set of skills to permit the restatement of financial statements, and thereby facilitate the particular informational needs of the credit or investment analyst.[4]

Related-party Transactions

A major distinction between companies of today and those of the 1960s and 1970s is the presence of significant intercorporate investments. It is extremely rare to find a company of the 1990s which does not hold a significant equity position in some subsidiary, affiliate company, or major supplier or customer. Today's competitive market conditions almost require that such investments be made in order to protect input and output markets.

Chapter 6 observed that, in most cases, profits on transactions involving subsidiary or affiliate companies are eliminated via the consolidation process used in preparing consolidated financial statements. However, where such investments are accounted for using the equity method, such as in the case of limited partnerships or joint ventures, profits on intercompany sales may not be effectively eliminated or offset in the current period. In the long run, of course, related-party profits reported in current period statements will be offset by higher inventory or depreciation charges

---

[4] Several financial researchers have investigated whether restating financial statements for alternative GAAP is worth the time and effort involved. In general, their results indicate that "LIFO/FIFO inventory differences and accelerated/straight-line depreciation differences do not affect net income or financial ratios significantly," except in some capital-intensive industries (e.g., steel and petroleum industries), but that restatement for unconsolidated subsidiaries (or joint ventures) and off-balance sheet debt (e.g., post-retirement benefits) is well justified as ratios are significantly affected. See J. Dawson, P. Neupert, and C. Stickney, "Restating Financial Statements for Alternative GAAP: Is It Worth the Effort?," *Financial Analysts Journal* (November/December, 1980).

in future periods. However, it is important for the analyst to note that current profits may be artificially inflated by significant related-party sales. Thus, for purposes of preparing pro forma financial statements, the analyst should consider eliminating the current profits associated with such related-party transactions, especially if such transactions are likely to be nonrecurring.

Accounting Changes

How a company chooses to present its financial results is substantially up to its chief executives. Thus, it is not surprising that, periodically, just as corporate executives change or retire, the particular accounting methods utilized by a company also change.

There are three types of accounting changes that analysts may confront: (1) a change in reporting entity, such as when two companies are merged; (2) a change in reporting method, such as a switch from LIFO to FIFO; or (3) a change in an accounting estimate, such as a revision in the expected useful life of a depreciable asset. All three types of changes may affect the level of reported results, and thus the analyst must be aware of where to locate information concerning such changes.

With respect to a change in reporting entity, Chapter 6 disclosed that in the case of a pooling of interests, all prior financial data (i.e., total assets, earnings, retained earnings) are effectively restated as if the two firms had been merged all along. In the case of a purchase, however, the financial statements are adjusted only for those periods subsequent to the purchase transaction. In either case, however, the analyst must recognize that all future statements, and thus the pro formas, must reflect the combined operations of the new entity.

With respect to a change in accounting method, not only will the auditor's report for the period involving a change alert the analyst that a change has occurred, but details of the method change must also be disclosed in the accompanying footnotes. Thus, if a company switches from accelerated depreciation to straight-line depreciation, the effect of the change on the current period earnings will be revealed in the footnotes, enabling the analyst to determine the level of earnings that would have been reported if the change had not occurred. Unfortunately, the effect of the change on reported profits need only be disclosed in the year of the change; hence, it is important for the analyst to review financial reports from prior years to determine if any method changes affecting reported earnings occurred.

Finally, with respect to accounting estimate changes, since this type of accounting change does not constitute an inconsistent application of GAAP, it will normally not be noted by the independent auditor in the audit report. However, like the accounting method change, the accounting estimate change and its effect on currently reported earnings must be disclosed in the financial statement footnotes. Thus, in the event that a company revises the expected useful life of its depreciable assets, the (usually positive) impact on current earnings must be disclosed. Unfortunately, such disclosure is only required in the period of change.

Cash Flows from Operations

If there is one measure that deserves careful review by the analyst, it is the cash flow from operations (CFFO). Without question, the CFFO is the most important indicator of credit and investment risk. So long as a company has a continuing positive CFFO, regardless of whether accrual earnings are positive or not, the company may be a sound credit or investment opportunity.

Under SFAS 95, the CFFO must be clearly identified in the statement of cash flows, and thus even the analyst with few skills can determine whether operations are a net positive (or negative) generator of cash. By comparing various required cash outflows, such as dividends, mandatory debt repayments, and depreciable asset replacements, with the CFFO, the analyst can determine a company's *discretionary cash flow*. The discretionary or "free" cash flow is the level of cash generated from operations that is available for special corporate goals, such as capital expansion or merger and acquisition. Obviously, the larger the discretionary cash flow position the better, thereby enabling a company to undertake self-financed capital expansion, merger or acquisition, or merely provide abnormal dividend returns to investors. Where discretionary cash flows are negative, the importance and reasonableness of the analyst's assumptions regarding future events and opportunities becomes highly magnified. Where the analyst truly earns his or her salary is in the analysis of credit and investment decisions involving companies with negative discretionary cash flows, and possibly even negative CFFO.

Managed Earnings

A major aspect of this book has been to review the ways that corporate executives can and do "manage" the level of reported assets, earnings, and cash flows. Because of the difficulty of effectively managing cash flows beyond a single period, the management of reported financial results tends to be principally focused on the balance sheet and the income statement. In Chapter 2, we saw that many companies manage revenues (and hence receivables) through a process called front-end loading. Revenues may be recognized early in a company's operating cycle, thereby causing earnings to be recognized sooner than perhaps is justified. Of concern to the analyst, then, is whether such sales will actually be consummated and whether the expected cash flows will be forthcoming.

In Chapter 3, we saw that some companies also manage earnings through a process called rear-end loading of expenses, or deferring the recognition of expenses that would otherwise have been matched with current period revenue. Like the front-end loading of revenues, the rear-end loading of expenses also produces a parallel increase in assets on the balance sheet, usually in the form of deferred assets or deferred expenses. We observed in Chapter 3 that rear-end loading could be achieved in many different ways: by choosing a slower write-off method for capitalized assets (e.g., straight-line depreciation), by selecting a longer write-off period, or by capitalizing certain costs (e.g., interest) that might otherwise be expensed.

In some cases, the management of earnings will be clearly identifiable in the footnotes to the financial statements, for example when a company makes an intuitively unsound accounting method change (e.g., switching from LIFO to FIFO during a period of rapid inflation) or accounting estimate change (e.g., increasing the depreciable life of assets facing technological obsolescence). In other cases, however, the question as to whether management is intentionally "managing" reported earnings and assets will be a judgment call, assisted only by a thorough knowledge of existing industry-accepted practice and of the effect of alternative GAAP on reported financial results.

Conclusions

As you reflect on the contents of this book, we hope that you do so with several emotions—anger, humor, pleasure, scepticism, and surprise. Anger is appropriate when one considers the numerous financial deceptions and instances of fraudulent reporting, usually the consequence of managerial greed, that have been perpetuated throughout the years. Humor is appropriate when one considers the methods used to perpetuate those deceptions. (Our favorite is the company that shipped bricks, rather than disk-drives, to its customers as a means to justify recording fraudulent sales.)

Surprise is an appropriate reaction when one considers the apparent magnitude of the fraudulent reporting problem, and that so many deceptions appear to escape early detection by the independent auditor. (But remember the old adage, "Where there is a will, there is a way.") And, scepticism that financial statements are ever fairly presented would also seem to be a reasonable reaction. But, most importantly, we hope that you experienced some pleasure, or perhaps it was relief from the knowledge that with a modicum of effort and a minimal accounting background, it is possible to make a reasonably well-informed assessment of a company's performance and its quality of reported earnings, assets, and cash flows.

APPENDIXES

Authoritative Accounting Pronouncements
The Alternative Minimum Tax
Analytical Software Instructions
Risk Analysis Profile Checklist
Suggested Reading

Authoritative Accounting Pronouncements

——————— **Accounting Principles Board (APB) Opinions** ———————

Number	Title	Date of Issuance
1.	New Depreciation Guidelines and Rules	November, 1962
2.	Accounting for the "Investment Credit"	December, 1962
3.	The Statement of Source and Application of Funds	October, 1963
4.	Accounting for the "Investment Credit" (Amending No. 2)	March, 1964
5.	Reporting of Leases in Financial Statements of Lessee	September, 1964
6.	Status of Accounting Research Bulletins	October, 1965
7.	Accounting for Leases in Financial Statements of Lessors	May, 1966
8.	Accounting for the Cost of Pension Plans	November, 1966
9.	Reporting the Results of Operations	December, 1966
10.	Omnibus Opinion—1966	December, 1966
11.	Accounting for Income Taxes	December, 1967

Number	Title	Date of Issuance
12.	Omnibus Opinion—1967	December, 1967
13.	Amending Paragraph 6 of the APB Opinion No. 9, Application to Commercial Banks	March, 1969
14.	Accounting for Convertible Debt and Debt Issued with Stock Purchase Warrants	March, 1969
15.	Earnings per Share	May, 1969
16.	Business Combinations	August, 1970
17.	Intangible Assets	August, 1970
18.	The Equity Method of Accounting for Investments in Common Stock	March, 1971
19.	Reporting Changes in Financial Position	March, 1971
20.	Accounting Changes	July, 1971
21.	Interest on Receivables and Payables	August, 1971
22.	Disclosure of Accounting Policies	April, 1972
23.	Accounting for Income Taxes—Special Areas	April, 1972
24.	Accounting for Income Taxes—Investments in Common Stock Accounted for by the Equity Method	April, 1972
25.	Accounting for Stock Issued to Employees	October, 1972
26.	Early Extinguishment of Debt	October, 1972
27.	Accounting for Lease Transactions by Manufacturer or Dealer Lessors	November, 1972
28.	Interim Financial Reporting	May, 1973
29.	Accounting for Nonmonetary Transactions	May, 1973
30.	Reporting the Results of Operations—Reporting the Effects of Disposal of a Segment of a Business, and Extraordinary, Unusual and Infrequently Occurring Events and Transactions	June, 1973
31.	Disclosure of Lease Commitments by Lessees	June, 1973

——— Financial Accounting Standards Board (FASB) ——— Statements of Financial Accounting Standards

Number	Title	Date of Issuance
1.	Disclosure of Foreign Currency Translation Information	December, 1973
2.	Accounting for Research and Development Costs	October, 1974
3.	Reporting Accounting Changes in Interim Financial Statements (an amendment of *APB Opinion No. 28*)	December, 1974

Number	Title	Date of Issuance
4.	Reporting Gains and Losses from Extinguishment of Debt (an amendment of *APB Opinion No. 30*)	March, 1975
5.	Accounting for Contingencies	March, 1975
6.	Classification of Short-Term Obligations Expected to Be Refinanced (an amendment of *ARB No. 43*, Chapter 3A)	May, 1975
7.	Accounting and Reporting by Development Stage Enterprises	June, 1975
8.	Accounting for the Translation of Foreign Currency Transactions and Foreign Currency Financial Statements	October, 1975
9.	Accounting for Income Taxes—Oil and Gas Producing Companies (an amendment of *APB Opinions No. 11 and 23*)	October, 1975
10.	Extension of "Grandfather" Provisions for Business Combinations (an amendment of *APB Opinion No. 16*)	October, 1975
11.	Accounting for Contingencies—Transition Method (an amendment of *FASB Statement No. 5*)	December, 1975
12.	Accounting for Certain Marketable Securities	December, 1975
13.	Accounting for Leases	November, 1976
14.	Financial Reporting for Segments of a Business Enterprise	December, 1976
15.	Accounting by Debtors and Creditors for Troubled Debt Restructurings	June, 1977
16.	Prior Period Adjustments	June, 1977
17.	Accounting for Leases—Initial Direct Costs (an amendment of *FASB Statement No. 13*)	November, 1977
18.	Financial Reporting for Segments of a Business Enterprise—Interim Financial Statements (an amendment of *FASB Statement No. 14*)	November, 1977
19.	Financial Accounting and Reporting by Oil and Gas Producing Companies	December, 1977
20.	Accounting for Forward Exchange Contracts (an amendment of *FASB Statement No. 8*)	December, 1977
21.	Suspension of the Reporting of Earnings per Share and Segment Information by Nonpublic Enterprises (an amendment of *APB Opinion No. 15* and *FASB Statement No. 14*)	April, 1978

Number	Title	Date of Issuance
22.	Accounting for Leases—Changes in the Provisions of Lease Agreements Resulting from Refundings of Tax-Exempt Debt (an amendment of *FASB Statement No. 13*)	June, 1978
23.	Inception of the Lease (an amendment of *FASB Statement No. 13*)	August, 1978
24.	Reporting Segment Information in Financial Statements that are Presented in Another Enterprise's Financial Report (an amendment of *FASB Statement No. 14*)	December, 1978
25.	Suspension of Certain Accounting Requirements for Oil and Gas Companies (an amendment of *FASB Statement No. 19*)	February, 1979
26.	Profit Recognition on Sales-Type Leases of Real Estate (an amendment of *FASB Statement No. 13*)	April, 1979
27.	Classification of Renewals or Extensions of Existing Sales-Type or Direct Financing Leases (an amendment of *FASB Statement No. 13*)	May, 1979
28.	Accounting for Sales with Leasebacks (an amendment of *FASB Statement No. 13*)	May, 1979
29.	Determining Contingent Rentals (an amendment of *FASB Statement No. 13*)	June, 1979
30.	Disclosure of Information About Major Customers (an amendment of *FASB Statement No. 14*)	August, 1979
31.	Accounting for Tax Benefits Related to U.K. Tax Legislation Concerning Stock Relief	September, 1979
32.	Specialized Accounting and Reporting Principles and Practices in AICPA Statements of Position and Guides on Accounting and Auditing Matters (an amendment of *APB Opinion No. 20*)	September, 1979
33.	Financial Reporting and Changing Prices	September, 1979
34.	Capitalization of Interest Cost	October, 1979
35.	Accounting and Reporting by Defined Benefit Pension Plans	March, 1980
36.	Disclosure of Pension Information	May, 1980
37.	Balance Sheet Classification of Deferred Income Taxes (an amendment of *APB Opinion No. 11*)	July, 1980
38.	Accounting for Preacquisition Contingencies of Purchased Enterprises (an amendment of *APB Opinion No. 16*)	September, 1980

Number	Title	Date of Issuance
39.	Financial Reporting and Changing Prices: Specialized Assets—Mining and Oil and Gas (a supplement to *FASB Statement No. 33*)	October, 1980
40.	Financial Reporting and Changing Prices: Specialized Assets—Timberlands and Growing Timber (a supplement to *FASB Statement No. 33*)	November, 1980
41.	Financial Reporting and Changing Prices: Specialized Assets—Income-Producing Real Estate (a supplement to *FASB Statement No. 33*)	November, 1980
42.	Determining Materiality for Capitalization of Interest Cost (an amendment of *FASB Statement No. 34*)	November, 1980
43.	Accounting for Compensated Absences	November, 1980
44.	Accounting for Intangible Assets of Motor Carriers (an amendment of Chapter 5 of *ARB No. 43* and an interpretation of *APB Opinions 17 and 30*)	December, 1980
45.	Accounting for Franchise Fee Revenue	March, 1981
46.	Financial Reporting and Changing Prices: Motion Picture Films	March, 1981
47.	Disclosure of Long-Term Obligations	March, 1981
48.	Revenue Recognition When Right of Return Exists	June, 1981
49.	Accounting for Product Financing Arrangements	June, 1981
50.	Financial Reporting in the Record and Music Industry	November, 1981
51.	Financial Reporting by Cable Television Companies	November, 1981
52.	Foreign Currency Translation	December, 1981
53.	Financial Reporting by Producers and Distributors of Motion Picture Films	December, 1981
54.	Financial Reporting and Changing Prices: Investment Companies (an amendment of *FASB Statement No. 33*)	January, 1982
55.	Determining Whether A Convertible Security Is A Common Stock Equivalent (an amendment of *APB Opinion No. 15*)	February, 1982
56.	Designation of AICPA Guide and Statement of Position (SOP)81-1 on Contractor Accounting and SOP 81-2 Concerning Hospital-Related Organizations as Preferable for Purposes of Applying *APB Opinion 20* (an amendment of *FASB Statement No. 32*)	February, 1982
57.	Related Party Disclosures	March, 1982
58.	Capitalization of Interest Cost in Financial Statements That Include Investments Accounted for by the Equity Method	April, 1982

Number	Title	Date of Issuance
59.	Deferral of the Effective Date of Certain Accounting Requirements for Pension Plans of State and Local Governmental Units (an amendment of *FASB Statement No. 35*)	April, 1982
60.	Accounting and Reporting by Insurance Enterprises	June, 1982
61.	Accounting for Title Plant	June, 1982
62.	Capitalization of Interest Cost in Situations Involving Certain Tax-Exempt Borrowings and Certain Gifts and Grants	June, 1982
63.	Financial Reporting by Broadcasters	June, 1982
64.	Extinguishments of Debt Made to Satisfy Sinking-Fund Requirements (an amendment of *FASB Statement No. 4*)	September, 1982
65.	Accounting for Certain Mortgage Banking Activities	September, 1982
66.	Accounting for Sales of Real Estate	October, 1982
67	Accounting for Costs and Initial Rental Operations of Real Estate Projects	October, 1982
68.	Research and Development Arrangements	October, 1982
69.	Disclosures About Oil- and Gas-Producing Activities	November, 1982
70.	Financial Reporting and Changing Prices: Foreign Currency Translation (an amendment of *FASB Statement No. 33*)	December, 1982
71.	Accounting for the Effects of Certain Types of Regulation	December, 1982
72.	Accounting for Certain Acquisitions of Banking or Thrift Institutions (an amendment of *APB Opinion No. 17*, an interpretation of *APB Opinions No. 16 and 17*, and an amendment of *FASB Interpretation No. 9*)	February, 1983
73	Reporting a Change in Accounting for Railroad Track Structures (an amendment of *APB Opinion No. 20*)	August, 1983
74.	Accounting for Special Termination Benefits Paid to Employees	August, 1983
75	Deferral of the Effective Date of Certain Accounting Requirements for Pension Plans of State and Local Governmental Units (an amendment of *FASB Statement No. 35*)	November, 1983
76.	Extinguishment of Debt (an amendment of *APB Opinion No. 26*)	November, 1983
77	Reporting by Transferors for Transfers of Receivables with Recourse	December, 1983

Number	Title	Date of Issuance
78.	Classification of Obligations that Are Callable by the Creditor (an amendment of *ARB No. 43*, Chapter 3A)	December, 1983
79.	Elimination of Certain Disclosures for Business Combinations by Nonpublic Enterprises (an amendment of *APB Opinion No. 16*)	February, 1984
80.	Accounting for Futures Contracts	August, 1984
81.	Disclosure of Postretirement Health Care and Life Insurance Benfits	November, 1984
82.	Financial Reporting and Changing Prices: Elimination of Certain Disclosures (an amendment of *FASB Statement No. 33*)	December, 1984
83.	Designation of AICPA Guides and Statement of Position on Accounting by Brokers and Dealers in Securities, by Employee Benefit Plans, and by Banks as Preferable for Purposes of Applying *APB Opinion 20*	March, 1985
84.	Induced Conversions of Convertible Debt (an amendment of *APB Opinion No. 26*)	March, 1985
85.	Yield Test for Determining Whether a Convertible Security Is a Common Stock Equivalent (an amendment of *APB Opinion No. 15*)	March, 1985
86.	Accounting for the Costs of Computer Software to be Sold, Leased, or Otherwise Marketed	August, 1985
87.	Employers' Accounting for Pensions	December, 1985
88.	Employers' Accounting for Settlements and Curtailments of Defined Benefit Pension Plans and for Termination Benefits	December, 1985
89.	Financial Reporting and Changing Prices	December, 1986
90.	Regulated Enterprises—Accounting for Abandonments and Disallowances of Plant Costs (an amendment of *FASB Statement No. 71*)	December, 1986
91.	Accounting for Nonrefundable Fees and Costs Associated with Originating or Acquiring Loans and Initial Direct Costs of Leases	December, 1986
92.	Regulated Enterprises—Accounting for Phase-in Plans (an amendment of *FASB Statement No. 71*)	August, 1987
93	Recognition of Depreciation by Not-for-Profit Organizations	August, 1987
94.	Consolidation of All Majority-owned Subsidiaries (an amendment of *ARB No. 51*, with related amendments of *APB Opinion No. 18* and *ARB No. 43*, Chapter 12)	October, 1987

Number	Title	Date of Issuance
95.	Statement of Cash Flows	November, 1987
96.	Accounting for Income Taxes	December, 1987
97.	Accounting and Reporting by Insurance Enterprises for Certain Long-Duration Contracts and for Realized Gains and Losses from the Sale of Investments	April, 1988
98.	Accounting for Leases	August, 1988
99.	Deferral of the Effective Date of Recognition of Depreciation by Not-for-Profit Organizations	January, 1989
100.	Accounting for Income Taxes-Deferral of the Effective Date of *FASB Statement No. 96*	March, 1989
101.	Regulated Enterprises—Accounting for the Discontinuation of Application of *FASB Statement No. 71*	March, 1989
102.	Statement of Cash Flows—Exemption of Certain Enterprises and Classification of Cash Flows from Certain Securities Acquired for Resale	April, 1989
103.	Accounting for Income Taxes—Deferral of Effective Date of FASB Statement No. 96	December, 1989
104.	Statement of Cash Flows—Net Reporting of Certain Cash Receipts and Cash Payments and Classification of Cash Flows from Hedging Transactions	December, 1989
105.	Disclosure of Information About Financial Instruments with Off-Balance-Sheet Risk and Financial Instruments with Concentrations of Credit Risk	March, 1990
106.	Employers Accounting for Postretirement Benefits Other Than Pensions	December, 1990

The Alternative Minimum Tax

Until the advent of the corporate Alternative Minimum Tax (AMT), created by the Tax Reform Act (TRA) of 1986, little connection existed between federal tax regulation and corporate financial reporting. There were, of course, some exceptions such as the LIFO inventory compliance rule and certain tax issues surrounding business combinations; but, in general, the analyst could ignore tax regulations in the analysis of financial statements. This is not to suggest that tax considerations were unimportant to credit and investment decisions, but rather that the financial reporting system was essentially insulated from most of these considerations.

With the arrival of the corporate AMT, however, accounting for income taxes and their financial reporting became considerably more complex. As the analyst may have observed in Chapter 4, the provision for income taxes under SFAS 96 is dependent upon the deferral of income taxes and the actual tax liability.[1] Consequently, the calculation of the AMT may affect

---

[1] Under APB 11, the amount of taxes deferred is dependent upon the provision for income taxes and the actual tax liability. Consequently, under either SFAS 96 or APB 11, the tax liability calculation will affect financial reporting when and if the AMT is applicable.

this provision through the tax liability (i.e., the amount owed) if the AMT is applicable.

Calculation of the AMT

The AMT is a mandatory alternative tax liability calculation such that if higher than the tax liability assessed under existing tax regulations, it represents the amount that will ultimately be paid by a corporation. Before the TRA of 1986, corporations were subject to an add-on minimum tax on certain tax preference items. Nonetheless, the perception still existed among many governmental officials and individual taxpayers that certain corporations did not pay sufficient income taxes. Thus, the TRA of 1986 created a 20 percent flat rate AMT designed to ensure that all corporations would pay at least 10 percent of their book income as taxes.[2]

In its simplest form, the AMT for taxable years through 1989 is calculated as follows:

> Taxable Income calculated per existing regulations
>
> + Tax Preference Items
>
> + ½ (Difference between AMTI and pretax financial reported income)[3]
>
> ---
>
> Alternative Minimum Taxable Income (AMTI)
> − Exemption
>
> ---
>
> Adjusted AMTI
> × .20
>
> ---
>
> AMT
> − Foreign Tax Credits/pre-1986 ITC carryover[4]
>
> ---
>
> AMT to be compared to tax computed under regular tax system

The exemption used to adjust the AMTI is maximally $40,000 at AMTI values of $150,000 or less, and is reduced to $0 at $310,000 at a rate of $.25 per AMTI dollar. Thus, if regular taxable income were $0, pretax financial income $500,000, and there are no preference items, the AMT would be

---

[2] As the calculation shows, this 10 percent minimum results only if the Alternative Minimum Taxable Income (AMTI) is above $310,000 and no other adjustments (e.g., net operating losses or investment tax credits) exist.

[3] AMTI is, at this stage of the calculation, the regular taxable income plus any preference items.

[4] Investment tax credits were effectively eliminated by the TRA of 1986, and this adjustment will ultimately be eliminated from the AMT calculation.

$50,000, or ½ ($500,000 – $0) × .20. The effective tax rate on pretax financial income would thus be $50,000/$500,000, or the minimum 10 percent.

For tax years after 1989, the AMT calculation will no longer involve a comparison of the difference between AMTI and income reported for financial statement purposes. The book income adjustment, as it is known, will be replaced by an *adjusted current earnings* (ACE) concept. Any excess of the ACE over the pre-ACE AMT will force an adjustment of AMTI by 75 percent. Thus, for taxable years after 1989, the AMT calculation is as follows:

	Taxable Income calculated per existing regulations
+	Tax Preference Items
–/+	³/₄ (ACE – AMTI before this adjustment)
	Alternative Minimum Taxable Income (AMTI)
–	Exemption
	Adjusted AMTI
×	.20
	AMT
–	Foreign Tax Credits/pre-tax 1986 ITC carryover
	AMT to be compared to tax computed under regular tax system

The ACE calculation is dependent upon a statutory adjustment to regular taxable income, rather than being tied to accounting income. Congress found that the earlier AMT calculation could induce a managerial decision to lower reported earnings as a means to minimize the potential AMT. The new ACE should avoid that undesirable effect.

A noted difference between the pre-1989 calculation of AMT and the revised calculation is that the ACE adjustment can reduce the AMT whereas the book income adjustment used in 1989 and before could only increase AMT. Moreover, the effective tax rate on pretax financial income will no longer be minimally 10 percent.

Financial Reporting and the AMT

The AMT affects the financial reporting of taxes by creating a minimum tax liability which, in turn, affects the amount of deferred taxes calculated under APB 11 and the provision for income taxes under SFAS 96. This, however, should not alter the analyst's interpretation of income tax numbers as outlined in Chapter 4.

On the other hand, and more importantly, the TRA of 1986 made the AMT dependent upon the difference between regular taxable income and reported financial income in years 1989 and before.[5] One can only conjecture, but the manipulation of reported corporate income was an expected event (at least in the opinion of these authors), and Congress introduced the ACE adjustment for 1990 and years thereafter to overcome that manipulative response. Since calculation of regular taxable income is regulated by existing tax rules, a corporation desiring to minimize its AMT will now have to minimize the difference between regular taxable income and the ACE. Thus, tax planning will, of necessity, also involve the planning of adjusted current earnings.

During the period 1987 to 1989, the analyst could have expected the current portion of the income tax provision to be at least 10 percent of the reported pretax income. If this were not true, and if no apparent adjustments for net operating loss carryforwards or pre-1986 ITCs existed, then the corporation may not have been calculating and paying its correct tax liability. This type of finding can be significant in both credit and investment decisions, since claims against corporate assets by either a lender or an investor would be subordinated to this IRS tax liability.

As with most tax issues, more complications arise than can be discussed and changes occur regularly, as witnessed by ACE. If an AMT problem is suspected, the analyst should seek advise from a specialist.[6]

---

[5] Congress generated a list of rank-ordered sources to be used in identifying financial pretax income for years 1987 to 1989. The list, in descending order, is:

(1) Financial statements filed with the SEC.

(2) Financial statements audited and certified by a CPA that have been used as a report or statement for credit purposes, issued to shareholders, or used for any other substantial nontax purposes.

(3) Financial statements provided to the federal government or its agencies.

(4) Financial statements provided to a state government or its agencies (or a political subdivision).

(5) A noncertified report or financial statement actually used for credit purposes, sent to shareholders, or used for any other substantial nontax purpose.

[6] For a more detailed discussion of this topic, the reader is referred to R. Kay and G. Searfoss, *Handbook of Accounting and Auditing,* (Warren, Gorham; 1990).

Analytical Software Instructions

The computer disk accompanying this book contains two programs which can be used to perform both traditional and nontraditional financial analysis.[1] Both types of analysis are described in Chapter 12. **THE AUTHORS MAKE NO EXPLICIT OR IMPLICIT WARRANTY ABOUT THE SOFTWARE CONTAINED ON THE DISK. WHILE EVERY ATTEMPT HAS BEEN MADE TO INSURE THE ACCURACY OF FORMULAS, ETC., ANY DECISIONS MADE USING THE SOFTWARE ARE THE SOLE RESPONSIBILITY OF THE USER.**

The discussion contained in this appendix is limited to the operation of the computer software. If the user is unfamiliar with the MS DOS 3.X or higher (disk operating system) instruction set, a copy of the operating system manual accompanying his/her computer should be obtained. The hardware needed to run these programs is an IBM or IBM-compatible 286 or

---

[1] All programs on this disk are copyrighted by Kirk Lee Tennant. Any use of these programs outside the context of this book and its agreements are explicitly prohibited except by permission of Kirk Lee Tennant. Inquiries can be made to Kirk Lee Tennant at the Cox School of Business, Southern Methodist University, Dallas, Texas 75275.

386, with at least 640 K memory and an EGA or higher resolution monitor running the DOS operating system. The programs contained on the noncopy-protected disk may be duplicated for the exclusive use of the purchaser of this book. Also, the purchaser is free to copy the programs from one media to the next (i.e., to a hard drive or 5¼" floppy disk).

——— Analytical Algorithms for Summary Financial ——— Statements (ANALYST)

The ANALYST program may be used to create a direct method cash flow statement, perform traditional ratio analysis or cost-volume-profit analysis, and create data files for use in the FACES program. The program is completely menu driven and supplies the user with many reports about a given firm. The user may also store and utilize industry data for comparisons with various ratios, by period and for multiple SIC categories.

ANALYST utilizes a program which interfaces with a set of three database files. The program must know the location of these database files either through the DOS path command or be resident with the program files in the same drive/directory. The six files necessary to run ANALYST are:

ANALYST.EXE

ANALYST.MSG

ANALYST.OVL

ANALYST1.RBF

ANALYST2.RBF

ANALYST3.RBF

If any of the six files is missing the program will not execute.

Unless the program is being run on a hard drive, the limited storage capacity of a floppy disk will constrain the amount of company information that can be input. Since data cannot be deleted from a disk, only edited, it is recommended that the user prepare a backup copy of any original database files (extension.RBF) used to replace a floppy disk once it is full.

Running ANALYST

To run the program, the user simply types **ANALYST** at the DOS prompt (i.e., A> or C>) and presses the **ENTER** or **RETURN** key. The main menu for the ANALYST program will appear. At the menu, the user simply moves the highlight using the cursor keys or a mouse to the option desired and hits RETURN. The mouse is not supported by this program so the cursor keys and return are used to point and select a menu item, respectively.

Options in ANALYST

The main menu of the ANALYST program contains two options:

1. Financial Statement Analysis Tools
2. Risk Analysis Profile (RAP) Checklist

Financial Statement Analysis Tools

The first of the main menu options provides a convenient program for storing financial data from both individual companies and industries for use in subsequent financial statement analysis. Also, reports detailing cash flows, ratio analysis, and cost-volume-profit analysis may be generated.

Upon choosing this option, a submenu containing the following options will be displayed:

1. INPUT\EDIT ENTITY DATA
2. INPUT\EDIT INDUSTRY DATA
3. PRINT ENTITY DATA
4. PRINT INDUSTRY DATA
5. PRINT LIST OF ENTITIES AND INDUSTRIES
6. EXIT TO MAIN MENU

Option 1, **Input\Edit Entity Data**, will require the user to input the balance sheet and income statement items. For Option 2, the user will need to input or edit industry data to be used in comparisons with firm data. Option 3 will display a menu of the various reports that can be printed for any company, and likewise, Option 4 displays a menu of the various reports detailing industry data available to the user. Option 5 simply provides a list of the companies and industries covered by the current database. Option 6 returns the user to the main menu.

To circumnavigate the menu system of ANALYST, the user need only remember that the ESC(ape) key will take the user to a menu one level higher than the current position. Choosing a menu item and pressing ENTER will take the user one level deeper in the menu system. At the main menu level, ESC will take him/her to the operating system DOS prompt and end the program ANALYST.

ANALYST provides many options which the user will need to explore. Hopefully, ANALYST will be a useful tool in analyzing the financial statements of any company for either a credit or investment decision.

Risk Analysis Profile (RAP) Checklist

The second of the main menu options is a computerized checklist of key numbers, relationships, footnotes, and financial statement items that may help the user in the analysis and review of any set of financial statements. A hard copy of this checklist is contained in Appendix 4, and may be copied from the appendix by any user. The computerized version contained in ANALYST prompts the user for any necessary data to complete the checklist—a hard copy of which can be printed on the user's computer printer.

The submenu for the RAP checklist contains six menu options:

1. Input RAP Checklist Data
2. Edit RAP Checklist Data
3. List RAP Checklist Data
4. Print RAP Checklist Data
5. Instructions
6. Exit

These menu items are self-explanatory. The RAP checklist provides a convenient way to store information about an entity from period to period, and the questions on the checklist are referenced (where appropriate) to pages in this book so the user may quickly explore the significance of any given issue to the financial statements at hand.

————Financial Analysts' Caricature Evaluation System———— (FACES)

Running FACES

The use of the FACES program outlined in Chapter 12 involves two separate files—the program file and the data file. To start the program, the user needs to ensure that the program file (called FACES.EXE on the disk) is in the current directory or can be accessed from the current directory (either through the DOS path command or drive designation). The user need only type FACES at the A> or C> or include its drive and directory designation (i.e., D:\FA\FACES where the program is on drive D and in directory FA). The completely menu-driven software will appear on the screen at that time. Although this program was written in C and executes rather rapidly, it does take a minute to load from disk to memory.

The data file is an ASCII file[2] which contains the raw ratios (up to 19 for as many as 24 periods) for a given company. The ASCII file is delimited by blanks (more about this later) and corresponds to the structure of a file exported by any of the many spreadsheet programs.

The data file may contain industry averages as well as company data with which to make comparisons. A particular data file can be called from within the program by using the (R)ead command. After entering (R)ead, the program will prompt the user for the data file name (be sure to include any drive and directory designations if the data file is not in the current drive and directory). An easier way to load a data file is at the same time the FACES program is executed. To accomplish this, the user simply includes the name of the data file with the program name FACES. For example, assume that the FACES program is stored on drive C in a directory called FA and a data file CHILIS.DAT (an actual file on the enclosed disk) is located in drive A. To run the FACES program and load the CHILIS.DAT file assuming the current directory is the root directory of drive C, the following command would be entered:

C>C:\FA\FACES A:CHILIS.DAT

It is important to remember that the blank space between the word FACES and the drive designation or start of the data file name must be typed or the program will not execute.

Options in FACES

Once the program FACES has been executed, a series of commands is available. The commands and their functions are:

Command	Function
(A)ttrib	Option assigns facial features (listed later in this appendix) to the rows in the data file.
(B)ackward	Option scrolls the graphic faces toward the beginning of the data periods.
(C)olors	Option assigns one of 15 colors to the various facial features (hair, eyebrows, etc.)
(D)raw	Option refreshes the graphics screen if a DOS error (i.e., write protect enabled when program attempts to write to disk) over–writes the graphics screen.
(F)orward	Option scrolls the graphic faces toward the end of the data periods.

---

[2] An ASCII (American Standard Code for Information Interchange) code is a format wherein the letter A is represented by a particular number (i.e., 65). A computer reading a file of ASCII characters will recognize that when it reads the number 65, the user really means the letter A. The ASCII format is used here because most word processors, spreadsheet packages, and other computer software can create a file in this format. A computer screen will not display the ASCII numbers but instead translates them into identifiable characters.

Command	Function
(H)elp	Option provides help on any command in FACES.
(L)oad	Option loads a previously saved FACES file. This is not an ASCII file and is only useful to the FACES program. FACES works faster with this type of file rather than with the ASCII file.
(M)eans	Option displays the deviation in terms of percent from mean value. The display features do not relate magnitude change (only direction) and this option allows the user to see what magnitude of change a particular attribute has.
(N)ormalize	Option sets the period that is to be used to establish the standard for comparison of ratio movement. Usually period 1 is the best period to observe changes over time.
(P)rint	Option prints faces to either an IBM Proprinter (or other com-patible printer) or an EPSON compatible printer.
(Q)uit	Option terminates program and returns user to DOS prompt.
(R)ead	Option reads an ASCII file (usually created by a spreadsheet or word-processing program) containing the ratio data.
(S)ave GCA	Option saves currently displayed facial data to a special file which can be used later by loading it with the (L)oad command.
(T)oggle	Option displays a second page of six faces.
(Z)oom	Option allows the comparison of two individual faces on a larger scale than the six-face page.

The user must only press the key of the capitalized character of each com-mand for that command to be executed. For example, to move forward through the faces one at a time, the user simply presses the F key on the keyboard. For some options like (Z)oom, the first time the Z key is pressed the comparison of two larger faces appears on the computer screen. A sec-ond pressing of the Z key returns the six face screen.

Structure of the Data File

As stated earlier in this appendix, the data file is an ASCII file delimited by blank spaces which contain the 19 ratios (not all need to be used) that others have found useful in financial analysis. To make the data file useful to the program it must have a particular format. The first number of the first line of the file contains the number of periods of data that the data file contains, whereas the second number is either 0 if no industry data exists or 1 if indus-try data does exist. The next rows of data contain the raw ratio numbers for the 19 ratios (0 if that ratio is not being used) for the stated number of periods.

For example, the matrix of data from the data file CHILIS.DAT is shown in Exhibit A3.1 and reveals that the data file contains 6 periods of firm data, as well as industry data. Rows 2 to 20 contain financial ratio data for Chili's, whereas rows 21 to 39 contain industry data for the same ratios (see Exhibit A3.2). If industry data had not been available, a 0 would have been placed in row 1 after the number 10 (number of periods) and the additional 19 rows of ratios for the industry would not be contained in the file.

The features that can be associated with various ratios are:

1. Face Width
2. Face Height
3. Shape of Top of Head
4. Shape of Bottom of Head
5. Location of Ears
6. Diameter of Ears
7. Coverage of Hair
8. Height of Hair
9. Position of Part
10. Beard Width at the Chin
11. Beard Length
12. Angle of Eyebrows
13. Radius of Eyes
14. Radius of Pupils
15. Length of Nose
16. Width of Nose
17. Distance of Mouth from Nose
18. Mouth Width
19. Mouth Curvature

Remember that the features can be associated with different ratios through the FACES (A)ttribute option.

Exhibit A3.1

CHILI'S RATIOS FOR 1985-1990 AS ORIGINALLY STATED AND INDUSTRY RATIOS FOR SIC# 5812

1985	1986	1987	1988	1989	1990	
6	1					
43.490	43.680	43.970	44.100	59.080	81.730	NET SALES/ACCOUNTS RECEIVABLE
1.220	1.160	1.280	1.310	1.312	1.110	NET FIXED ASSETS/NET WORTH
2.970	2.780	3.620	3.620	3.630	2.620	NET SALES/NET WORTH
47.700	45.050	6.900	48.120	-48.710	-18.880	NET SALES/WORKING CAPITAL
1.220	1.240	2.890	1.240	0.800	0.560	CURRENT ASSETS/CURRENT LIABILITIES
0.410	0.440	0.100	0.670	-0.748	-0.190	INVENTORY/WORKING CAPITAL
4.103	2.284	0.439	2.734	-3.570	-1.491	NET INCOME BEFORE TAX/WORKING CAPITAL
0.086	0.062	0.064	0.057	0.073	0.079	NET INCOME BEFORE TAX/NET SALES
0.256	0.172	0.230	0.206	0.266	0.207	NET INCOME BEFORE TAX/NET WORTH
0.280	0.250	0.280	0.310	0.367	0.320	CURRENT LIABILITIES/NET WORTH
0.770	0.640	0.890	0.720	0.958	0.160	TOTAL DEBT/NET WORTH
7.710	6.240	1.680	9.510	-7.930	-0.660	LONG-TERM DEBT/WORKING CAPITAL
11.180	9.360	5.100	6.080	6.600	11.840	CURRENT LIABILITIES/INVENTORY
0.200	0.270	0.350	0.180	0.150	0.120	CURRENT ASSETS/TOTAL ASSETS
0.082	0.130	0.630	0.230	0.149	0.090	QUICK ASSETS/NET WORTH
0.539	0.580	0.410	0.520	0.680	1.880	CFFO/TOTAL DEBT
0.139	0.132	0.100	0.100	0.110	0.110	CFFO/NET SALES
31.790	28.210	19.110	20.270	18.970	28.960	COST OF GOODS SOLD/INVENTORY
20.807	15.123	7.260	4.643	8.188	13.857	NET INCOME BEFORE TAX AND INTEREST/INTEREST

Exhibit A3.1 (Continued)

CHILI'S RATIOS FOR 1985-1990 AS ORIGINALLY STATED AND INDUSTRY RATIOS FOR SIC# 5812

1985	1986	1987	1988	1989	1990	
57.100	90.100	68.600	64.600	140.000	153.500	NET SALES/ACCOUNTS RECEIVABLE
1.659	1.793	1.361	1.144	2.289	1.501	NET FIXED ASSETS/NET WORTH
5.715	3.608	4.013	2.888	5.425	3.442	NET SALES/NET WORTH
-40.800	-93.300	98.600	41.800	-21.600	-45.900	NET SALES/WORKING CAPITAL
0.800	0.900	1.100	1.200	0.700	0.700	CURRENT ASSETS/CURRENT LIABILITIES
-2.030	-1.063	-17.000	1.946	-0.436	-0.812	INVENTORY/WORKING CAPITAL
-1.813	-0.545	-27.446	2.737	-0.543	-1.996	NET INCOME BEFORE TAX/WORKING CAPITAL
0.030	0.013	0.046	0.072	0.038	0.062	NET INCOME BEFORE TAX/NET SALES
0.243	0.104	0.230	0.207	0.104	0.193	NET INCOME BEFORE TAX/NET WORTH
0.777	0.462	0.502	0.464	0.844	0.490	CURRENT LIABILITIES/NET WORTH
2.200	2.700	1.600	0.900	1.900	1.600	TOTAL DEBT/NET WORTH
-11.515	-14.250	-110.000	7.757	-3.692	-6.896	LONG-TERM DEBT/WORKING CAPITAL
4.045	5.059	4.392	3.139	5.098	5.641	CURRENT LIABILITIES/INVENTORY
0.238	0.140	0.221	0.263	0.143	0.172	CURRENT ASSETS/TOTAL ASSETS
0.433	0.237	0.330	0.347	0.231	0.258	QUICK ASSETS/NET WORTH
0.188	0.133	0.137	0.284	0.197	0.295	CFFO/TOTAL DEBT
0.061	0.062	0.042	0.104	0.082	0.105	CFFO/NET SALES
24.900	18.300	20.600	11.700	11.100	30.500	COST OF GOODS SOLD/INVENTORY
2.400	1.500	2.500	2.300	1.400	1.800	NET INCOME BEFORE TAX AND INTEREST/INTEREST

Exhibit A3.2 _____

FINANCIAL RATIOS FOR CHILI'S DATA FILE

Row	Formula	Common Name	Category*
2	Net Sales/Accounts Receivable	Receivable Turnover	T
3	Net Fixed Assets/Net Worth		CS
4	Net Sales/Net Worth		P
5	Net Sales/Working Capital		L
6	Current Assets/Current Liability	Current Ratio	L
7	Inventory/Working Capital		L
8	Net Income Before Tax/Working Capital		L
9	Net Income Before Tax/Net Sales	Return on Sales	P
10	Net Income Before Tax/Net Worth	Return on Equity	P
11	Current Liabilities/Net Worth		L
12	Total Debt/Net Worth	Debt to Equity Ratio	CS
13	Long-term Debt/Working Capital		DSC
14	Current Liabilities/Inventory		L
15	Current Assets/Total Assets		L
16	Quick Assets/Net Worth		L
17	CFFO/Total Debt		CF
18	CFFO/Net Sales		CF
19	Cost of Goods Sold/Inventory	Inventory Turnover Ratio	T
20	(Net Income Before Tax + Interest)/Interest	Coverage Ratio	DSC

* The categories for the various ratios are discussed in Chapter 12. T-turnover, L-liquidity, CS-capital structure, CF-cash flow, DSC-debt service coverage, P-profitability.

Risk Analysis Profile Checklist

Entity Code:

Name of Entity:

Date of Financial Statements:

Audited?

Auditor:

Time Period:

Major Business Line:

SIC Class:

THE CONTROL ENVIRONMENT

☐ What degree of risk does management's philosophy and operating style present to the quality of earnings?

☐ What degree of risk does the entity's organizational structure present to the quality of earnings?

☐ What is the risk that the board of directors will not provide adequate organizational oversight?

☐ What degree of risk does the method of assigning authority and responsibility present to the quality of earnings?

☐ What degree of risk does management's control system present to the quality of earnings?

☐ What degree of risk do external forces (e.g., a shrinking market) present to the quality of earnings?

THE ACCOUNTING SYSTEM

☐ What degree of risk exists that not all valid transactions have been recorded in the accounting system?

☐ What degree of risk does management's ability to shift accounting transactions between periods present to the quality of earnings?

THE CONTROL PROCEDURES

☐ What degree of risk does improper transaction authorization present to the quality of earnings?

☐ What degree of risk does management override of accounting control present to the quality of earnings?

GENERAL CONSIDERATIONS

☐ What degree of risk does the entity's size present to the quality of earnings?

☐ What degree of risk does the entity's type of ownership present to the quality of earnings?

☐ What degree of risk does the nature of the entity's business present to the quality of earnings?

☐ What degree of risk does the entity's lack of diversification present to the quality of earnings?

☐ What degree of risk do legal and regulatory requirements present to the quality of earnings?

☐ What degree of risk does the method of data processing present to the quality of earnings?

———————————— INSTITUTIONAL RISK ————————————

Audit Report Type:

☐ What degree of risk does the auditor's report suggest?

☐ Was there an auditor change?

☐ If yes, for what reason?

☐ If yes, does this change suggest an increase in risk?

☐ If yes, what degree of risk is suggested by the change?

☐ Were there any departures from GAAP?

☐ If yes, what departures?

☐ If yes, what degree of risk do these departures suggest for the quality of earnings?

☐ Was there any mention of uncertainties or contingent liabilities?

☐ If yes, what were they?

☐ If yes, what degree of risk do these uncertainties present to the quality of earnings?

☐ What were the significant accounting principles used by the entity for:

- Inventory:
- Depreciation:
- Other:

☐ In general, what level of risk is suggested by the entity's choice of these methods?

———————————— INCOME STATEMENT RISK ————————————
REVENUE RECOGNITION

☐ What revenue recognition method is used?

☐ What degree of risk does this method present to the quality of earnings?

☐ What is your best estimate of the length of the working capital cycle (i.e., the length of time from when cash goes out for the purchase of inventory to the return of cash through the collection of receivables from sales)?

☐ Is the length of this cycle consistent with the industry?

☐ What degree of risk does the entity's working capital cycle present to the quality of earnings?

☐ Does the entity sell its products or services to a wholesaler or to the ultimate consumer?

☐ If sales are via a wholesaler, what degree of risk does this present to the quality of earnings?

☐ What are the typical terms of the entity's credit policy?

☐ What degree of risk do the terms of the entity's credit policy present to the quality of earnings?

☐ What was last period's average days receivables outstanding?

☐ What is this period's average days receivables outstanding?

☐ What risk does the change in the average days receivable outstanding present to the quality of earnings?

☐ What was the change in the total accounts receivable outstanding from last period to the current period?

☐ What was the change in sales from the last period to the current period?

☐ What is the ratio of the change in accounts receivable over sales for the period?

☐ Is the ratio of change in accounts receivable to the change in sales greater than 10%?

☐ What risk does the change in accounts receivable present to the quality of earnings?

———————— THE COST OF OPERATIONS ————————

☐ Is absorption or direct costing used in the calculation of cost of goods sold?

☐ What inventory cost-flow approach is used to cost inventory?

☐ If LIFO was used, what is the value of the LIFO reserve?

☐ What is the ratio of the LIFO reserve to the current inventory value?

☐ Can the entity pass inflationary increases in inventory costs to its customers?

☐ If LIFO was used, did the entity experience any LIFO liquidations?

☐ If so, in what amount?

☐ What risk does the entity's choice of inventory method present to the quality of earnings?

☐ Which depreciation method is the entity using?

☐ Has the entity implemented any change in the cstimated life of any long-term productive asset?

☐ If yes, what was the dollar impact change on current earnings?

☐ What risk does the entity's choice of depreciation method and changes in accounting estimates (if any) present to the quality of earnings?

———————— DEFERRED AND REAL TAXES ————————

☐ Is the entity using APB 11 or SFAS 96 to account for income taxes?

☐ What was the reported income tax expense for the current period?

☐ What was the current portion of the income tax expense for the current period?

☐ What is the net income before taxes (NIBT)?

☐ What is the ratio of the current portion of the income tax expense to the NIBT?

☐ What was the change in the total deferred income tax account for the current period?

☐ What were the major types (reversals, deferrals) of changes in deferred taxes, their reason, and the amounts involved?

☐ Is it likely that these changes will recur again in future periods?

☐ How much, if any, does the entity have in net operating losses (NOLs) to carryforward to subsequent years?

☐ Is the entity due any tax refund for previous periods?

☐ What risk does the entity's accounting for income taxes present to the quality of earnings?

━━━━━━━━━━━━ BALANCE SHEET RISK ━━━━━━━━━━━━

Cash, Marketable Securities, and Receivables

☐ Is the cash balance an overdraft?

☐ Were there any realized gains and losses on the sale of marketable securities?

☐ What method was used, if any, to calculate the allowance for uncollectible accounts?

Inventory

☐ Was an L.C.M. adjustment made for inventory?

☐ If so, what was the amount?

☐ What was the inventory turnover last period?

☐ What was the inventory turnover this period?

Prepaids

☐ Are the prepaid assets in excess of 10% of total assets?

☐ If yes, are the prepaids potentially being used to manipulate earnings?

Current Liabilities

☐ What was the average payable period in the last accounting period?

☐ What is the average payable period in the current accounting period?

☐ Is the average payable period in line with terms offered to the entity on inventory and other purchases?

☐ If no, the likely reason:

Notes Payable

☐ Are trade notes frequently used in the entity's industry?

☐ If so, is the interest rate charged appropriate?

Accrued Expenses Payable

☐ Is the ratio of accrued expenses payable greater than 10 percent of the outstanding liabilities?

☐ If yes, are accrued expenses payable potentially being used to manipulate earnings?

Current Portion of Long-Term Debt

☐ Has the current portion of any long-term liability (e.g., bonds, leases, etc.) been appropriately recognized?

☐ What level of risk to the quality of earnings is implied by the reporting of working capital accounts?

———— NONCURRENT ASSET ACCOUNTS ————

Intercompany Investments

☐ Does the company have any investments at cost?

☐ Does the company have any equity investments reported on a one-line consolidation basis?

☐ What percent of the entity's revenue is from subsidiary earnings?

☐ Has the company made an acquisition in the current year?

☐ If yes, did the entity use the purchase method of accounting?

☐ Did the entity use the pooling-of-interests method of accounting?

☐ What level of risk to the quality of earnings is implied by the entity's accounting for intercompany investments?

Noncurrent Operating Assets

☐ Has the value of any noncurrent assets been impaired?

☐ Has interest been capitalized in the current period?

☐ If yes, what is the ratio of capitalized interest to total interest?

☐ Are there any R & D projects in process?

☐ If yes, were the R & D costs expensed in the current period?

☐ If yes, describe the project and its likely impact on future earnings?

☐ What is the ratio of intangible assets to total assets?

☐ Are the intangible assets worth the amount reported?

☐ Why?

☐ Does the entity own any natural resources?

☐ If yes, what basis does the entity use to account for these resources?

☐ Are the entity's cost centers decentralized?

☐ What level of risk to the quality of earnings is implied by the reporting of noncurrent assets?

————— NONCURRENT LIABILITY ACCOUNTS —————

Long-Term Debt

☐ Has the entity issued any zero-coupon bonds?

☐ Has the entity defeased any long-term debt?

☐ Has the entity extinguished any debt before maturity?

☐ Has the entity restructured any troubled-debt?

Contingencies or Commitments

☐ Does the entity have any of the following contingencies or commitments?

- Lawsuits:
- Recourse Loans:
- Recourse Receivables:
- Working Capital Maintenance Agreements:
- Take-or-Pay Contracts:
- Leveraged Employee Stock Ownership Plans:
- Other Contractual Agreements:
- Other Commitments:

☐ Does the entity make use of operating leases?

☐ If yes, what is the present value of future committed cash flows?

☐ What is the ratio of operating leases to other liabilities?

☐ Are any pension funds underfunded, and, if so, what is the underfunded amount?

☐ Is the entity exposed to any other post-employment benefits besides pensions?

☐ If yes, what is the reported amount?

☐ What level of risk to the quality of earnings is implied by the reporting of noncurrent liabilities?

————— EQUITY ACCOUNTS —————

☐ Is the entity exposed to any foreign currency transactions and translation problems?

☐ Does the entity have a long-term adjustment to equity for any impaired long-term investments?

☐ Does the entity have dilutive securities, such as warrants or convertible debt, outstanding?

☐ Are any dividends in arrears on any equity issue?

☐ Has the entity undergone a quasi-reorganization in the past five years?

☐ Does the entity follow a policy of purchasing treasury stock to support its stock price?

☐ Does the entity use stock dividends or splits to manage the high-end of the market price of its stock?

☐ What level of risk to the quality of earnings is implied by the reporting of the owners' equity accounts?

———————— ANALYSIS OF CASH FLOW ————————

☐ What was the entity's prior period CFFO?

☐ What is the entity's current period CFFO?

☐ Does the entity have free cash flow?

☐ If yes, in what amount?

☐ What are the entity's five major sources of cash?

    1.

    2.

    3.

    4.

    5.

☐ What are the entity's five major uses of cash?

    1.

    2.

    3.

    4.

    5.

☐ What level of risk to the quality of earnings is implied by the cash flow from operations?

ANALYTICAL MODELS

Ratio Analysis Results:

Historical Results of DuPont Model:

(Asset turnover) × (Financial Leverage) × (Operating Leverage) = ROE

$$\frac{\text{Sales}}{\text{Average Assets}} \times \frac{\text{Average Assets}}{\text{Average Equity}} \times \frac{\text{Net Income}}{\text{Sales}} = \frac{\text{Net Income}}{\text{Average Equity}}$$

1. _____   _____   _____ = _____
2. _____   _____   _____ = _____
3. _____   _____   _____ = _____
4. _____   _____   _____ = _____
5. _____   _____   _____ = _____

Cost-Volume-Profit Analysis:

Estimates of Cost Structure:

Variable Cost as a % of each sales dollar: _____

Fixed cash costs: _____

Breakeven in $: _____

Current Sales Level _____

Margin of Safety _____

☐ What level of risk to the quality of earnings is implied by the analytical analysis?

Suggested Reading

Chapter 1: The Institutional Environment

American Institute of Certified Public Accountants, *Understanding Audits and the Auditor's Report: A Guide for Financial Statement Users* (AICPA, 1989).

D. Akst, *Wonder Boy, Barry Minkow—The Kid Who Swindled Wall Street* (Scribner's, 1990).

D. R. Beresford, "The 'Balancing Act' in Setting Accounting Standards," *Accounting Horizons* (March, 1988).

T. R. Dyckman and D. Morse, *Efficient Capital Markets and Accounting: A Critical Analysis* (Prentice-Hall, Inc., 1986).

B. G. Malkiel, *A Random Walk Down Wall Street* (W. W. Norton & Co., Inc., 1973).

K. A. Merchant, *Fraudulent and Questionable Financial Reporting: A Corporate Perspective* (Financial Executives Research Foundation, 1987).

K. Wishon, "Plugging the Gaps in GAAP: The FASB's Emerging Issues Task Force," *Journal of Accountancy* (June, 1986).

Chapter 2: Revenue Recognition

A. J. Briloff, *More Debits Than Credits* (Harper & Row Co., 1976).

A. J. Briloff, *Unaccountable Accounting* (Harper & Row Co., 1972).

E. R. Brownlee, K. R. Ferris, and M. E. Haskins, *Corporate Financial Reporting: Text and Cases* (BPI/Irwin, 1990).

G. Hector, "Cute Tricks on the Bottom Line," *Fortune* (April 24, 1989).

F. S. Worthy, "Manipulating Profits: How It's Done," *Fortune* (June 25, 1984).

Chapter 3: The Cost of Operations

K. Bendis, "Cute Tricks on the Bottom Line," *Fortune* (April 24, 1989).

E. R. Brownlee, K. R. Ferris, and M. E. Haskins, *Corporate Financial Reporting: Text and Cases* (BPI/Irwin, 1990).

R. Reilly, "LIFO Adoption and a Firm's Ability to Meet Indenture Covenant Restrictions, *Credit and Financial Management* (September, 1982).

R. Reilly, "LIFO Adoption and Its Effect on the Firm's Financial Position and Debt Capacity," *The Ohio CPA Journal*, (Summer, 1982).

R. Taylor, "Liquidation of LIFO Inventories," *Management Accounting* (April, 1978).

H. Wallich and M. Wallich, "Profits Aren't As Good As They Look," *Fortune* (March, 1974).

D. Wechsler, "Earnings Helper," *Forbes* (June 12, 1989).

R. Welton, G. Friedlob, F. Gray, and J. Sloan, "LIFO/FIFO: A Simple Solution to Inventory Disclosure Problems, *Management Accounting* (October, 1987).

Chapter 4: Income Taxes

B. M. Abbin, "How Will the New Corporate AMT Affect Financial Statement Income?" *Financial Executive* (November/December, 1987).

J. L. Carpenter and N. L. Wilburn, "New Rules in Income Tax Accounting: Implications for Financial Statement Users." *Journal of Commercial Bank Lending* (December, 1988).

Financial Accounting Standards Board, *Statement of Financial Accounting Standards No. 96: Accounting for Income Taxes* (Stamford, CT: 1987).

D. C. Jeter and P. K. Chaney, "A Financial Statement Analysis Approach to Deferred Taxes." *Accounting Horizons* (December, 1988).

H. Nurnberg, "Changes in Tax Rates Under the Deferred and Liability Methods of Interperiod Tax Allocation." *Accounting Horizons* (September, 1987).

H. Nurnberg, "Income Tax Allocation Under SFAS 96." *CPA Journal* (July, 1988).

M. van Breda and K. R. Ferris, "Accounting for Deferred Income Taxes: Understanding the New Approach." *Journal of Managerial Issues* (Fall 1989).

Chapter 5: Working Capital

H. Gilman, "Wholesalers Caught in a Squeeze by Retailers," *The Wall Street Journal* (May 29, 1986).

D. Grinnel and C. Norgaard, "Reporting Rules for Marketable Equity Securities, *Financial Analysts Journal* (Vol. 36, No. 1).

J. Lesta, "Validating Accounts Receivable: Back to Basics, *Journal of Commercial Bank Lending* (April 1990).

K. Nebel, "Working Capital Financing: A Dual Approach to Generating Funds," *Journal of Commercial Bank Lending* (May 1990).

C. Rumble, "So You Still Have Not Adopted LIFO," *Management Accounting* (October 1983).

R. Wilner, "SA Fury Mounts Over Retailers' Changebacks," *Woman's Wear Daily* (February 1, 1989)

Chapter 6: Intercorporate Investments

F. Beams, *Advanced Accounting* (Prentice Hall, 1990).

W. De Moville and A. G. Petrie, "Accounting for a Bargain Purchase in a Business Combination," *Accounting Horizons* (September 1989).

J. Heian and J. Thies, "Consolidation of Finance Subsidiaries: $230 Billion in Off-Balance-Sheet Financing Comes Home to Roost," *Accounting Horizons* (March 1989).

H. Sklenar, "Mergers and Acquisitions: Trends, Scandals and Opportunities," *The Ohio CPA Journal* (Winter 1983).

Chapter 7: Noncurrent Operating Assets

J. Colley and A. Volkan, "Accounting for Goodwill," *Accounting Horizons* (March 1988).

E. Brownlee, K. Ferris, M. Haskins, *Corporate Financial Reporting* (BPI/Irwin, 1990).

K. R. Ferris and M. E. Barrett, "Assessing the Quality of Reported Earnings in the Oil and Gas Industry: Some Guidance for Credit Analysts," *The Journal of Commercial Lending* (February 1984).

K. Means and P. Kazenski, "SFAS 34: A Recipe for Diversity," *Accounting Horizons* (September 1988).

H. Nurnberg, "Annual and Interim Financial Reporting of Changes in Account-ing Estimates," *Accounting Horizons* (September 1988).

T. Pouschine, "Reel Assets," *Forbes* (December 29, 1986).

L. Saunders, "Drilling for Information," *Forbes* (July 28, 1986).

Chapter 8: Long-term Debt

R. Billingsley, R. Lany, and G. Thompson, "Valuation of Primary Issue Con-vertible Bonds," *Journal of Financial Research* (Fall 1986).

L. Jereski, "Invisible Debt," *Forbes* (February 9, 1987).

R. Klein, "Eliminating Debt by Defeasance," *Business Magazine* (October/De-cember 1984).

J. Peavy III and J. Scott, "A Closer Look at Stock-for-Debt Swaps," *Financial Analysts Journal* (May/June 1985).

A. Phillips and S. Moody, ""The Effects of Defeased Debt on Loan Decisions," *Journal of Commercial Bank Lending* (February 1989).

P. Wang, "The Unlevel Accounting Field," *Forbes* (November 28, 1988).

Chapter 9: Special Topics in Debt Valuation

M. Austin, B. Strawser, and N. Mixon, "Contingencies and Unasserted Claims: Adequate Answers?" *The CPA Journal* (September 1985).

W. B. Barrett, "Term Structure Modeling for Pension Liability Discounting," *Financial Analysts Journal* (Vol. 44, No. 6).

P. Miller, "The New Pension Accounting: Part 1," *Journal of Accountancy* (January 1987).

P. Miller, The New Pension Accounting: Part 2," *Journal of Accountancy* (February 1987).

L. Murphey, "Employer's Accounting for Pensions-A Lender's Perspective." *Journal of Commercial Bank Lending* (March 1990).

B. Rudolph, "You Better Believe," *Forbes* (July 30, 1985).

A. Sannella, "The Capitalization of Operating Leases: The Discounted Cash Flow Approach," *Journal of Commercial Bank Lending* (October 1989).

E. Shoenthal, "Contingent Legal Liabilities," *The CPA Journal* (March 1976).

C. Volk, "The Risks of Operating Leases," *Journal of Commercial Bank Lending* (May 1988).

Chapter 10: Owner's Equity

P. Asquith and D. Mullins, Jr., "Signalling with Dividends, Stock Repurchases, and Equity Issues," *Financial Management* (Vol. 15, No. 3).

J. Byrne, "The Cure that Kills," *Forbes* (November 5, 1984).

J. Coughlan, "Anomalies in Calculating Earnings Per Share," *Accounting Horizons*, (December 1988).

C. Gibson, "Quasi-reorganizations in Practice," *Accounting Horizons* (September 1988).

R. Greene, "What, and Whose, Bottom Line?" *Forbes* (October 7, 1985).

A. Hershman, "The Spreading Wave of Stock Buybacks," *Dun's Business Month* (August 1984).

L. Jereski, "Better than Free," *Forbes* (June 15, 1987).

Chapter 11: Cash Flow Analysis

C. Casey and N. Bartczak, "Cash Flow—it's not the Bottom Line," *Harvard Business Review* (July-August, 1984).

C. Chastain, S. Cianciolo and A. Thomas, "Strategies in Cash Flow Management," *Business Horizons* (May-June, 1986).

Ernst & Whinney, "Statement of Cash Flows—Understanding and Implementing FASB Statement No. 95," Financial Reporting Developments (January, 1988).

D. Giacomino and D. Mielke, "Using the Statement of Cash Flows to Analyze Corporate Performance," *Management Accounting* (May, 1988).

R. Greene, "Are More Chryslers in the Offing?" *Forbes* (February 2, 1981).

L. Heath, "Cash Flow Reporting: Bankers Need a Direct Approach," *Journal of Commercial Bank Lending* (February 1987).

C. Malburg, "Strategies for Optimal Cash Management." *The Practical Accountant* (May, 1988).

J. Riggs, *Engineering Economics* (McGraw-Hill, 1982).

B. Thomas, "The Perils of Ignoring Cash Flow," *Directors & Boards* (Fall, 1983).

Chapter 12: Alternative Models of Financial Analysis

G. Foster, *Financial Statement Analysis, 2/E* (Prentice-Hall, 1986).

R. Garrison, *Managerial Accounting*, 5/E (BPI, 1988).

H. Heymann, R. Bloom, and R. Auster, "Cost-volume-profit analysis applied to cash management," *Cashflow* (July/August, 1984).

S. Moriarity, "Communicating Financial Information Through Multi-dimensional Graphics" *Journal of Accounting Research* (Spring, 1979).

T. Selling and C. Stickney, "Disaggregating the Rate of Return on Stockholders' Equity: A New Approach," *Accounting Horizons* (December, 1990).

Chapter 13: Assesing the Quality of Earnings and Assets

L. A. Bernstein and J. G. Siegel, "The Concept of Earnings Quality," *Financial Analysts Journal* (July/August, 1979).

L. Berton and J. Schiff, *The Wall Street Journal on Accounting* (Dow Jones/Irwin, 1990).

E. E. Comisky, "Assessing Financial Quality: An Organizing Theme for Credit Analysts," *The Journal of Commercial Bank Lending* (December, 1982).

J. P. Dawson, P. M. Neupert, and C. P. Stickney, "Restating Financial Statements for Alternative GAAPs: Is It Worth the Effort?," *Financial Analysts Journal* (November/December, 1980).

T. L. O'glove, *Quality of Earnings* (Free Press, 1987).

M. V. Sever and R. E. Boilclair, "Financial Reporting in the 1990s," *Journal of Accountancy* (January 1990).

F. S. Worthy, "Manipulating Profits: How It's Done," *Fortune* (June 25, 1984).

Index

299